I0017887

The Complete Guide to Advertising on Amazon Prime

Maximize Your Sales, Master the Platform, and
Drive Success Today

Valentia Bras

DISCLAIMER

While every precaution has been taken in the preparation of this book, the publisher assumes no responsibility for errors or omissions, or for damages resulting from the use of the information contained herein.

The Complete Guide to Advertising on Amazon Prime: Maximize Your Sales, Master the Platform, and Drive Success Today

First edition.

TABLE OF CONTENTS

PART 1

Understanding the Amazon Advertising Ecosystem

INTRODUCTION
AMAZON ADVERTISING FOR PRIME PRODUCTS

THE POWER OF AMAZON PRIME AND ITS AUDIENCE

Amazon Prime is more than just a subscription service—it's a carefully crafted ecosystem, one that has quietly but profoundly reshaped how consumers shop, engage with content, and make purchasing decisions. With over 200 million global members and counting, Amazon Prime has become a household staple, creating a captive and committed audience that offers businesses an extraordinary opportunity for growth. Understanding the power of this platform means recognizing not just its technological infrastructure or shipping perks, but the depth of customer loyalty and behavioral patterns it has nurtured over time.

At its core, Amazon Prime is built on a foundation of convenience, speed, and value. The promise of two-day shipping initially drew millions of customers into its orbit, but it's the continuous expansion of benefits— Prime Video, Prime Music, Prime Reading, exclusive deals, and more— that has transformed it into an all-encompassing lifestyle service. This bundling of offerings doesn't just add value; it strengthens retention. Members become deeply integrated into Amazon's world, building habits around shopping, entertainment, and consumption that naturally align with Amazon's marketplace.

The audience Amazon Prime attracts is distinctively engaged and conversion-ready. These aren't casual browsers—they are loyal, high-intent customers who trust Amazon's ecosystem. Their buying behavior reflects this. Studies consistently show that Prime members spend significantly more than non-members—sometimes nearly double— because they trust the platform, expect fast delivery, and are routinely exposed to Amazon's personalized recommendation engines. These shoppers are conditioned to act quickly, enticed by flash deals, limited-time offers, and algorithmically tailored suggestions. For advertisers, this means marketing to an audience that not only spends more but does so faster, with fewer barriers to purchase.

The psychological advantage Amazon holds over traditional retail and even other digital platforms is its sheer familiarity and integration. Prime members don't just shop on Amazon—they live on it. They stream movies while browsing for home goods. They listen to music while adding groceries to their cart. This continuous exposure multiplies opportunities for brand messaging. Advertising on such a platform taps into a user base that is already immersed, already emotionally and financially invested. The trust built over years of consistent service translates directly into higher click-through rates, greater brand engagement, and faster sales cycles.

One of the most powerful aspects of Amazon Prime's audience is their openness to discovery. While they often arrive with intent—to restock household goods, to find the next binge-worthy show—they are also receptive to new suggestions. Amazon's interface is built to promote discovery at every turn, from the "Customers who bought this also bought..." sections to the increasingly sophisticated ad placements across product pages and Prime Video streams. For emerging brands, this creates a rare chance to appear side-by-side with household names, leveling the playing field in a way few other platforms can offer.

Equally important is the sheer volume of data Amazon collects and uses to optimize user experience. Every click, search, view, and purchase feeds a vast network of insights that power the advertising engine. This means advertisers can target Prime users not just by demographics but by purchase history, browsing behavior, and even streaming habits. An ad campaign here isn't a shot in the dark—it's a precision-guided message tailored to meet a customer at exactly the right moment. The result is relevance at scale, which drives performance beyond what traditional advertising can deliver.

Furthermore, the Amazon Prime audience skews favorably in terms of demographics. Prime members often represent a financially stable, digitally savvy consumer group. They include busy professionals, families looking for convenience, tech-forward shoppers, and entertainment enthusiasts. They are people willing to pay a premium for access, speed, and ease, and that willingness carries over into their buying patterns. Premium-priced products, subscription services, and value-driven brands all perform well within this space because they match the expectations and preferences of the audience.

The role of Prime Video cannot be underestimated in expanding the power of Amazon's audience. With tens of millions of users consuming content on Prime Video, Amazon has blurred the line between content consumption and product discovery. Ads can now appear not just during a shopping session, but in the middle of a binge-watch session, creating new, immersive touchpoints for brands. This fusion of entertainment and commerce is a paradigm shift. It turns passive viewers into active consumers and introduces new ways for brands to connect emotionally through storytelling, visuals, and context.

Another unique dimension of Amazon Prime is the platform's ability to shorten the buyer's journey. Traditional ad funnels often stretch across multiple platforms and touchpoints—discovery on one channel, research on another, conversion somewhere else. But on Amazon, everything is compressed. A user might see an ad while watching a series, click through to a product page, read reviews, and make a purchase—all within minutes, and without ever leaving the platform. This end-to-end seamlessness removes friction and increases the chances of impulse buying. Brands can capitalize on this with high-converting creatives and strategic placements that align with shopper intent and behavior.

It's also worth noting the culture of trust Amazon has cultivated among its Prime members. The consistent delivery of value—be it in the form of fast shipping, customer service, easy returns, or transparent reviews—has created a comfort zone for shoppers. When Prime members see a product advertised within the Amazon ecosystem, it carries an implicit credibility. This is a huge advantage for advertisers. Unlike on social media or other websites, where skepticism often accompanies sponsored content, ads on Amazon are perceived more as helpful suggestions than sales pitches. The context of the platform itself validates the message, which dramatically increases conversion rates.

As competition for consumer attention intensifies, platforms that offer both reach and receptivity become increasingly vital. Amazon Prime is not just a marketplace; it's a marketplace with a built-in, loyal audience that is primed—pun intended—to discover, engage, and buy. The relationship between Amazon and its Prime members is symbiotic and sticky. Shoppers get unmatched convenience and value; in return, Amazon gets their attention, trust, and data. For advertisers, this ecosystem offers an opportunity not merely to sell, but to build lasting brand relationships.

The potential for long-term customer loyalty is particularly high within this environment. When customers are already spending a significant portion of their digital lives on one platform, and when that platform rewards repeated engagement, it becomes far easier for brands to secure repeat purchases and foster brand affinity. Subscribe & Save programs, personalized recommendations, and retargeting through on-platform ads all play a role in making sure once a customer finds your product, they come back again and again. In essence, Amazon doesn't just help you sell to a customer—it helps you keep them.

The future of advertising will increasingly revolve around platforms that merge commerce with content, data with delivery, and reach with relevance. Amazon Prime is at the forefront of this convergence. Its audience represents not just a large consumer base but a curated, loyal, and highly responsive community. Brands that learn to navigate this space with authenticity, precision, and strategic creativity will not only reach more customers—they'll build relationships that last. In the world of modern digital advertising, few audiences are as powerful or as ready to engage as the one already living inside the Amazon Prime ecosystem.

WHY ADVERTISING ON AMAZON PRIME IS CRUCIAL FOR SELLERS

Advertising on Amazon Prime is no longer a strategic luxury—it is a business imperative. As the lines between entertainment, shopping, and digital engagement blur, the Amazon Prime platform emerges as one of the most powerful spaces for brand visibility and conversion. Sellers who want to stay relevant and competitive in today's saturated marketplace must begin to view Amazon Prime not just as a channel, but as a dynamic ecosystem designed to drive consumer behavior. The importance of this platform lies not only in its reach but in the depth of influence it holds over its users.

At the heart of Amazon Prime is an audience that is loyal, high-spending, and deeply entrenched in the Amazon ecosystem. With well over 200 million members worldwide, this subscription base represents a highly targeted market segment that trusts Amazon as both a retailer and a recommender. These are not passive viewers or casual browsers—they are informed shoppers who rely on Amazon's infrastructure to make confident purchasing decisions. The moment a product is promoted within this environment, it gains a level of credibility that other platforms struggle to offer.

This credibility stems from the relationship Amazon has built with its Prime members. Years of reliable two-day shipping, excellent customer service, and consistently positive user experiences have conditioned customers to trust what they see on the platform. Unlike ads on social media or other websites, which may be met with skepticism, an ad seen on Amazon carries the authority of the brand itself. This immediate sense of trust helps eliminate a major barrier in the path to purchase. The product doesn't have to fight for legitimacy; it already possesses it by association.

Moreover, advertising on Amazon Prime allows sellers to position themselves directly in the flow of a consumer's natural behavior. Instead of disrupting an activity to place an ad in front of the user, Amazon integrates advertising into the user experience itself. Whether a customer is watching Prime Video, searching for a household item, or browsing recommended products on their homepage, ads become part of the discovery process. They feel less like interruptions and more like relevant suggestions. This seamless integration drastically improves the chance of engagement and conversion.

What makes this even more potent is Amazon's unmatched access to consumer data. Every search, every click, every purchase feeds into a vast, constantly evolving system that helps refine the targeting capabilities available to advertisers. Sellers can reach audiences not just by basic demographics, but by intent, behavior, and interest. This level of granularity ensures that the right product reaches the right person at the right time. Sellers no longer have to rely on broad strokes or assumptions—they can build campaigns informed by the very actions of their ideal customers.

The power of visual storytelling also comes into play with advertising on Amazon Prime, particularly through Prime Video. Here, brands can do more than simply display a product—they can tell stories, create emotional connections, and deliver rich, immersive experiences. A compelling video ad placed before or during a streaming session can leave a deeper impression than a standard product listing ever could. This is where sellers begin to differentiate themselves, not only as retailers but as brands with personality, value, and resonance.

Competition in the e-commerce space is intense, and standing out requires more than just having a good product. Visibility is everything. Products that are buried deep within search results or that lack any promotional push often go unnoticed, regardless of quality. Advertising on Amazon Prime puts products in front of millions of potential buyers, many of whom are ready to act. With the right combination of creative strategy and targeting, a product can leap from obscurity to best-seller status. This isn't just theory—it's a common reality for brands that harness Amazon's promotional tools effectively.

Another key advantage is the shortened sales funnel. On other platforms, consumers often have to move through several steps before reaching a purchase decision. They might see an ad on social media, follow it to a landing page, research reviews on a third-party site, and then navigate to a different platform to buy. Each step introduces potential drop-off. Amazon removes these extra layers. A customer sees an ad, clicks on it, reads verified reviews, and purchases—often within minutes and without leaving the platform. This frictionless experience boosts conversion rates and allows sellers to capture intent at the moment it arises.

Return on ad spend is also higher on Amazon Prime compared to many other digital platforms. Because ads are being shown to a high-intent audience that is already conditioned to buy, every dollar spent works harder. The environment filters out a large portion of uninterested traffic. Sellers are not throwing wide nets and hoping for bites; they are using precision tools to target users who are already in a buying mindset. This results in lower cost-per-clicks, better conversion metrics, and ultimately, more efficient marketing budgets.

Sellers also benefit from Amazon's built-in infrastructure of customer trust. Amazon is known for fast shipping, generous return policies, and an overall frictionless buying experience. When a customer sees an ad on the platform, they don't need to worry about delivery timelines or complicated returns—they know what to expect. This peace of mind translates to increased willingness to click, engage, and purchase.

Sellers can focus on showcasing the value of their product 'rather than defending their legitimacy or reassuring customers about fulfillment.

Another layer of value lies in the insights sellers gain from advertising performance on Amazon Prime. Every campaign provides detailed analytics—who clicked, when they clicked, what they bought, how much they spent, and what else they viewed. These insights don't just help refine future campaigns—they inform product development, inventory planning, and pricing strategies. The data loop that Amazon creates empowers sellers with actionable intelligence that can drive decisions across their entire business.

The opportunity to scale is also uniquely accessible. Amazon's platform is global, and Prime membership stretches across continents. A campaign that performs well in one region can be replicated and adapted for others. Sellers with scalable fulfillment models can expand their reach dramatically by simply optimizing their campaigns for international audiences. Advertising on Prime is not bound by the same limitations as brick-and-mortar retail or even some online marketplaces. The digital infrastructure allows for rapid growth when paired with strong execution.

There is also an invaluable brand-building component. Advertising on Amazon Prime allows sellers to create a presence that goes beyond the product page. Sponsored Brands, video ads, and enhanced content provide tools to build brand identity within the platform itself. Over time, customers don't just remember the product—they remember the brand, its voice, and its story. This emotional connection pays dividends over the long term, translating into repeat purchases and word-of-mouth referrals.

As the digital landscape continues to evolve, sellers who hesitate to embrace Amazon Prime advertising risk falling behind. The marketplace is moving fast, and those who do not proactively invest in visibility and engagement will find it increasingly difficult to gain ground. This isn't about jumping on a trend; it's about adapting to a new standard in consumer behavior. Buyers are making decisions based on what they see in trusted digital spaces—and for millions, that space is Amazon Prime.

Timing, of course, plays a crucial role. Early adopters of new ad formats or targeting strategies often enjoy disproportionate returns. Whether it's interactive video ads, streaming promotions, or integrated product placements within Prime Video content, being among the first to experiment can yield substantial benefits. Sellers who recognize these shifts and move quickly are often the ones who end up owning the conversation in their niche.

Ultimately, the digital shelf is just as competitive—if not more— than the physical one. In order to be chosen, a product must be seen, trusted, and desired. Amazon Prime advertising provides all the tools necessary to achieve that trifecta. Sellers who make the most of these tools don't just sell more—they build stronger brands, gain deeper customer insights, and future-proof their business in a marketplace that's evolving faster than ever. The question is no longer whether sellers can afford to advertise on Amazon Prime—it's whether they can afford not to.

OVERVIEW OF AVAILABLE AD TYPES

Navigating the world of advertising within the Amazon ecosystem begins with understanding the different types of ads available to sellers and brands. Each ad type offers a unique approach to visibility, targeting, and customer engagement, and knowing how to leverage them effectively can be the difference between simply existing on the platform and dominating your niche. Amazon's advertising suite is designed to reach customers at different stages of their shopping journey, and it delivers remarkable flexibility for advertisers of all sizes. From individual sellers to global brands, the system is built to amplify presence and drive results, both on and off the platform.

Sponsored Products form the backbone of Amazon's advertising infrastructure. These ads promote individual product listings and appear directly within search results or on product detail pages. Their power lies in their simplicity and precision. When a shopper types in a search query, Sponsored Products are often the first listings they see—blended in seamlessly with organic results but clearly labeled as "sponsored." This gives advertisers a crucial edge. The consumer's attention is directed toward promoted products before they even scroll. Because Sponsored Products look like regular listings, they benefit from a sense of trust and familiarity, reducing resistance and increasing the likelihood of clicks.

The real strength of Sponsored Products is in the intent of the shopper. These ads target customers who are actively searching for items to purchase, making them incredibly valuable for conversion. The targeting can be keyword-based, allowing advertisers to align their products with specific search terms, or product-based, enabling ads to appear on competitor listings or complementary product pages. The control over bids, budget, and placement makes this format ideal for performance-driven strategies, especially when trying to increase sales volume, boost product visibility, or gain traction with new listings.

Moving beyond individual product promotion, Sponsored Brands offer a more immersive experience. These ads promote a collection of products under a single brand and appear prominently in search results, often featuring the brand's logo, a custom headline, and multiple products. This format is less about immediate conversion and more about brand storytelling and discovery. It introduces shoppers to the breadth of a product catalog, and it elevates brand presence by putting a name and narrative in front of the customer.

Sponsored Brands create opportunities to establish identity and recall. With customizable messaging and creative options, advertisers can communicate value propositions, highlight seasonal promotions, or push new product launches in a visually engaging format. These ads also link directly to a branded storefront or a custom landing page within Amazon, guiding users into a curated brand experience rather than a single product detail page. For brands seeking to increase awareness and build long-term recognition, this format offers a dynamic space to make a lasting impression.

Sponsored Display is where things begin to move beyond the boundaries of traditional search advertising. These ads are designed for cross-channel visibility and retargeting. They can appear on Amazon's own properties—like product detail pages, customer review pages, and the homepage—but also extend across third-party websites and apps through Amazon's network. This is a powerful tool for reinforcing brand exposure beyond the immediate moment of product search. It's particularly effective for recapturing the attention of shoppers who have previously viewed a product but haven't yet made a purchase.

One of the standout features of Sponsored Display is its ability to deliver behavior-driven targeting. Advertisers can reach audiences based on past engagement, interests, or shopping behaviors, allowing for a more personalized marketing approach. If a customer viewed a product, added it to a cart, or browsed similar items, Sponsored Display can keep the product front-of-mind even as they navigate other areas of the web. This type of advertising is essential for building customer touchpoints throughout the purchase funnel, nurturing awareness and nudging conversions over time.

Amazon DSP, or Demand-Side Platform, represents the most advanced and expansive level of advertising on Amazon. It allows advertisers to programmatically buy video, audio, and display ads at scale, not only on Amazon-owned properties like IMDb and Prime Video, but across thousands of third-party websites, mobile apps, and streaming services. This is where brand-building meets big data. Through DSP, advertisers access deep audience segmentation tools based on Amazon's vast repository of first-party consumer data.

What sets Amazon DSP apart from other advertising tools is its reach and intelligence. Advertisers can build highly detailed audience profiles based on shopping behavior, media consumption, lifestyle interests, or demographic information. These profiles allow brands to reach both new prospects and returning customers with unprecedented precision. The platform supports advanced ad formats including OTT (over-the-top) video ads, display banners, and audio ads that run across

Amazon Music and Alexa-enabled devices. It integrates seamlessly with Amazon's measurement tools, giving advertisers full visibility into campaign performance across various touchpoints.

For brands with larger budgets and long-term growth strategies, DSP opens up a new realm of possibility. It moves advertising into the realm of brand positioning, emotional storytelling, and large-scale audience engagement. It is especially useful for launching new product lines, entering new markets, or reinforcing a brand's image through repeated exposure across media. While it requires a more substantial investment than the self-service ad types, the returns are proportional to the effort and scale.

Together, these four ad types create a powerful ecosystem. Sponsored Products capture immediate purchase intent, driving volume through search results. Sponsored Brands elevate the entire brand identity, offering a richer and more comprehensive introduction to a seller's offerings. Sponsored Display extends reach across platforms and keeps products top-of-mind through intelligent retargeting. Amazon DSP takes everything to a higher level, giving brands the tools to run complex, multi-layered campaigns that move far beyond the point of sale.

Success lies in knowing how to balance and integrate these tools. A seller launching a new product might start with Sponsored Products to gain quick traction and test market response. As data comes in, layering in Sponsored Brands can help scale that product's presence while introducing other offerings. Sponsored Display can then be used to follow up with interested customers and increase retargeting efficiency. Once the brand has gained momentum and built enough demand, DSP can be employed to tell a broader story and fuel long-term growth with strategic placements across digital channels.

Mastering these ad formats also requires a deep understanding of campaign management, analytics, and budget optimization. Each type serves a different function and performs differently depending on the product category, customer intent, and creative quality. Advertisers must continuously monitor and adjust bids, creatives, and targeting parameters to stay ahead. What works for one product or audience segment may not work for another, which is why testing and iteration are essential.

In a crowded marketplace where every inch of visibility counts, knowing the distinctions and strengths of each ad format provides a competitive edge. It empowers advertisers to be agile and responsive, to test hypotheses and scale what works, and to build a brand presence that isn't just seen—but remembered. The Amazon advertising landscape is vast, but it's also structured, strategic, and responsive to data. With the right approach, these ad types aren't just tools—they're levers that can shift a product's trajectory, amplify brand voice, and transform a business's presence in the digital marketplace.

UNDERSTANDING THE CUSTOMER JOURNEY ON AMAZON PRIME

Understanding the customer journey on Amazon Prime is essential for any brand seeking to thrive within the world's most powerful digital marketplace. This journey isn't a straight line. It doesn't follow a single path from interest to purchase. Instead, it's a dynamic, multi-touch experience influenced by discovery, trust, convenience, and value—factors that Amazon has meticulously designed its platform around. The key to advertising success lies in understanding each step of this journey and aligning ad strategies to meet the customer where they are, with the right message at the right moment.

The first phase of this journey often begins before the customer consciously decides to make a purchase. This is the awareness stage, and in Amazon's world, it can take place anywhere within its massive digital ecosystem. It might start with a product recommendation while browsing, a sponsored video ad on Prime Video, or even through content streamed on Fire TV or Alexa-enabled devices. This stage is subtle, driven by algorithms that predict what a customer might be interested in based on past behavior, search patterns, or shopping history. A well-placed ad here isn't just presenting a product—it's planting a seed.

What makes this moment so influential is the passive trust users have in the platform. Amazon Prime members, in particular, are deeply embedded in the Amazon universe. They rely on it for everything from entertainment to household goods, making them uniquely receptive to the ideas and suggestions served to them. At this stage, they aren't necessarily looking for a specific product, but they are open to discovering something that catches their interest. Brands that invest in visually compelling, emotionally resonant ads—especially through formats like Sponsored Brands or video ads—can stand out by capturing attention without being invasive.

As the journey progresses, the customer moves into the consideration stage. Here, intent becomes clearer. They begin typing keywords into the search bar, browsing categories, reading product titles, glancing at reviews, and comparing price points. This is where data-driven targeting becomes critical. Amazon's powerful advertising tools ensure that the products most relevant to the customer's intent rise to the top. Sponsored Products are particularly effective here because they show up as native listings, seamlessly blending with organic search results and offering a natural next step for the customer.

During consideration, the customer isn't just evaluating a product—they're evaluating a seller. Brand presence becomes crucial. Customers pay attention to ratings, review volume, shipping times, and even the visual quality of a listing. Advertisers who have invested in

Sponsored Brands, branded storefronts, and enhanced product content create a more immersive and reassuring experience. A professional presentation signals legitimacy and trustworthiness. When a customer sees a consistent brand story across multiple touchpoints, their confidence grows. They may not click "Buy Now" immediately, but the brand gains mental real estate.

This phase also involves a lot of back-and-forth. Customers may add products to their cart and leave them there for days. They may browse on a mobile device during a commute and then revisit the same product later on a desktop. They might search for related items to compare or click on ads that take them to complementary product categories. All of this digital behavior creates a cloud of intent that advertisers can tap into using retargeting tools like Sponsored Display and Amazon DSP. These ads remind the customer of what they liked and encourage them to return and complete the purchase.

Then comes the decision-making stage—the tipping point. Here, the customer has moved from passive curiosity to active buying mode. They're no longer looking for information; they're confirming their choice. Small details become large influencers: delivery time, Prime shipping eligibility, price competitiveness, number of five-star reviews, and ease of return. If a brand has done its job in previous stages, this decision becomes a formality. The product already feels familiar. The seller feels reliable. The customer clicks the purchase button with confidence, often influenced by a subtle mix of targeted advertising and built-in Amazon benefits.

What sets Amazon Prime apart is the speed and efficiency of this decision-making process. Thanks to one-click buying, saved payment methods, and free two-day shipping, customers can go from consideration to purchase in a matter of seconds. Unlike other platforms that might require multiple redirects or verifications, Amazon makes the transaction almost frictionless. This rapid execution means brands need to have their infrastructure and advertising strategies tightly aligned. There's no time for second impressions.

But the journey doesn't end at the sale—it evolves into post-purchase engagement. Customers return to Amazon to track their order, read follow-up emails, leave reviews, and in many cases, purchase related items. This creates a new opportunity for advertisers. Brands that use Sponsored Display or DSP to target previous buyers with complementary products can increase customer lifetime value. For example, someone who buys a camera may soon be shown ads for lenses, tripods, or editing software. Amazon's ecosystem is built for this kind of fluid, ongoing marketing cycle. Each interaction feeds into the next, forming a loop rather than a line.

Reviews also play a critical role in this stage. Happy customers become brand advocates, whether they realize it or not. Their ratings and testimonials influence future buyers in the awareness and consideration phases. That's why customer satisfaction must be a core part of any advertising strategy. The journey might start with a well-placed ad, but it's sustained by a product that delivers on its promise and a brand that follows through on its messaging.

Beyond product-specific journeys, Amazon Prime also fosters brand loyalty. A customer who has a positive experience with a seller is more likely to return to that brand in the future, even for unrelated products. That's the silent power of brand consistency within Amazon. When advertising, listings, shipping, and customer service all align, the brand becomes a trusted name within the buyer's personal marketplace. Over time, repeat customers begin skipping search altogether. They go straight to the brand's storefront, knowing exactly what they're looking for. That's not just a conversion—it's a transformation of buyer behavior.

The journey also varies across devices and times of day. Customers may first discover a product while watching Prime Video on their smart TV, then search for it again on their phone, and finally purchase it through a desktop interface. Each touchpoint requires consistency in messaging, visual branding, and user experience. Sellers must think holistically, not just about the ad that gets the click, but about the experience that keeps the customer moving forward regardless of how or when they interact with the platform.

This multi-device, multi-moment customer journey is where Amazon's unified ecosystem shines. It's not just about having products listed or running ads—it's about participating in an environment where entertainment, shopping, and information are interwoven. The customer's path to purchase is fluid and often unpredictable, but Amazon's tools give sellers the ability to stay visible, relevant, and persuasive at every step.

Understanding this journey means thinking like a customer while acting like a strategist. It requires seeing the platform not as a vending machine, but as a living, breathing marketplace where habits are formed, preferences evolve, and brands are built over time. Advertising on Amazon Prime is about more than selling a product—it's about guiding a customer through a complete experience, from curiosity to conversion, and ideally, to lasting loyalty. When that journey is respected, understood, and nurtured, the results speak not just in revenue, but in brand equity and long-term success.

SETTING CLEAR ADVERTISING GOALS AND KPIS

No advertising campaign on Amazon—or anywhere else—can thrive without a clear understanding of what it is meant to achieve. Without direction, data loses its meaning. Metrics become noise instead of insight. Spending spirals without control. The cornerstone of successful advertising is the intentional setting of goals and the careful selection of Key Performance Indicators, or KPIs, to track progress. These are not just business buzzwords. They are the navigational tools that ensure every dollar spent moves the brand closer to a tangible result. They transform advertising from a gamble into a strategy.

Advertising goals must be more than vague aspirations. "Increase sales" or "get more clicks" may sound good, but they lack the specificity necessary to guide meaningful action. A well-defined goal goes deeper. It describes a precise outcome, a timeline for achieving it, and a rationale for why it matters. For some brands, the goal might be to launch a new product and achieve a specific number of units sold within the first three months. For others, it might be to boost brand visibility in a crowded category, capture new-to-brand customers, or increase the average order value. Each of these objectives requires a different approach, a different message, and a different measure of success.

Clarity of goals begins with self-awareness. Sellers must ask fundamental questions about where they are in their growth journey. Is the brand in its infancy, trying to establish a presence and attract initial reviews? Is it in a scaling phase, trying to capture greater market share and outpace competitors? Or is it in a maturity phase, seeking to optimize return on ad spend while maintaining a dominant position? Each phase demands different strategies and, by extension, different goals.

Once the purpose of the campaign is locked in, KPIs become the scoreboard. These are the metrics that will tell the story of performance. But not all KPIs are created equal. The key is to select those that align directly with the goal, offering a clear cause-and-effect relationship between the actions taken and the results achieved. If the goal is to drive awareness, then impressions, reach, and click-through rate may be the most telling metrics. If the goal is to increase conversions, then conversion rate, cost-per-click, and ACoS (Advertising Cost of Sales) come into sharper focus.

ACoS, in particular, is one of the most critical KPIs in the Amazon advertising landscape. It represents the percentage of sales that are spent on advertising. A low ACoS suggests efficiency; a high ACoS may signal over-investment or poor targeting. However, ACoS must be understood within context. A high ACoS may be acceptable—or even strategic—when launching a new product or entering a competitive market. In such cases, the focus may be on visibility and sales velocity, not short-term profitability. Understanding this nuance is essential. A campaign can be technically "inefficient" but strategically brilliant if it accomplishes a broader objective, such as boosting organic rankings or winning the Buy Box more frequently.

Another vital KPI is ROAS—Return on Advertising Spend. While similar to ACoS, ROAS flips the equation to show how much revenue is generated for each dollar spent on ads. It's a favorite metric among finance-focused marketers because it ties performance directly to the bottom line. But like ACoS, ROAS must be interpreted in the light of campaign intent. Chasing a high ROAS at the expense of growth or brand exposure can lead to overly conservative strategies that stunt momentum.

Click-through rate (CTR) is yet another critical indicator, offering insights into how compelling the ad creative is and how well it matches customer intent. A low CTR may indicate poor keyword selection, uninspiring product images, or irrelevant messaging. A high CTR means the ad is capturing attention—but it must be followed by solid conversion performance to be meaningful. CTR alone cannot carry a campaign; it simply opens the door. What happens after the click matters even more.

Conversion rate, then, becomes the next focal point. This metric reveals how effectively a product page turns traffic into buyers. It ties directly to the quality of the listing—images, descriptions, bullet points, A+ content, pricing, shipping options, and reviews. If conversion rates are lagging, even the most well-targeted and well-funded campaign will fail to deliver satisfactory returns. Advertising and product presentation must work hand-in-hand, with the former driving traffic and the latter closing the deal.

Beyond these core KPIs, there are other valuable metrics that serve more nuanced purposes. New-to-brand customer rate, for instance, helps sellers understand whether their campaigns are attracting first-time buyers or simply recycling existing ones. This is especially important for brands looking to expand their reach or launch new product lines. Similarly, detail page views can indicate how effective an ad is at driving deeper engagement, while time-on-page and bounce rate—measured through Amazon Attribution and DSP tools—can offer deeper behavioral insights for off-Amazon campaigns.

The timing of goal-setting and KPI selection is as crucial as the metrics themselves. These elements should be locked in before a campaign goes live—not after the fact. Too often, advertisers look at whatever data is available post-launch and try to retrofit a narrative around it. This backward approach leads to vanity metrics and misaligned expectations. Instead, campaigns should be architected with intent. The goals dictate the strategy, the strategy informs the tactics, and the KPIs validate the execution.

Goals also need timelines. Without a time horizon, performance cannot be properly evaluated. A campaign designed to build brand awareness over six months should not be judged by its sales volume after one week. Likewise, a promotional push for a holiday weekend should be monitored in real-time with rapid adjustments to bidding, targeting, and creative. KPIs are not static—they must be read in rhythm with the campaign's lifecycle.

Flexibility is also essential. As campaigns progress, goals may evolve based on market response, competitive activity, or internal business shifts. Smart advertisers revisit their objectives regularly, asking whether the original goal still holds or whether new priorities have emerged. A flexible mindset allows for dynamic optimization. Budgets can be reallocated to high-performing campaigns. Keywords can be refined. Creative can be refreshed. KPIs can be adjusted to reflect changing realities without losing sight of the larger mission.

Above all, setting clear advertising goals and KPIs empowers accountability. It creates transparency across teams, aligning marketers, executives, and product managers around a shared definition of success. It also supports better decision-making. When campaigns are driven by clear objectives and measured by meaningful data, it becomes easier to justify spending, defend strategy, and refine execution. Conversations move from gut instinct to grounded analysis.

Even in failure, there is value. When a campaign underperforms, having clear goals and KPIs allows advertisers to diagnose the issue. Was it a targeting problem? A creative mismatch? A pricing disadvantage? With the right framework in place, answers come faster, and recovery becomes possible. Data turns into insight. Insight leads to innovation. Innovation, over time, fuels mastery.

In the rapidly evolving world of Amazon advertising, where algorithms shift and competitors multiply, clarity is the anchor. Goals keep the focus sharp. KPIs keep the performance honest. Together, they form the language of intelligent advertising—a language that separates the hopeful from the strategic, the passive from the proactive, and the ordinary from the exceptional. With these tools, advertisers stop shooting in the dark. They begin building with purpose.

CHAPTER 1
NAVIGATING THE AMAZON ADVERTISING CONSOLE

ACCOUNT SETUP AND STRUCTURE

Getting your advertising account properly set up and structured on Amazon is the first crucial step toward building a campaign that doesn't just function, but performs with precision and purpose. This foundational layer determines how easily you can track performance, scale your advertising efforts, troubleshoot problems, and make smart, timely decisions. While many sellers rush into launching campaigns to generate immediate traffic and sales, skipping over or underestimating the setup and organizational strategy often leads to chaos later—fragmented data, unclear budget allocation, and disjointed reporting that can blur the line between growth and guesswork.

Everything begins with gaining access to Amazon's advertising console. For third-party sellers, this typically means being enrolled in Amazon's Brand Registry. Without this verification, your ability to run advanced ad types—like Sponsored Brands and Sponsored Display—is limited. Brand Registry not only opens the doors to more powerful advertising tools, but also provides a suite of brand-building features, including enhanced content and access to Amazon Stores, which can dramatically improve the customer's shopping experience. For vendors or first-party sellers, the process may differ slightly, but access to the advertising console remains consistent in terms of its interface and structure.

Once inside the console, the real work begins. How you structure your advertising account is a direct reflection of your business logic. If your campaigns don't mirror your product lines, goals, and audience segments, your performance data will be messy and unmanageable. Imagine walking into a retail store where all products are thrown together in one pile— apparel, electronics, kitchen supplies, all jumbled with no sense of category or purpose. That's what a poorly organized ad account looks like from the inside. You can still make sales, but you'll never know what's working, what's underperforming, or where to invest your budget for the best returns.

At the campaign level, organization should reflect your strategic priorities. Campaigns are the highest-level containers in your account. Each one should represent a major initiative—perhaps a product category, a seasonal push, or a specific goal such as customer acquisition or clearance of slow-moving inventory. The name of the campaign should be both descriptive and consistent, ideally following a naming convention that includes the product or brand name, the ad type, and the objective. For example, a campaign titled "Kitchenware_SponsoredProducts_Launch" instantly tells you what it's about, helping you maintain clarity as your account grows.

Inside each campaign, you'll find ad groups, which allow for more granular targeting and budget control. Ad groups work best when they are tightly focused around a single theme—like a specific product type, customer demographic, or keyword set. The closer the alignment within an ad group, the more relevant your ads will be to the shopper's search intent, which can lead to higher click-through rates and better conversions. Ad groups are also where keyword bidding happens in Sponsored Products and Sponsored Brands, and where audience targeting is configured for Sponsored Display. Treating ad groups as strategic sub-divisions rather than catch-all containers leads to cleaner data and more precise optimizations.

Budgeting is another core part of account structure, and it deserves as much thought as campaign naming or keyword strategy. Amazon gives advertisers the option to set budgets at the campaign level, which makes planning straightforward—but it also introduces the risk of uneven spend if the structure isn't logical. For instance, if a single campaign includes both high-performing products and those still in testing, the weaker performers might cannibalize the budget. Splitting these out into separate campaigns or even accounts, if necessary, can ensure your best assets always receive adequate investment.

A well-structured account also makes performance analysis far more efficient. When each campaign and ad group is labeled accurately and built with a clear purpose, reviewing results becomes a simple matter of filtering. You can quickly answer questions like: How is our new product line performing? Are Sponsored Display ads outperforming Sponsored Products in the holiday season? Which keywords are driving conversions for our most competitive category? This clarity helps marketers respond faster and more accurately, whether they're scaling a winning campaign or cutting losses on underperformers.

Product targeting is another area where structure plays a critical role. For Sponsored Display and Sponsored Products campaigns that use ASIN targeting, grouping similar products together within a campaign ensures that cross-promotions are logical and beneficial. For example, if you're advertising a range of wireless earbuds, keeping all variations of that product within the same campaign allows you to analyze consumer preferences more holistically. It also gives you the opportunity to test different ad creative or copy tailored to specific models while maintaining a unified performance view.

Seasonal or event-based campaigns benefit from a slightly different organizational mindset. These should be treated as time-boxed projects with a clear start and end date, often with a dedicated budget and a focused product selection. Think Prime Day, Black Friday, or a back-to-school promotion. Building standalone campaigns for these efforts allows for clean measurement of promotional impact without contaminating the data from your always-on campaigns. Once the event is over, you can pause or archive these campaigns, leaving behind a dataset that's easy to revisit for planning future events.

An advanced but increasingly relevant layer of structure involves separating branded and non-branded traffic. In many categories, customers search either by brand name or by generic keywords. By creating separate campaigns to target each, advertisers gain greater control over how budget is allocated and how success is measured. Branded campaigns often convert at higher rates and deliver better ROAS, but they may not contribute to customer acquisition if shoppers were already looking for your brand. Non-branded campaigns, though typically more competitive and expensive, are where brand growth happens. Segmenting them allows you to scale more intelligently.

Account structure also influences team collaboration and reporting. As your business grows and multiple team members get involved in campaign management, naming conventions, folder hierarchies, and documentation practices become critical. Everyone needs to understand what each campaign is trying to do, which products it covers, and how success is defined. This shared understanding reduces errors, speeds up decision-making, and supports alignment between marketing, product, and executive teams.

Even more advanced advertisers may use portfolios—Amazon's feature for grouping campaigns under a single organizational unit. Portfolios can reflect brand divisions, business units, or regional markets. They are especially helpful for businesses running dozens or hundreds of campaigns at once. With portfolios, advertisers can apply budget caps, track spending by brand or product family, and streamline reporting. While not essential for every seller, portfolios become invaluable as complexity grows.

Maintaining the integrity of your account structure isn't a one-time event—it requires discipline over time. As new products launch, seasons change, and goals evolve, campaigns need to be reviewed and updated. Legacy campaigns that no longer serve a purpose should be archived. Ad groups with overlapping keywords should be reviewed for cannibalization. Budgets should be rebalanced based on performance. This is where having a solid foundation pays off. An organized account is easier to audit, optimize, and scale.

Ultimately, the way your account is set up speaks volumes about how you run your business. A scattered structure reflects a reactive mindset, while a streamlined, intentional setup demonstrates strategy and foresight. When campaigns, ad groups, and targeting strategies are aligned with your brand's goals, everything runs smoother—ads perform better, budgets stretch further, and reporting becomes a source of insight rather than confusion.

Getting the setup right from the beginning saves time, money, and frustration. It's the infrastructure that supports every impression, every click, and every sale that follows. In a platform as dynamic and data-rich as Amazon, clarity in structure is more than a best practice—it's a competitive advantage. The brands that succeed aren't just the ones with great products or big budgets. They're the ones that build their advertising operations with purpose, discipline, and long-term thinking from the very first step.

UNDERSTANDING THE DASHBOARD AND KEY METRICS

When navigating the advertising landscape on Amazon, the dashboard is your control center. It is where data flows in real time, campaigns are managed, insights are interpreted, and decisions take form. Understanding this dashboard and the key metrics it offers isn't just helpful—it's essential. Without a firm grasp of what the numbers mean, how they interconnect, and what they signify in context, any strategy will be built on guesswork rather than grounded insight. The dashboard is not simply a panel of statistics; it is the lens through which advertisers see how their investment performs and where their efforts need adjustment.

At first glance, the Amazon Ads dashboard can seem overwhelming, especially for those new to the platform. It features numerous performance indicators, filters, timelines, and visualizations that paint a multifaceted picture of campaign health. However, when dissected with care and attention, it reveals a clear and powerful narrative. Every chart, number, and percentage is a sentence in the story of how your products are competing, how your audience is engaging, and how your marketing dollars are returning—or not returning—value.

Central to this dashboard is the campaign manager, the hub where all running and past campaigns are listed. From this view, advertisers can monitor performance at a high level or drill down into the specifics of each campaign, ad group, and ad type. The dashboard is highly customizable, allowing you to filter by date range, ad type, targeting method, and even specific product ASINs. This flexibility is crucial because it lets advertisers extract exactly the data they need depending on their goals, be it brand awareness, product launches, or return on ad spend.

Among the most closely monitored metrics is impressions, which indicates how many times your ad has been shown to customers. While impressions don't guarantee engagement, they reveal the visibility your campaign is generating. A high impression count may suggest strong keyword alignment or broad targeting, whereas low impressions could signal an overly narrow audience or poor ad placement. But impressions alone are never enough to evaluate success. They must be weighed alongside engagement metrics to determine whether visibility is leading to meaningful action.

Click-through rate, or CTR, is one of those engagement metrics and serves as a litmus test for ad relevance. It tells you how many people who saw your ad actually clicked on it. A high CTR usually means your ad copy, product image, and placement are resonating with your audience. Conversely, a low CTR might indicate that your messaging is off, your images aren't compelling, or your ad is showing up for irrelevant searches. CTR, in this sense, becomes a diagnostic tool, helping you refine your creative and targeting strategies.

Then there's the all-important cost-per-click, or CPC, which is what you pay each time someone clicks on your ad. On Amazon's auction-based system, CPC can fluctuate widely depending on competition, keyword popularity, and ad relevance. While a lower CPC can mean more traffic for less spend, it doesn't always translate to profitability. In some categories, higher CPCs are justified if they lead to higher conversion rates. Understanding this balance is key. A successful campaign isn't always the cheapest; it's the one that generates profitable, sustainable sales.

Conversion rate is the next vital metric to watch. It measures how many clicks turn into purchases. A strong conversion rate typically reflects alignment between the shopper's intent and the product offering. It can also signal trust in the brand, competitive pricing, and high-quality product detail pages. When conversion rates are low, it usually indicates a problem beyond the ad itself—perhaps with the product title, images, pricing, reviews, or availability. Conversion rate tells you whether your ads are simply generating curiosity or actually closing the sale.

Another cornerstone of the dashboard is Advertising Cost of Sales, or ACoS. This percentage-based metric compares the amount you've spent on ads to the revenue those ads have generated. If you spent $100 and made $500 in sales, your ACoS would be 20%. It's a key indicator of profitability and efficiency. A low ACoS suggests a high return on investment, while a high ACoS may mean you're overspending for each sale. However, interpreting ACoS requires nuance. In a product launch phase, you may accept a higher ACoS to gain traction. For mature products, a lower ACoS might be the goal. ACoS is not a one-size-fits-all metric—it varies by product margin, lifecycle stage, and business objective.

For brands focused on long-term growth rather than immediate profit, Amazon also offers metrics related to New-to-Brand (NTB) sales. These indicate how many of your conversions came from customers who hadn't purchased from your brand in the last twelve months. This is a valuable lens through which to view acquisition strategies. If your campaign is bringing in a high number of new-to-brand customers, it may be more valuable than one with a lower ACoS but only repeat buyers. NTB data empowers marketers to balance short-term revenue with long-term customer acquisition goals.

In addition to the core metrics, the dashboard offers valuable data on spend, orders, units sold, and total sales generated by advertising. Each of these metrics contributes to the full picture of how ads are impacting your business. For example, tracking total sales helps tie your advertising performance back to overall business goals. Are your ads responsible for 10% or 60% of your revenue? Are certain campaigns leading to more units per order or higher average order values? These questions can be answered when you interpret the data in context.

Time-based trends are another powerful element of the dashboard. By selecting different date ranges, you can identify seasonality, promotional impact, or campaign fatigue. If a campaign suddenly drops in performance, looking at its historical data can help pinpoint when and why the change occurred. Perhaps a competitor entered the market. Maybe customer interest dipped post-holiday. The dashboard doesn't just show you where you are—it helps you understand how you got there and where you might be headed next.

Geographic performance is also accessible, allowing advertisers to see which regions are driving the most impressions, clicks, and sales. This information can inform not just your advertising strategy but also inventory planning and fulfillment priorities. If your ads are overperforming in a certain area, it might make sense to focus your budget there or increase local stock. The dashboard acts like a compass, helping you navigate not just where your customers are, but where your business should lean next.

Another often overlooked area is keyword and search term analysis. Within the dashboard, you can access the specific terms shoppers used that triggered your ads. This is incredibly valuable for refining targeting. It shows you which keywords are converting, which are wasting spend, and which new ones might be worth testing. Smart advertisers use this information to fine-tune their match types, add negative keywords to filter out irrelevant traffic, and identify long-tail opportunities that competitors might be ignoring.

The dashboard enables export functionality, letting you download reports in bulk. This allows for even deeper analysis in external tools like Excel or third-party analytics platforms. It also makes it easier to build presentations, run A/B tests, and build case studies for internal stakeholders. While the dashboard offers real-time insights, exports allow you to take that data further—to segment, pivot, compare, and strategize at a deeper level.

Understanding the Amazon Ads dashboard and the metrics it surfaces is not a matter of checking in now and then. It's about developing an ongoing relationship with your data. It means learning to spot trends early, diagnose problems quickly, and measure success meaningfully. Every number tells a story—not just about the ad, but about the customer, the market, the product, and the brand. When you treat the dashboard as a dynamic feedback loop rather than a static report, you unlock its true power—not just as a tracker, but as a roadmap to performance, profitability, and growth.

CAMPAIGN MANAGER OVERVIEW: NAVIGATION AND FEATURES

The Campaign Manager serves as the operational headquarters for every advertiser seeking success on Amazon. It's more than just a panel of numbers and buttons—it is the command center where strategies are launched, refined, and scaled. For anyone serious about mastering the platform, learning how to navigate this tool and understand its features is non-negotiable. Whether you're running a single Sponsored Products campaign or managing a robust portfolio across Sponsored Brands, Sponsored Display, and Amazon DSP, this interface provides the controls, the insights, and the real-time feedback that determine how effectively your advertising efforts will convert into sales and sustainable growth.

When logging into Amazon's advertising platform, the Campaign Manager is typically the first page you land on. At a glance, it offers a panoramic view of all your campaigns—active, paused, archived, or scheduled. The layout is built for clarity and responsiveness, allowing users to toggle between summary metrics and deep dives into performance. The interface, while powerful, is designed to be intuitive even for newcomers. A clean sidebar on the left organizes navigation, while the main panel populates with campaign data based on filters, timeframes, and metrics selected.

The default view showcases your campaigns in a table format, with each row representing an individual campaign and each column showing a different key performance indicator. This layout is fully customizable. You can choose which columns to display—such as impressions, clicks, spend, sales, ACoS, ROAS, CTR, and CPC—based on what's most relevant to your goals. The sort and filter functionalities further streamline the experience. Want to see only Sponsored Brands campaigns that have spent over $500 in the last week? Or perhaps identify which Sponsored Products campaigns are underperforming on ACoS? With a few clicks, the data reshapes to meet your inquiry, allowing for efficient oversight and decision-making.

Each campaign listed in the overview is clickable, serving as a gateway to more granular data. Drilling down into a specific campaign reveals its ad groups, each of which functions as a subset with its own keywords, bids, budget allocations, and performance metrics. From here, you can examine exactly how different parts of the campaign are performing. Perhaps one ad group is driving most of the conversions while another is consuming budget without delivering results. This nested hierarchy allows for micro-level adjustments without disrupting the overall campaign framework.

One of the most valuable features within Campaign Manager is the real-time performance tracker. Unlike some advertising platforms that have significant data delays, Amazon's interface updates frequently, allowing you to monitor the immediate impact of changes. This responsiveness supports an agile approach to campaign management. If you raise a bid, adjust a budget, or switch ad creatives, you don't have to wait days to gauge the result. The data reflects the outcome quickly, giving you the ability to double down on what's working or cut back on what's not.

Setting budgets and bids is another critical function embedded within the Campaign Manager. Budgets can be set at the campaign level, dictating the total amount to be spent over a day or the life of the campaign. Bids, on the other hand, can be managed at the keyword, product, or audience level, depending on the ad type. Amazon offers manual and automatic bidding strategies. In manual mode, advertisers have complete control over how much they're willing to pay per click. In automatic mode, Amazon's algorithm adjusts bids based on the likelihood of conversion. The platform even offers dynamic bidding options—up and down, down only, or fixed—to help advertisers better align spend with performance potential.

Another essential part of the Campaign Manager interface is the search term report access. Through this feature, advertisers can view the exact search terms customers used to trigger their ads. This information is critical for optimizing keyword strategy. High-performing search terms can be promoted to exact match in new campaigns, while irrelevant or costly ones can be added as negative keywords to avoid future waste. The data offers more than just tactical value; it reveals how your audience thinks, what language they use, and what they're truly seeking. Over time, this shapes not just ads, but product listings, content strategies, and even future product development.

Beyond performance and targeting, the Campaign Manager provides control over ad creatives. For Sponsored Brands and Sponsored Display, where visuals and messaging play a larger role, the interface allows advertisers to upload logos, customize headlines, and select landing pages or Store destinations. These elements can be previewed directly in the dashboard, ensuring the user experience aligns with your brand message. Having this creative control within the same system where performance is monitored closes the loop between design and data.

Campaign Manager also integrates reporting and export capabilities for deeper analysis. While the dashboard view offers on-the-fly insights, downloading reports allows advertisers to build trend lines, calculate month-over-month changes, and segment data across larger timeframes or product categories. Exported files can be opened in Excel, Google Sheets, or specialized analytics tools for custom evaluation. This becomes especially valuable when presenting performance to stakeholders, developing quarterly strategies, or building out attribution models.

For those managing multiple brands, regions, or product portfolios, the Campaign Manager supports organizational tools like portfolios and tags. Portfolios allow advertisers to group related campaigns together, making budgeting, tracking, and reporting more streamlined. For instance, if you're managing campaigns for two separate product lines—say electronics and home appliances—you can place each within its own portfolio, allocate a distinct budget, and analyze performance independently. Tags serve as flexible labels, helping categorize campaigns based on objectives, channels, or audience types. These organizational layers make it easier to scale operations while maintaining order.

Another significant feature is the campaign scheduler, which allows you to plan and automate your advertising calendar. You can create campaigns in advance and set them to activate or pause on specific dates. This is especially useful for time-sensitive promotions like seasonal sales, product launches, or holiday pushes. By scheduling campaigns in advance, you ensure timely execution without the need for manual intervention. This also helps prevent lapses in visibility during key revenue periods, giving your campaigns continuity and consistency.

Alerts and notifications are built into the interface as well. These provide real-time warnings when something goes wrong—a campaign runs out of budget, a product goes out of stock, or performance drops below a threshold. Such alerts act as guardrails, ensuring you can respond quickly to issues that could otherwise silently erode your return on investment. With the platform constantly monitoring itself, advertisers are free to focus on strategy without worrying about missing critical operational signals.

Moreover, the Campaign Manager provides a holistic view across different ad types. Instead of siloing Sponsored Products, Sponsored Brands, and Sponsored Display into separate tools, the interface unites them. This enables comparative analysis, helping you determine which ad types are most effective for each stage of the funnel or each type of product. For example, you might find that Sponsored Brands are best for new launches, while Sponsored Products deliver better results for established bestsellers. Seeing all of these campaigns side by side promotes smarter allocation of ad spend and more cohesive messaging across touchpoints.

User permissions and access levels are another thoughtful aspect of Campaign Manager, particularly for teams. Account owners can assign different roles to users, such as administrators, analysts, or creatives. This protects sensitive settings while still allowing for collaborative management. With the ability to share access without compromising control, Campaign Manager becomes scalable across departments, agencies, or brand partners.

Ultimately, mastery of the Campaign Manager comes from using it not just as a tool, but as a platform for experimentation, feedback, and iteration. It's where creativity meets logic, where strategy meets execution. By exploring its features fully, advertisers unlock more than visibility—they unlock control. And with that control comes the power to transform budgets into breakthroughs, clicks into customers, and insights into sustained growth. Every campaign launched through this interface is a test, a message, and a move in the larger game of e-commerce. Knowing how to use the dashboard is the first step; knowing how to interpret and act on what it reveals is where mastery truly begins.

BILLING AND PAYMENT INFORMATION

Navigating the billing and payment system within Amazon's advertising platform is crucial for maintaining a smooth and effective advertising strategy. Whether you are a small business owner, a large enterprise, or an agency managing multiple accounts, understanding how billing works is essential to ensure that your campaigns continue running without interruption, and your financial management is transparent and organized. The billing system on Amazon Ads is designed to be flexible and accessible, but to harness its full potential, it's important to familiarize yourself with its structure, how payments are processed, and how to manage your account to avoid unnecessary surprises.

At its core, the billing structure for Amazon advertising operates on a pay-per-click (PPC) model for most ad types, meaning you only pay when a customer clicks on your ad. This model ensures that advertisers are only spending money on actual engagement, rather than just for ad impressions. This kind of performance-based pricing helps ensure that your budget is spent more efficiently, as you are not paying simply for visibility, but for actual interactions with your products. Other ad types, such as display ads and video ads, may have different payment models, but the concept remains similar: payment is tied to performance metrics, either clicks, impressions, or video views, depending on the ad format and your campaign settings.

The first thing to understand when managing billing for your Amazon Ads account is the payment method. Amazon offers several options for funding your account, typically through credit cards, debit cards, or bank accounts. You'll need to link one or more payment methods to your account in order to activate and run campaigns. Amazon typically allows for flexibility in terms of the payment method you use, but it's important to note that your account will need to be fully funded in order to avoid campaign pauses due to insufficient funds. Having an active, up-to-date payment method linked to your account is critical to keeping your campaigns running smoothly.

Once you've linked your payment method, Amazon will bill your account based on your spending. The billing cycle can be either based on a pre-set daily budget or an overall monthly budget, depending on the way your campaign is structured. Each time your ad runs and accrues costs—whether through clicks, impressions, or other relevant metrics—the charges will accumulate. Amazon's platform operates on a threshold billing system, meaning that you are charged when your accumulated spending reaches a certain limit. Typically, this threshold is set to $1 for most advertisers, but this amount can vary depending on the country or region.

Billing cycles are typically monthly, but Amazon provides real-time updates on your balance and current spending, so you can track the performance and costs of your campaigns at any time. You can view your current spending, total budget, and how much you have left to spend within the Campaign Manager or billing dashboard. This transparency is crucial because it allows you to adjust your spending strategies in real time. If you notice that you're quickly reaching your budget limits or that certain campaigns are consuming funds faster than expected, you can pause or adjust bids to prevent overspending.

One of the benefits of Amazon's payment system is the ability to set a daily budget cap for each individual campaign. This means that you can control your ad spend by determining how much you are willing to spend on each campaign per day. If you have multiple campaigns running simultaneously, you can also set different daily budgets for each. This gives you granular control over how much money is allocated to each campaign based on its performance or importance. For example, if you're running a product launch campaign that you expect to generate a lot of traffic, you may set a higher daily budget for that particular ad. Conversely, if you have an underperforming ad, you may choose to lower its daily budget or pause it altogether until you can further optimize its performance.

Another critical aspect of the billing system is understanding how payments are processed and when they are due. Depending on your account history and reputation, Amazon may charge you on a rolling basis, or they may set a standard billing cycle based on your spend. Generally, if you're using a credit card as your payment method, Amazon will charge you automatically once your accumulated ad spend reaches the set billing threshold. For instance, if your total ad spend reaches $50, Amazon will charge your credit card for that amount. If your ad spend continues to increase, further charges will be processed in the same manner. This pay-as-you-go structure means that there are no upfront costs to worry about; instead, the cost of your advertising is spread out over the course of the month, depending on how quickly your ads generate clicks or impressions.

For users managing large-scale advertising campaigns with significant budgets, Amazon provides the option to apply for a monthly invoicing program. This program is typically available for advertisers who spend a certain minimum threshold on ads and have established a good payment history with Amazon. The monthly invoicing program provides the advantage of receiving a monthly statement and settling the balance at the end of the month, rather than having to make payments each time a billing threshold is reached. This can help businesses that have cash flow concerns or those who prefer to manage their advertising costs on a larger, more predictable scale.

Understanding invoicing is particularly important for advertisers who need detailed reporting for accounting or tax purposes. Amazon provides comprehensive invoicing and receipt documentation that you can access at any time through the billing section of the platform. These invoices will break down the costs associated with each campaign, ad group, and individual ad, showing you how much was spent on clicks, impressions, or any other payment-triggering event. For businesses that need to reconcile advertising costs with broader financial reporting, these invoices serve as an essential tool.

In the case that your account accrues unpaid balances, Amazon's system has safeguards in place to prevent further campaigns from running. If your account reaches a state of overdue payments, Amazon will pause all active campaigns until the outstanding balance is settled. It's critical to stay on top of your billing to avoid these disruptions. The dashboard will provide alerts if your payment method is invalid, or if you're nearing your credit limit. This allows you to resolve payment issues quickly before they impact the performance of your campaigns.

Refunds are another important consideration within Amazon's billing system. While refunds aren't commonly issued for advertising costs, there are situations where Amazon may provide credit if there is an issue with the ad placement, or if there are discrepancies due to technical issues. For example, if your ad ran in a location that violated Amazon's advertising policies or if there was an error that resulted in overcharging, Amazon may issue a refund or credit to your account. In these cases, the platform will typically send you an email notification outlining the refund or credit process.

For advertisers managing multiple accounts or brands, Amazon provides the option to set up consolidated billing. This allows you to manage several campaigns under one single payment method, simplifying the process of tracking and paying for advertising costs across multiple accounts. This can be particularly useful for agencies or large organizations managing numerous product lines or regions. With consolidated billing, all advertising charges across accounts are aggregated into one statement, making it easier to manage financial reporting and streamline payments.

It's also worth noting that Amazon's billing system supports multiple currencies, making it a globally accessible platform for advertisers. Whether you are running campaigns in the U.S., the UK, Japan, or India, the billing system accommodates different currencies and ensures that exchange rates are applied accurately. This is particularly valuable for businesses with international reach or those advertising across multiple regions, as it reduces the complexity of dealing with foreign exchange rates and simplifies payment management.

Managing billing and payment for Amazon Ads requires careful attention to ensure that your campaigns continue to run smoothly and that there are no surprises when it comes to costs. By understanding the payment structure, setting budgets wisely, and staying on top of invoicing and payment schedules, advertisers can maintain control over their advertising spend and maximize the impact of their campaigns. With a clear understanding of how the billing system operates, you can focus on what matters most—optimizing your campaigns, growing your business, and achieving long-term success.

STAYING UPDATED WITH AMAZON ADVERTISING NEWS AND UPDATES

In the rapidly evolving world of digital advertising, staying updated with the latest trends, changes, and updates is crucial for any advertiser seeking to remain competitive, particularly on platforms as dynamic as Amazon. With new features, tools, and best practices constantly being introduced, keeping up with Amazon Advertising news and updates is not only important—it's essential for ensuring that your campaigns are optimized and your strategy remains aligned with the platform's ever-evolving landscape.

The first step in staying updated is understanding the pace at which Amazon's advertising platform evolves. Amazon continuously adds new advertising products, refines existing features, and makes adjustments to its algorithms. These updates can directly impact how your ads perform, how your targeting is applied, and how you can optimize your campaigns. Missing out on these updates can result in missed opportunities or, worse, advertising inefficiencies that cost you money. To stay ahead of the curve, it's important to make staying informed a regular part of your advertising strategy.

One of the most reliable ways to stay updated with Amazon Advertising changes is by subscribing to Amazon's official communication channels. The Amazon Advertising blog is a primary resource where the platform announces new features, best practices, and case studies. It provides an in-depth look at changes to ad formats, updates to bidding strategies, and tips for advertisers looking to maximize their performance on the platform. Regularly checking this blog will keep you well-informed about any significant shifts in advertising policies or new tools that could benefit your campaigns.

Amazon also maintains a dedicated help and support section for advertisers, which provides detailed guides, FAQs, and troubleshooting information. As updates are made to the platform, this support hub is often the first place to reflect those changes. It's especially helpful when you need to dive into the specifics of how a new feature or tool works. Additionally, Amazon's help section offers educational content on how to better use its advertising tools, making it an indispensable resource for both beginners and seasoned professionals.

To complement these official sources, industry-specific websites and forums can provide valuable insights. Websites that cover e-commerce and digital marketing, such as Search Engine Journal, Marketing Land, and WordStream, regularly report on changes within Amazon Advertising. These platforms offer expert commentary, analyses, and recommendations based on their research and experience with the platform. Following these sources will help you understand not only the "what" and "how" of Amazon's updates, but also the "why" behind them, which can be critical for adapting your strategy effectively.

Beyond news sites, there are communities and forums where Amazon advertisers frequently discuss updates and share their experiences. These forums can be particularly helpful because they offer real-world examples of how updates impact actual campaigns. Platforms like Reddit, in particular, have active communities dedicated to e-commerce and Amazon advertising. These forums provide a space for users to ask questions, share successes and failures, and discuss the most recent updates. By engaging in these communities, you can learn from the experiences of others and apply that knowledge to your own campaigns.

Another way to stay ahead of Amazon's updates is by following key influencers and thought leaders in the e-commerce and digital advertising space. Many of these individuals or organizations specialize in Amazon advertising and frequently share their insights through social media channels like Twitter, LinkedIn, and YouTube. Some run newsletters or post regular blog updates with a focus on Amazon's ad ecosystem, providing actionable tips and strategies for staying on top of the latest trends.

Moreover, Amazon hosts a variety of events and webinars that provide in-depth looks at upcoming features, tools, and best practices. Events such as the Amazon Ads Summit and various training programs give advertisers an opportunity to interact with Amazon's own team and gain firsthand knowledge about new product features or strategies. These events are often exclusive, providing early access to information that could give you a competitive advantage in your advertising campaigns. They also offer a space for networking, which can be invaluable for discussing strategies and solutions with other advertisers in the same industry.

For advertisers managing large or complex campaigns, leveraging third-party advertising software or platforms can be an additional way to stay updated. Many of these tools integrate with Amazon Advertising and offer their own news feeds, alerts, or insights. For instance, platforms like Helium 10, Jungle Scout, and Sellics provide not only tracking and analytics features but also news updates and educational resources tailored to Amazon sellers and advertisers. By using these tools, you can receive notifications about updates and changes to the Amazon Advertising platform in real time, ensuring that you're always working with the most current data and tools.

The importance of staying updated goes beyond simply knowing what's new on the platform. Understanding how these changes impact your campaigns is just as important. For example, if Amazon introduces a new targeting option or bidding strategy, knowing how to implement it effectively can make a significant difference in your ad performance. Changes to Amazon's algorithm may affect how your ads are ranked or when they are shown, so being aware of these updates will allow you to optimize your bidding strategies or adjust your creative content in response. Additionally, understanding changes to Amazon's reporting tools or analytics features can help you interpret performance data more effectively, giving you the ability to make informed decisions and further refine your strategy.

A key component of staying updated is also anticipating future changes and trends. While Amazon doesn't always disclose what updates are coming down the pipeline, you can often spot emerging patterns based on past behavior and market demands. For example, as Amazon continues to prioritize voice search and Alexa-enabled devices, advertisers may see new opportunities to target customers through voice-enabled ads or more granular location-based targeting. By observing how Amazon is positioning itself within the broader e-commerce ecosystem, you can start to prepare your strategy for potential changes.

Additionally, as Amazon Advertising becomes more integrated with other Amazon services, such as Amazon Prime Video or Amazon Fresh, advertisers should stay informed about how these integrations can be leveraged for more comprehensive advertising strategies. For instance, Amazon Prime Video advertising may be an increasingly important channel for advertisers seeking to capture the attention of viewers on the platform. Understanding how to combine different advertising formats across Amazon's ecosystem will allow you to create more holistic campaigns that reach customers across various touchpoints, from search results to streaming content.

One of the most critical aspects of staying updated is implementing what you learn into your campaigns. Even if you're constantly consuming news and updates, putting that information into action is what ultimately moves the needle. Whether it's adjusting your bidding strategy based on a new feature, trying out a new ad format, or reevaluating your targeting based on updated insights, continuously testing and optimizing your campaigns based on the latest trends is essential. Amazon Advertising gives you the tools to make these adjustments in real-time, and by staying informed, you ensure that you're not just keeping up with the competition—you're staying ahead of it.

It's important to stay consistent in your efforts to stay updated. Set aside time regularly to read up on the latest updates, attend relevant webinars, and engage with the community. With Amazon Ads constantly evolving, the effort you put into staying informed will pay off in improved campaign performance, better ad spend efficiency, and ultimately, more sales. Being proactive about updates and adapting your strategies in response is what separates successful advertisers from those who struggle to keep up with the platform's pace.

CHAPTER 2
DEFINING YOUR TARGET AUDIENCE ON AMAZON PRIME

UNDERSTANDING PRIME DEMOGRAPHICS AND BUYING BEHAVIORS

To fully capitalize on the power of Amazon Prime for advertising, it's essential to understand the platform's demographics and buying behaviors. Amazon Prime members represent a highly valuable and engaged audience, and gaining insights into their habits, preferences, and purchasing patterns can significantly enhance the effectiveness of your advertising strategy. These consumers are not just casual shoppers; they are loyal, motivated buyers who demonstrate specific behaviors that set them apart from non-members. Understanding these nuances can help you tailor your ads in ways that resonate with Prime members, leading to higher conversions, more sales, and better return on investment (ROI).

Amazon Prime members are generally seen as the core of Amazon's most loyal customer base. With a vast and expanding membership, Prime customers have a number of key characteristics that are important to understand. One of the most significant traits of Prime members is their purchasing frequency. Prime members tend to shop more often and spend more on average than non-members. This heightened engagement is largely due to the exclusive benefits that come with a Prime membership, such as free shipping, access to Prime Video and Prime Music, and exclusive discounts. As a result, Prime members are conditioned to shop frequently and with fewer barriers, making them a highly desirable target for advertisers.

Understanding the typical demographic profile of Prime members is crucial for targeting ads more effectively. While Prime has a broad and diverse user base, certain trends have emerged that can guide your advertising strategy. For instance, Prime members are generally more affluent than non-members, with a significant portion of them falling within higher income brackets. Studies have shown that a majority of Prime members earn above-average household incomes, which can indicate a higher disposable income for spending on products advertised through Amazon. As such, products that cater to higher-end markets or offer premium features tend to perform better with this demographic.

Age-wise, Prime members are typically in the 25 to 54 age range, a group that encompasses both young professionals and established individuals in their peak earning years. This age range suggests that Prime members are likely to be working adults with busy lifestyles who value convenience. They are accustomed to the speed and efficiency Amazon offers, and this preference for convenience often translates into purchasing behaviors that prioritize fast delivery options, ease of use, and competitive pricing. The increasing prevalence of family households within this demographic also means that Prime members often make purchasing decisions that impact the whole family, which could influence the types of products they are more likely to buy.

An essential aspect of understanding Prime member demographics is acknowledging the geographical spread of Prime users. While Amazon Prime is available in many countries, the demographics can vary from region to region. For instance, Prime members in urban areas tend to have different buying habits compared to those in rural areas. Urban consumers are often more tech-savvy and open to buying innovative products or services, while rural consumers may place higher value on products related to home and family needs. Recognizing these regional variations allows advertisers to tailor their campaigns to be more relevant and appealing to specific geographical areas.

When it comes to buying behavior, Prime members exhibit some notable trends. One of the most significant behaviors is the tendency to purchase with a sense of urgency, driven by the Prime benefits. Free two-day shipping and same-day delivery create an expectation for fast fulfillment, leading to quicker purchasing decisions. Prime members often make purchases based on the desire for immediate gratification, meaning they are more likely to buy items with minimal hesitation, especially when the purchase offers immediate utility or convenience.

Moreover, Prime members are more likely to make repeat purchases. The subscription model of Amazon Prime fosters a sense of loyalty, and members who have been subscribed for a longer period are often more inclined to return to Amazon for future purchases. This repeat behavior is further fueled by the fact that Prime members are often exposed to tailored recommendations based on their past buying history. Amazon's sophisticated recommendation engine makes it easier for Prime members to discover products that are in line with their interests and previous purchases, which drives higher conversion rates. By advertising to Prime members, you are often engaging with a consumer who has already shown a strong propensity to buy, making them more likely to act on targeted advertising.

In addition to these general purchasing behaviors, Prime members are also highly receptive to deals and discounts. While they are accustomed to the value that their membership offers, they are still motivated by additional savings. This is why promotions such as Amazon Prime Day and Lightning Deals can be especially effective when targeted toward Prime users. Advertising strategies that emphasize limited-time offers or exclusive discounts can be highly effective in driving conversions among this demographic. By leveraging the sense of exclusivity associated with Prime membership, you can create a sense of urgency that encourages members to act quickly.

Another key feature of Prime member behavior is the increasing trend toward voice shopping. With the growing adoption of Amazon's Alexa and other voice-activated devices, Prime members are becoming more comfortable making purchases through voice commands. This shift toward voice commerce is something advertisers need to be aware of when planning their campaigns. Creating ads that are optimized for voice search and integrating voice-friendly calls to action can help you capture the attention of Prime members who prefer using voice assistants to shop. Voice shopping is also changing the way customers discover products, as it allows users to place orders with minimal friction, making the entire process more seamless and convenient.

Prime members are also avid content consumers, particularly through Amazon Prime Video, which is one of the platform's most popular services. Many Prime members not only subscribe to enjoy movies and TV shows but also to gain access to original content that can't be found elsewhere. This opens up new opportunities for advertisers to place ads within Amazon's video ecosystem. Whether it's through pre-roll ads on Prime Video or within other content experiences such as Amazon Music or Audible, there are increasing opportunities for advertisers to engage with Prime members in ways that integrate seamlessly into their media consumption habits. Understanding that Prime members consume a substantial amount of content allows advertisers to craft campaigns that tap into these entertainment experiences, leveraging emotional connections or product placements within shows and movies to drive engagement.

As the shopping experience continues to evolve, Prime members are also showing a growing preference for mobile commerce. With smartphones and tablets becoming an integral part of daily life, more and more Prime members are making purchases directly from their mobile devices. This shift toward mobile shopping means that advertisers must ensure their campaigns are mobile-optimized, offering a smooth, user-friendly experience on smaller screens. Ads that are too complex or difficult to navigate on mobile devices will result in poor performance, so understanding mobile behaviors is essential for creating effective campaigns.

Additionally, Prime members are often highly influenced by user-generated content, such as reviews and ratings. Many Prime members will make their purchase decisions based on the experiences of others, so ensuring your products have positive reviews can significantly impact your ad performance. Prime members trust Amazon's review system, and the social proof provided by past customers can be a powerful factor in encouraging new purchases. When advertising to this audience, consider leveraging positive reviews, testimonials, or influencer endorsements to build trust and increase the likelihood of conversion.

To successfully target Prime members with advertising, it's important to understand these consumer behaviors and preferences in detail. The ability to tailor ads based on demographic insights—such as age, income, family status, location, and shopping habits—can significantly enhance the relevance of your messaging. Additionally, adapting your ads to align with the increasing preference for convenience, urgency, and seamless shopping experiences will increase the chances of driving higher engagement and conversion rates.

By understanding the demographics and buying behaviors of Amazon Prime members, you can craft highly targeted campaigns that resonate with this lucrative audience. With Prime members being more frequent, loyal, and engaged shoppers, they present an incredible opportunity for advertisers. The key to success lies in recognizing their unique characteristics, understanding their motivations, and delivering personalized, timely ads that align with their expectations. By doing so, you position yourself to not only capture their attention but also drive meaningful results from your advertising efforts on Amazon.

LEVERAGING AMAZON'S AUDIENCE TARGETING OPTIONS

When it comes to advertising on Amazon, understanding and leveraging the platform's audience targeting options is critical for maximizing the effectiveness of your campaigns. Amazon provides advertisers with a robust suite of tools to segment their audience in highly specific ways, allowing for the creation of customized and precise advertising strategies that speak directly to the needs and behaviors of potential customers. The platform's advanced targeting features empower advertisers to refine their reach, enhance engagement, and ultimately drive sales by connecting with the right audience at the right time. In this section, we will explore how you can make the most of Amazon's audience targeting options and implement them in a way that generates maximum impact for your campaigns.

Amazon's targeting capabilities are grounded in its vast data ecosystem, which includes invaluable insights into consumer behavior, purchasing habits, and search patterns. This data enables advertisers to segment their audience based on a range of factors, making it possible to create highly relevant and personalized advertising experiences. One of the most powerful aspects of Amazon's audience targeting options is its ability to target based on past behaviors—such as previous purchases, search activity, and viewing history—allowing for highly specific ad placements. By utilizing these insights, you can ensure that your ads are seen by users who are most likely to engage with your products, leading to higher conversion rates.

The first and perhaps most fundamental form of audience targeting available on Amazon is based on keywords. When creating ads on Amazon, you can target users based on the search terms they input into the platform. This type of targeting is especially effective for Sponsored Products campaigns, where your ads are shown in search results for relevant keywords. The more specific your keyword targeting, the more likely it is that your ads will appear to users who are actively searching for products similar to yours. In this way, you can capture the attention of shoppers who are already interested in purchasing items within your category, increasing the likelihood that they will click on your ad and make a purchase.

While keyword targeting is essential, Amazon offers several other targeting options that allow you to fine-tune your strategy even further. One of these is product targeting, which enables you to target your ads to specific products, categories, or brands. Product targeting works by placing your ads on product detail pages or in search results for specific products that are similar or complementary to yours. For example, if you are selling a kitchen appliance, you could target your ads to appear alongside other popular kitchen appliance listings or on the detail pages of related products. This type of targeting works well for cross-selling and up-selling, as it allows you to capture the attention of customers who are already in the process of making a purchase in a similar product category.

Another powerful targeting tool that Amazon provides is audience targeting, which focuses on customer demographics, behaviors, and interests. With audience targeting, you can zero in on specific consumer groups based on various criteria, such as age, income level, location, shopping behavior, and even lifestyle interests. Amazon segments its audience based on the information it collects through its vast array of services, including Prime membership, Amazon Fresh, Amazon Music, and Amazon Video. This rich data allows advertisers to segment their audience into distinct groups, such as frequent shoppers, tech enthusiasts, or eco-conscious consumers. By targeting these specific segments, you can craft ads that are much more relevant to the needs and desires of your audience, enhancing the chances that they will engage with your brand.

Remarketing is another highly effective form of audience targeting available on Amazon. Remarketing involves targeting customers who have previously interacted with your products or visited your product detail pages but did not complete a purchase. By displaying ads to these customers as they browse other areas of Amazon, you can remind them of your product and encourage them to return and complete their purchase. This strategy leverages the principle of recency, which suggests that customers are more likely to buy when reminded of a product they've already shown interest in. Remarketing can significantly increase your conversion rates because it targets individuals who are already familiar with your brand and have demonstrated intent to purchase.

For advertisers who want to dive even deeper into targeting options, Amazon also offers the ability to leverage Amazon's Audience Insights and Audience Insights reports. These reports provide valuable data on the shopping behaviors and preferences of different audience segments, allowing you to refine your targeting strategy even further. Audience Insights data can help you understand what types of products your audience is most likely to buy, what their browsing habits are, and which types of devices they are using to shop. By analyzing this data, you can identify patterns in your audience's behavior and make informed decisions about how to adjust your ads for maximum impact.

One of the most effective ways to leverage Amazon's targeting options is by combining multiple targeting methods to create a comprehensive and multi-faceted campaign. For example, you could target users based on keywords, while also honing in on specific product categories and applying audience-based targeting. This approach allows you to cast a wide net and reach a diverse set of consumers while ensuring that your ads remain highly relevant to the specific needs and interests of different segments. The more precise you are with your targeting, the higher the likelihood that your ads will convert into sales.

A key aspect of successful targeting is the use of A/B testing, which allows you to experiment with different targeting strategies to determine which ones perform best. Amazon provides the tools necessary to set up and run A/B tests on your campaigns, allowing you to test variations of your ads to see which keywords, audience segments, and creative elements generate the most clicks and conversions. By continuously testing and optimizing your campaigns, you can improve your targeting strategy over time and ensure that your ads are always reaching the most relevant audience.

Another important consideration when leveraging Amazon's targeting options is the allocation of your advertising budget. Because some targeting options—such as product targeting or audience targeting—may be more competitive than others, you'll need to carefully manage your budget to ensure you're getting the best return on investment. This might involve adjusting bids for certain keywords or targeting methods based on the performance of each individual segment. Amazon's advertising dashboard provides real-time reporting on your ad performance, allowing you to track metrics like click-through rates (CTR), conversion rates, and cost-per-click (CPC). By monitoring these metrics closely, you can make data-driven decisions about how to allocate your budget to the most effective targeting options.

It's also essential to consider the mobile experience when leveraging Amazon's audience targeting. A significant percentage of Amazon shoppers make purchases via mobile devices, so it's critical that your ads are optimized for mobile screens. Mobile users tend to shop differently, often making quicker, more impulsive decisions. This means that ads targeting mobile users should be concise, visually appealing, and easy to interact with. By tailoring your ads for mobile devices, you can better capture the attention of users who are on the go and increase the chances of a successful conversion.

One of the most exciting developments in Amazon's targeting options is the ability to use Amazon's Demand-Side Platform (DSP) for more advanced audience segmentation and programmatic buying. The DSP allows advertisers to access Amazon's vast data pool and target consumers across Amazon-owned sites and other third-party platforms. With DSP, advertisers can target users based on very specific behaviors, such as past purchase history, website visits, and demographic information. DSP also offers advanced retargeting features, enabling you to target customers who have engaged with your brand but have not yet made a purchase.

By combining all of these audience targeting options, advertisers can create highly effective campaigns that are designed to reach the right customers at the right time. Leveraging Amazon's audience targeting tools is not just about reaching a broad group of people; it's about reaching the *right* people. With the platform's comprehensive targeting options, advertisers can ensure that their ads are seen by those who are most likely to engage with their products, resulting in higher conversions, more sales, and a better overall return on advertising spend. In today's competitive online retail environment, mastering audience targeting is one of the most powerful ways to set your business apart and succeed on Amazon.

IDENTIFYING YOUR IDEAL CUSTOMER PROFILE FOR PRIME PRODUCTS

In the world of e-commerce, understanding your ideal customer profile (ICP) is critical to the success of your business. This principle applies not only to traditional marketing but to advertising on platforms like Amazon Prime, where precision and relevance in targeting your audience can significantly impact your sales and brand visibility. Identifying your ideal customer profile is the foundation upon which successful advertising campaigns are built. It ensures that every marketing effort is directed toward the right people—those most likely to engage with your product, make a purchase, and become repeat customers. In the case of Prime products, knowing your ICP is essential for maximizing the effectiveness of your advertising on Amazon and for creating a connection with your audience that drives long-term success.

The first step in identifying your ideal customer profile is to develop a deep understanding of who your product is meant for. You need to think beyond basic demographic information like age, gender, or income level. Instead, focus on the specific characteristics, behaviors, needs, and desires that align with your product. For example, if you sell high-end skincare products, your ICP might include consumers who prioritize self-care, have a preference for premium brands, and are willing to invest in products that promise quality and results. By identifying the deeper motivations and preferences of your customers, you can create more compelling and targeted advertising that resonates with their needs.

Amazon Prime is a powerful tool for reaching potential customers who are already engaged with the platform, making it an ideal place to refine and implement your customer profile. Prime members are highly engaged, and their purchasing behavior tends to be more consistent and often driven by convenience. However, not all Prime members are the same. Within this broad group, there are distinct sub-segments based on various factors such as shopping habits, preferences, and product categories. Therefore, your task is to identify the specific group of Prime members who are most likely to find value in your product and tailor your advertising to this audience.

To start building an effective ICP, you should consider both demographic and psychographic factors. Demographic information includes basic details about your audience such as age, gender, income, and location. These details are helpful for segmenting your target audience into manageable groups. For example, if your product is a children's toy, you would want to target parents, especially those with young children, as they are most likely to make a purchase. On the other hand, if you are selling fitness equipment, your ideal customers might include individuals interested in health and wellness, ranging from young adults to middle-aged professionals who are focused on improving their physical fitness.

Psychographics, however, go beyond basic demographic data and delve into the deeper motivations, interests, and lifestyle choices of your audience. This aspect of the ideal customer profile is crucial because it helps you identify why someone would choose to buy your product. Do they value sustainability and eco-friendliness? Are they looking for convenience and time-saving solutions? Do they prioritize technology and innovation? Understanding these psychographic elements allows you to create advertising messages that speak directly to these values, making your campaigns much more effective in attracting the right customers.

Once you have a clear picture of the demographic and psychographic characteristics of your ideal customer, you can start looking at behavioral factors. These factors are especially important on Amazon, where consumers' buying behaviors can be easily tracked. Prime members, for instance, tend to have a history of frequent purchases, so their past buying behavior can offer valuable insights. Are your ideal customers more likely to purchase items through the Amazon app, or do they tend to use desktop computers for their shopping? Do they often browse for products in your category, or do they prefer browsing other categories? By analyzing behavioral data from Amazon's platform, you can get a clearer understanding of how your ideal customer interacts with the marketplace and tailor your advertising to those behaviors.

Amazon offers advertisers a wealth of tools to help them analyze customer behavior and identify patterns that will help in targeting the right audience. Tools like Amazon's Audience Insights and reports from the Campaign Manager provide real-time data on customer demographics, interests, shopping behaviors, and more. By using these insights, you can build a more granular and targeted approach to identifying your ideal customer. These tools allow you to segment your audience in ways that go beyond traditional demographic breakdowns, helping you find the customers who are most likely to engage with your product based on their actual behavior on the platform.

Another essential aspect of defining your ideal customer profile is understanding where your product fits in the larger context of Amazon's marketplace. The platform features millions of products, and positioning your product correctly is crucial for attracting the right buyers. By examining how your product fits into existing categories, which products it competes with, and what types of shoppers are buying similar products, you can better define your ICP. For example, if you're selling tech gadgets, your ideal customers might include early adopters and tech enthusiasts who are frequently on Amazon looking for the latest innovations. Understanding the competitive landscape on Amazon will give you a better sense of who your ideal customer is and how to reach them effectively.

Once you have a clear understanding of your ideal customer's demographics, psychographics, and behaviors, it's time to consider how to apply this information to your advertising campaigns. Amazon offers several advertising solutions that allow you to target specific audience segments. Sponsored Products, for instance, is an excellent tool for targeting shoppers who are actively searching for products similar to yours. By using relevant keywords, you can ensure that your product shows up in search results for potential customers who are already expressing an interest in similar items. Additionally, Sponsored Brands allows you to promote your brand and a set of products directly in the search results, giving you a broader reach while still targeting the right demographic.

Another feature to consider when setting up your campaigns is Amazon's audience targeting. This feature allows you to refine your ads based on customer interests, past behaviors, and even income levels. By taking advantage of these targeting options, you can ensure that your ads are being seen by those who are most likely to convert, increasing the overall efficiency of your advertising spend. You can also use tools like remarketing to target customers who have previously interacted with your products but haven't completed a purchase, increasing your chances of securing the sale.

As you continue to refine your advertising strategy, it's essential to regularly evaluate and update your ideal customer profile. Customer preferences and behaviors can change over time, and so should your approach. Use the data you gather from your advertising campaigns to fine-tune your ICP. Amazon's detailed reporting and analytics make it easy to track the performance of your ads and see how different audience segments are responding. By analyzing this data and adjusting your strategy accordingly, you can ensure that you're always reaching your most profitable audience and adapting to shifting trends in customer behavior.

Building a comprehensive and accurate ideal customer profile is an ongoing process that involves continuously gathering data, analyzing customer behaviors, and adapting to changes in the marketplace. In the context of Prime products, this process becomes even more crucial, as Prime members are an engaged and loyal customer base with specific shopping patterns. By identifying and targeting your ideal customers within this group, you can create more effective, targeted campaigns that drive higher engagement, greater sales, and long-term customer loyalty.

UTILIZING FIRST-PARTY AND THIRD-PARTY DATA FOR AUDIENCE INSIGHTS

In the competitive world of online advertising, especially on a platform as vast and dynamic as Amazon, understanding your audience is the key to crafting successful campaigns. To maximize the impact of your ads, you must leverage accurate, actionable data. This is where first-party and third-party data become crucial assets. Both types of data provide valuable insights that can refine your audience targeting, improve your campaign performance, and ultimately drive sales. The effective use of both first-party and third-party data allows for a comprehensive approach to audience segmentation and helps marketers make informed decisions based on real-world behaviors and preferences.

First-party data refers to the information that you, as a seller or advertiser, collect directly from your own interactions with customers. This data is considered highly valuable because it comes directly from the people who have interacted with your business, whether through your website, social media, email subscriptions, or past purchases. First-party data is specific to your business and is often the most accurate and reliable source of customer insights. By analyzing this data, you can understand your customers' buying habits, preferences, and engagement patterns in a way that's unique to your brand.

When advertising on Amazon Prime, first-party data becomes even more important. Amazon provides various tools that help you access and utilize this data, especially through your Seller Central account. You can gain insights into customer behavior, such as which products customers are searching for, what they add to their shopping carts, and which items they ultimately purchase. This information allows you to refine your audience segmentation and create highly tailored ad campaigns that speak directly to the needs and desires of your customers. For example, if you have a returning customer who frequently purchases kitchen gadgets, you can target that customer with a campaign highlighting your newest kitchen products or exclusive deals on similar items.

First-party data also provides an opportunity for businesses to personalize their interactions with customers. Personalization is one of the most effective ways to engage and retain customers, as it makes them feel valued and understood. On Amazon, using first-party data to personalize your advertising efforts can lead to higher conversion rates. Personalized ads are more likely to catch a customer's attention because they are relevant to their interests and previous purchasing behaviors. This form of targeted advertising not only enhances the customer experience but also improves the return on investment (ROI) for advertisers.

Third-party data, on the other hand, is collected from external sources and can provide broader insights into the behaviors and preferences of audiences that may not have interacted directly with your business. Third-party data typically comes from data brokers, market research firms, and other external providers that gather and aggregate information from a wide variety of sources. This data can include demographic information, psychographics, browsing habits, and purchase history, providing a more comprehensive view of your target market and helping you reach a wider audience.

While first-party data gives you a detailed view of your existing customers, third-party data can help you expand your reach and identify potential customers who may not yet be familiar with your brand. By understanding how different audience segments behave outside of your immediate customer base, you can refine your targeting strategy and reach individuals who exhibit characteristics similar to your best customers. For example, if your brand sells organic skincare products, third-party data may reveal that consumers who purchase organic food products also show a strong interest in natural beauty items. With this insight, you can target these consumers with ads for your skincare line, even if they have never interacted with your brand before.

Combining both first-party and third-party data provides a comprehensive view of your audience, helping you identify opportunities that may have otherwise been missed. By blending internal data with external insights, you can improve both the precision and the reach of your campaigns. First-party data gives you an understanding of customer behavior and loyalty, while third-party data expands your view to include broader trends, helping you uncover new audience segments that are aligned with your product offerings. For example, a business selling outdoor gear might use first-party data to identify loyal customers who frequently purchase hiking boots and backpacks. Third-party data might reveal a growing interest in camping and hiking among a particular demographic group, prompting the business to launch a targeted ad campaign to reach these potential customers.

When it comes to utilizing both first-party and third-party data for Amazon advertising, it's important to take advantage of the platform's robust suite of tools. Amazon provides advanced targeting capabilities that allow you to use both types of data effectively. For instance, Amazon's Audience Insights tool allows you to segment your audience based on demographic factors such as age, location, and purchase history. This tool can integrate first-party data from your previous customers and combine it with third-party insights to create an accurate and comprehensive customer profile. By using this tool, you can ensure that your ads are shown to the right people at the right time, increasing the likelihood of conversions and sales.

In addition to Audience Insights, Amazon provides other targeting options that let you further refine your audience. For example, Sponsored Products ads allow you to target keywords that your customers are searching for, based on first-party data from previous interactions with your listings. Similarly, Sponsored Display ads allow you to retarget users who have shown interest in your products but have not yet completed a purchase. By leveraging both first-party and third-party data in these ad types, you can refine your messaging and tailor your approach to specific audience segments, increasing the effectiveness of your campaigns.

Moreover, third-party data can also help with competitive analysis. By understanding your competitors' audience, you can identify areas where you can differentiate your product offerings and craft more compelling ad campaigns. For instance, third-party data might reveal that your competitor's customers are primarily interested in a specific feature of their product. Armed with this information, you can highlight unique features of your product that your competitors might not emphasize, giving you a competitive edge.

Despite the many benefits of utilizing both first-party and third-party data, it's important to be mindful of privacy regulations and the ethical use of data. Both types of data must be collected and used in compliance with data protection laws such as the General Data Protection Regulation (GDPR) in Europe or the California Consumer Privacy Act (CCPA). These regulations are designed to protect consumer privacy, and businesses must ensure they are transparent about how they collect, store, and use customer data. Failing to comply with these regulations can lead to legal repercussions and damage to your brand's reputation. It's crucial, therefore, to maintain transparency with customers and ensure that all data usage is ethical and compliant with applicable laws.

By leveraging both first-party and third-party data, you can create more effective, targeted advertising campaigns that drive sales and boost customer engagement. First-party data gives you deep insights into your existing customers, while third-party data provides a broader view of potential customers and market trends. Combining these data sources enables you to refine your targeting strategy, personalize your ads, and reach a wider audience that is more likely to convert. As you continue to optimize your campaigns using both data types, you'll be able to fine-tune your audience insights and make informed decisions that maximize the success of your Amazon advertising efforts.

CREATING CUSTOMER PERSONAS TO INFORM YOUR ADVERTISING STRATEGY

Creating customer personas is one of the most effective ways to ensure your advertising strategy is not only targeted but also resonant with the right audience. A customer persona, often referred to as a buyer persona, is a semi-fictional representation of your ideal customer, based on real data and insights. By developing customer personas, you are essentially creating detailed profiles that allow you to tailor your marketing efforts to meet the specific needs, behaviors, and pain points of different audience segments. In the context of Amazon advertising, this strategy becomes even more crucial because the platform provides an opportunity to reach a vast and diverse customer base. Understanding who your customers are and how they think can significantly enhance your ability to craft campaigns that capture attention, foster engagement, and ultimately drive sales.

The process of creating customer personas starts with gathering data. While you may have a general idea of who your customers are, the real insights come from analyzing data sources such as your previous sales, website analytics, social media insights, and even feedback from existing customers. Amazon's own tools, like Seller Central and its associated reports, provide invaluable data about customer behavior on your listings. This data can help you understand customer demographics, purchasing patterns, and even which products they view most frequently. Collecting and analyzing this data allows you to segment your audience based on shared characteristics, which is essential for building accurate and actionable customer personas.

Once you have gathered data, the next step is to identify key segments within your audience. These segments could be based on factors like age, gender, income, geographic location, buying habits, or even psychographic attributes such as values and lifestyle choices. For instance, if your product is a high-end fitness tracker, your ideal customer persona might include individuals who are health-conscious, tech-savvy, and have disposable income. Alternatively, if you sell budget-friendly home essentials, your customer persona might include young families or first-time homeowners looking for affordable solutions. Identifying these key segments allows you to understand not only who your customers are but also how they approach the buying process.

It's essential to move beyond basic demographics and delve deeper into understanding your personas' motivations, challenges, and goals. For example, why do they purchase your product? What problems are they trying to solve, and how does your product offer a solution? These insights help shape your advertising messages. If you understand that your fitness tracker persona is motivated by health and wellness goals, your advertisements should emphasize the product's features that promote improved fitness, better sleep, and long-term health benefits. On the other hand, if your persona values affordability and practicality, your messaging should focus on value for money and the product's efficiency rather than high-end features. By aligning your messaging with the persona's motivations, you increase the chances of resonating with them and driving conversions.

In addition to motivations and challenges, understanding a persona's decision-making process is crucial for informing your advertising strategy. Some customers may prioritize product reviews and social proof, while others may be influenced by product features or the reputation of the brand. Knowing how your target audience makes decisions allows you to craft more effective campaigns. For example, if your customer persona values social proof, incorporating user-generated content, reviews, and ratings in your ads will help build trust and credibility. If your target audience is driven by convenience and quick delivery, highlighting Amazon's Prime benefits or fast shipping options may be more compelling.

To create highly effective customer personas, it's also important to consider the different stages of the buying journey. Customers are at different points in their decision-making process when they encounter your ads, and your advertising strategy should address their needs at each of these stages. For instance, some customers may only be in the awareness stage, meaning they're just beginning to learn about their problem and potential solutions. For these customers, educational ads that introduce your product as a solution to a common pain point might be more effective. On the other hand, customers who are in the consideration or decision stage may require more detailed information, such as comparisons to competing products or testimonials from satisfied customers. Creating personas that include these stages allows you to craft ads that speak directly to the customer's current mindset, increasing the likelihood of a conversion.

Developing customer personas also means identifying where your target audience spends their time online and how they consume content. This is particularly important for advertising on Amazon Prime, where shoppers may be browsing while watching a TV show or scrolling through product listings. Knowing where your persona engages with content—whether through video, articles, social media, or in-depth product descriptions—enables you to create ads that fit seamlessly into these behaviors. For example, video ads are a powerful tool for storytelling and can be highly effective for audiences who engage with visual content. If your customer persona tends to engage with written content, then detailed product descriptions and customer reviews will be more compelling. The goal is to meet your audience where they are and deliver your message in the format that resonates best with them.

Another crucial aspect of customer persona development is understanding their values and preferences, especially when it comes to brand loyalty and social causes. Many consumers today care deeply about the ethical stance of the brands they support, whether that's in relation to sustainability, social justice, or corporate responsibility. If your product or brand has a strong value proposition related to one of these areas, it can be helpful to include that in your customer personas. For example, if your brand is known for using environmentally friendly materials, your persona might consist of individuals who prioritize sustainability in their purchasing decisions. Similarly, if your target audience is highly engaged with social causes, emphasizing your company's charitable efforts or ethical practices can strengthen the connection between your brand and the customer persona.

Once you've developed a set of customer personas, it's essential to integrate them into your advertising strategy. The key here is personalization. Ads that are personalized to speak directly to a customer persona's unique characteristics and needs have a higher chance of resonating and driving conversions. For example, if you've created a persona for young professionals who value style and functionality, your ad copy should highlight how your product complements their lifestyle, focusing on time-saving features, modern design, and convenience. In Amazon advertising, this personalization can be reflected in your choice of targeting, ad format, and even the keywords you use to trigger your ads.

Leveraging customer personas also allows you to test different approaches and refine your advertising campaigns. By analyzing the performance of your ads with respect to each persona, you can identify which segments respond best to certain messages or offers. Over time, you can optimize your ad campaigns by allocating your budget to the personas that yield the highest returns, while tweaking your approach to better meet the needs of underperforming segments.

Ultimately, customer personas serve as a foundation for creating highly relevant, personalized ad campaigns that speak directly to the needs, behaviors, and preferences of your ideal customers. By developing a deep understanding of who your customers are and what drives their purchasing decisions, you can ensure that your advertising strategy on Amazon is not only effective but also delivers a compelling, value-driven experience that encourages loyalty, engagement, and long-term success.

PART 2

Mastering Amazon Sponsored Products Ads

CHAPTER 3
KEYWORD RESEARCH FOR SPONSORED PRODUCTS

UNDERSTANDING KEYWORD MATCH TYPES: BROAD, PHRASE, AND EXACT

When it comes to advertising on Amazon, understanding keyword match types is a crucial element in ensuring the success of your campaigns. The way keywords are selected and matched in your ads directly impacts who sees your product, the relevancy of your ads, and ultimately, how well your ads convert. Amazon offers different types of keyword match options—broad, phrase, and exact—that give advertisers varying degrees of control over the targeting of their ads. Understanding the nuances of each match type and how to use them strategically can significantly improve the performance of your ads and help you achieve your advertising goals more effectively.

At the heart of Amazon's keyword matching system lies the goal of connecting your products with the right customers. Keywords are the bridge between what shoppers are searching for and what your product offers. However, how those keywords are matched with search queries can make a substantial difference in terms of ad visibility, relevance, and cost-efficiency. The three match types—broad, phrase, and exact—offer different levels of precision and flexibility, and each one can be used in a variety of ways to achieve specific advertising objectives.

Broad match is the most flexible keyword match type and is ideal for advertisers looking to cast a wide net. When you use broad match, your ad can appear for any search term that includes your targeted keyword, as well as any variations of that keyword, including synonyms, misspellings, and related terms. For example, if your keyword is "running shoes," your ad might show for searches like "sneakers," "athletic footwear," or "sports shoes," even if those terms weren't explicitly part of your original keyword phrase. Broad match allows your ad to reach a larger audience by displaying it for a variety of search queries that may be relevant to your product, even if the exact phrasing differs. This level of flexibility is valuable when you're looking to generate impressions, build brand awareness, or drive traffic to your listings, as it can help you attract potential customers who may not have searched for your exact product but are still interested in related items.

One of the main benefits of broad match is its reach. By allowing your ads to show up for a wide array of search terms, it increases the chances that your ad will be seen by more shoppers, which can help boost your overall visibility. However, with this broad reach comes the risk of irrelevance. Since your ad can show for a wide range of search queries, it might also be displayed for search terms that are not closely related to your product. This can lead to wasted spend if your ads are shown to people who have no intention of purchasing your product. To mitigate this risk, it's essential to continuously monitor your campaign performance and make adjustments as needed. For example, you might want to add negative keywords to prevent your ads from showing for terms that aren't relevant to your product, ensuring that your advertising budget is being spent efficiently.

Phrase match is a more controlled match type that offers a middle ground between broad match and exact match. With phrase match, your ad will appear for search queries that contain your exact keyword phrase, as well as additional words before or after it. However, the keyword phrase must appear in the search query in the same order that you specified, although other words may be included. For example, if your targeted keyword is "running shoes," your ad might show up for searches like "buy running shoes online," "best running shoes for men," or "running shoes for women," but it wouldn't show for searches like "shoes for running" or "men's athletic footwear." Phrase match allows for more control over who sees your ad by ensuring that the key elements of your keyword phrase are present in the search query, while still allowing for some flexibility in terms of the overall search phrase.

The advantage of using phrase match is that it strikes a balance between reach and relevance. While it doesn't have the broad reach of broad match, it still gives you the opportunity to capture a larger audience than exact match. Phrase match is particularly useful for advertisers who want to target a specific set of keywords but don't want to be too restrictive. It allows for variations in the way customers might phrase their searches while still ensuring that the core intent behind the search aligns with your product. This makes phrase match a good option when you want to target specific product categories or use longer, more descriptive keyword phrases that may capture shoppers in different stages of their buying journey. However, similar to broad match, it's important to monitor your campaign performance and adjust your keyword list as necessary to ensure that your ads are shown to the most relevant audience.

Exact match is the most restrictive of the three match types, but it offers the highest level of precision. With exact match, your ad will only appear for searches that exactly match the keyword you've selected, with no additional words before or after it. For example, if your exact match keyword is "running shoes," your ad will only show for searches where the exact phrase "running shoes" is used. This can help ensure that your ads are shown only to shoppers who are searching for exactly what you offer, making it the best option for advertisers looking for highly targeted, high-converting traffic. Exact match is ideal for advertisers who have a strong understanding of their target audience and are looking to focus on a very specific set of search queries that closely align with their product offering.

The primary benefit of using exact match is its high level of relevance. By targeting only those search queries that exactly match your keyword, you can ensure that your ads are shown to the most qualified potential customers. This can lead to higher conversion rates, as the audience seeing your ad is already actively searching for the exact product you offer. However, the downside of exact match is that it limits the reach of your ads. Since your ad will only show for exact searches, there is a greater risk of missing out on potential customers who might be searching for slightly different variations of your keyword. This is why exact match is typically used in conjunction with other match types, such as broad or phrase match, to ensure that you strike the right balance between precision and reach.

Choosing the right keyword match type for your Amazon advertising campaigns requires a clear understanding of your objectives. If your goal is to increase brand awareness and reach a large audience, broad match may be the best option, as it allows your ads to be shown to a broad range of shoppers. If you're looking to target a more specific audience while still maintaining some flexibility in how the search term is phrased, phrase match provides a good middle ground. For highly targeted campaigns with a focus on conversion, exact match is the ideal choice. However, to maximize the effectiveness of your campaigns, it's often beneficial to use a combination of these match types, depending on your goals and the stage of the customer journey you are targeting.

Ultimately, understanding keyword match types—broad, phrase, and exact—is key to running effective and efficient advertising campaigns on Amazon. By choosing the right match type for your specific goals, you can ensure that your ads are reaching the most relevant audience and driving the best results. As with any advertising strategy, it's important to continuously monitor performance, test different approaches, and refine your targeting to achieve the best return on investment. By mastering the use of keyword match types, you can optimize your Amazon ads to increase visibility, improve targeting, and drive more sales for your business.

UTILIZING AMAZON'S SEARCH TERM REPORTS FOR KEYWORD DISCOVERY

Understanding and utilizing Amazon's search term reports is an essential strategy for any seller aiming to enhance their advertising performance on the platform. These reports provide detailed insights into the actual search terms that lead customers to click on your ads, enabling you to make informed decisions about your keywords, bidding strategies, and overall campaign optimization. By leveraging these valuable data points, sellers can discover new keyword opportunities, refine their targeting, and ultimately drive better results from their Amazon advertising efforts.

When you run a pay-per-click (PPC) campaign on Amazon, you are paying for clicks based on keywords that you target. However, the search term reports provide you with additional data about how customers are interacting with your ads beyond the keywords you've selected. These reports break down the search terms that users entered when they clicked on your ad, giving you a clearer picture of how your keywords are performing in real-world searches. This data is invaluable, as it can highlight new keyword opportunities, expose irrelevant search terms, and guide you in adjusting your advertising strategy to better align with customer behavior.

One of the main advantages of using Amazon's search term reports is the ability to identify keywords that you may not have initially considered. Often, customers use search terms that are closely related to your product, but you might not have targeted those exact phrases in your campaigns. The search term report allows you to see these additional variations of keywords that are driving traffic to your listings, and this can lead to the discovery of highly relevant terms that you might have overlooked. For example, if you're selling "organic dog food," you may not have specifically targeted terms like "natural pet food" or "grain-free dog food," but the search term report could reveal that these terms are driving clicks to your ad. By adding these newly discovered keywords to your campaigns, you can expand your reach and increase the chances of capturing potential customers who are searching for these terms.

Moreover, the search term report can help you identify negative keywords—terms that are irrelevant to your product and could be wasting your advertising budget. When a search term appears in your report that has no relevance to your product or is not likely to convert, you can add it to your negative keyword list. This prevents your ads from showing up for irrelevant searches, which helps reduce unnecessary spending and improves the efficiency of your campaigns. For example, if your product is a high-end coffee maker and you're seeing that clicks are coming from searches like "cheap coffee makers" or "coffee maker reviews," these terms might not be relevant to your target audience. By excluding these terms, you can focus your budget on keywords that are more likely to lead to conversions.

Another benefit of Amazon's search term reports is that they allow you to assess the performance of your keywords based on actual user behavior. The report includes data on impressions, clicks, conversions, and the cost associated with each search term. This level of detail enables you to understand which keywords are generating the most clicks and which ones are actually converting into sales. By analyzing these metrics, you can identify which search terms are providing the best return on investment (ROI) and adjust your campaigns accordingly. For example, if a keyword is generating a lot of impressions but few conversions, it might indicate that the keyword is not as relevant as you initially thought, and you may need to refine your targeting or adjust your bids.

Additionally, you can use the search term report to assess the effectiveness of your bidding strategy. If certain search terms are driving significant traffic but the conversion rate is low, it might be worth experimenting with higher bids for those keywords to improve visibility and drive more qualified traffic. Conversely, if certain terms are underperforming, you can reduce your bids or exclude them altogether to optimize your budget. The ability to continuously fine-tune your bidding strategy based on real-time data from the search term report is one of the key advantages of using Amazon's advertising platform.

When leveraging the search term report for keyword discovery, it's also important to remember that this data should be analyzed regularly. Customer behavior can shift over time, and new trends can emerge, so it's essential to stay on top of your search term reports to ensure that your campaigns remain relevant and effective. By frequently reviewing your search term data, you can quickly identify shifts in customer interest, seasonal trends, or new keywords that may be gaining traction, allowing you to adapt your campaigns in real time.

In addition to discovering new keywords, Amazon's search term reports can also help you fine-tune your ad copy and product listings. If you notice that certain search terms are driving traffic but your ads aren't converting as well as expected, it could be a sign that your product listing or ad copy isn't aligned with what customers are looking for. By adjusting your product descriptions, titles, or images to better match the search terms, you can increase the likelihood of conversions. For instance, if a search term like "eco-friendly kitchenware" is driving clicks but not conversions, you may want to highlight the eco-friendly features of your product more prominently in your ad copy or product description.

To effectively utilize Amazon's search term reports, it's essential to have a system for organizing and analyzing the data. A common approach is to export the search term report regularly and sort the data based on performance metrics such as impressions, clicks, and conversions. By doing so, you can quickly identify high-performing keywords, as well as terms that need to be excluded or refined. Additionally, consider using tools like Amazon's Campaign Manager to automate the process of adding new keywords or negative keywords to your campaigns, making it easier to act on the insights from the search term report.

The search term report is also a valuable tool for long-term campaign optimization. As you gather more data over time, you can start to identify patterns in consumer behavior that can inform your broader marketing strategy. For example, if you notice that certain keywords consistently generate high conversion rates, it may be worth investing more heavily in those terms across different campaigns or targeting those keywords in a more granular way. Alternatively, if you find that some search terms are consistently underperforming, you can reallocate your advertising budget to more profitable keywords.

Amazon's search term reports provide a wealth of information that can significantly improve the effectiveness of your advertising campaigns. By using the reports to discover new keyword opportunities, identify negative keywords, and refine your bidding strategies, you can ensure that your ads are reaching the most relevant audience and driving the best possible results. Moreover, by regularly reviewing and acting on the insights provided by the search term report, you can stay ahead of shifting customer behavior, optimize your campaigns in real time, and achieve a better return on investment. Whether you're a new seller or an experienced advertiser, mastering the use of search term reports is essential for maximizing the impact of your Amazon advertising efforts.

LEVERAGING KEYWORD RESEARCH TOOLS

Keyword research is a cornerstone of any successful advertising strategy, especially when it comes to Amazon. With millions of products competing for attention, targeting the right keywords can make all the difference between a successful campaign and one that falls flat. To effectively reach your target audience and increase conversions, leveraging advanced keyword research tools is crucial. These tools provide a wealth of insights, allowing you to discover high-performing keywords, assess competition, and refine your advertising strategy. Among the most powerful and widely used tools are Amazon Brand Analytics, Helium 10, and Jungle Scout, each offering unique features that can elevate your keyword research efforts.

Amazon Brand Analytics is an incredibly valuable tool for any seller using Amazon's platform. Available to professional sellers enrolled in the Amazon Brand Registry, this tool gives access to a range of data-driven insights that can guide your keyword strategy. One of the key features of Amazon Brand Analytics is its "Search Terms" report, which reveals the most frequently searched terms for products within specific categories. By using this report, you can identify trending keywords, discover new search terms to target, and even analyze customer search behavior in your niche. This can be especially helpful for discovering long-tail keywords that may not be immediately obvious but could drive high-quality traffic to your listings. By analyzing the search volume and competition for these terms, you can prioritize which keywords to target in your PPC campaigns.

Another powerful feature within Amazon Brand Analytics is the "Market Basket Analysis." This allows you to see which products are frequently bought together, providing you with valuable insights into customer purchasing behavior. By understanding what other products customers are buying alongside your own, you can identify additional keywords and product combinations to target, further expanding your reach. The "Item Comparison" report is also incredibly helpful, as it reveals which competing products customers are considering in comparison to your own. This gives you a competitive advantage by showing you the keywords that your competitors are ranking for, allowing you to adjust your advertising and SEO strategies to capture a larger share of the market.

While Amazon Brand Analytics offers robust data, other third-party tools like Helium 10 and Jungle Scout also provide critical insights that can further enhance your keyword research efforts. Helium 10 is a comprehensive suite of tools designed specifically for Amazon sellers, with one of its standout features being the "Magnet" tool. Magnet helps you generate keyword ideas by providing a list of high-traffic keywords relevant to your product or niche. What sets Helium 10 apart is its ability to provide keyword suggestions based on actual Amazon search data, as well as its detailed metrics, such as search volume, competition level, and CPR (Cerebro Product Rank), which measures the ranking of your competitors' products for certain keywords. This allows you to fine-tune your keyword strategy by targeting keywords with high search volume but low competition, maximizing your chances of ranking for profitable terms.

Helium 10's "Cerebro" tool is another invaluable resource, providing detailed insights into the keywords your competitors are using. By entering a competitor's ASIN, you can uncover a comprehensive list of keywords that they are ranking for, along with data on their search volume and keyword performance. This level of competitive intelligence can help you identify gaps in your own keyword strategy and reveal opportunities to target terms that your competitors may have overlooked. By leveraging both the Magnet and Cerebro tools, you can create a highly optimized list of keywords that are tailored to your product, audience, and competition.

Jungle Scout is another powerful tool that specializes in Amazon keyword research and product analysis. One of its most useful features for keyword research is the "Keyword Scout" tool, which provides insights into keyword search volume, competition, and relevancy. What makes Jungle Scout stand out is its ability to filter keywords by their relevance to your product, ensuring that you are targeting terms that are directly related to your niche. Additionally, Jungle Scout offers a keyword tracking feature, allowing you to monitor the performance of specific keywords over time and track their ranking changes. This is especially helpful for understanding how your keyword strategy is evolving and whether your ads are consistently performing at their best.

Jungle Scout also provides insights into customer reviews and product listings, which can be invaluable for uncovering additional keywords to target. By analyzing the language customers use in their reviews, you can identify phrases and terms that potential buyers may be using but that might not show up in traditional keyword searches. This gives you an edge by allowing you to target highly specific, long-tail keywords that are highly relevant to your product but may not be immediately apparent.

While each of these tools offers unique features, they all share a common purpose: to help you discover the most effective keywords for your Amazon advertising campaigns. One of the primary benefits of using these keyword research tools is the ability to find keywords with the right balance of search volume and competition. When selecting keywords, it's important to avoid terms that are either too broad or too competitive. For example, targeting a highly competitive keyword like "laptop" may be too costly and difficult to rank for, while a term like "best laptop for students" may have a lower search volume but could lead to a more qualified audience with a higher likelihood of conversion. These tools help you strike that balance, identifying the most promising keywords that will drive relevant traffic to your listings.

In addition to keyword discovery, these tools provide insights into keyword trends, allowing you to adjust your strategy as market conditions change. By identifying seasonal shifts in search behavior or tracking the performance of emerging keywords, you can stay ahead of the competition and ensure that your campaigns remain relevant. For example, if a keyword related to a holiday season or special promotion starts gaining traction, you can quickly adjust your campaigns to target those terms before your competitors do. The ability to stay agile and adapt to market trends is a significant advantage in the fast-paced world of Amazon advertising.

Another benefit of using keyword research tools like Amazon Brand Analytics, Helium 10, and Jungle Scout is the ability to improve your overall Amazon SEO. The insights gained from keyword research can be applied not only to your advertising campaigns but also to your product listings. By optimizing your product titles, bullet points, and descriptions with high-performing keywords, you can improve your organic ranking on Amazon's search results, driving even more traffic to your listings. The synergy between paid ads and organic optimization creates a powerful strategy for maximizing visibility and conversions.

Leveraging advanced keyword research tools like Amazon Brand Analytics, Helium 10, and Jungle Scout is essential for any seller looking to succeed with Amazon advertising. These tools provide deep insights into keyword performance, competition, and customer behavior, allowing you to create highly targeted campaigns that drive relevant traffic and maximize conversions. By consistently using these tools to refine your keyword strategy, you can stay ahead of the competition, optimize your campaigns for the best possible results, and achieve long-term success on Amazon.

IDENTIFYING HIGH-INTENT KEYWORDS RELEVANT TO PRIME MEMBERS

When it comes to advertising on Amazon, understanding how to identify high-intent keywords that resonate with Prime members is one of the most crucial elements of a successful strategy. Prime members are not just any shoppers; they are loyal, often frequent, and engaged consumers who have demonstrated a willingness to pay for a superior shopping experience. As a result, targeting high-intent keywords relevant to this audience can significantly increase your chances of success. To truly unlock the potential of this valuable demographic, sellers must understand what motivates Prime members to make purchasing decisions and how to align their keywords with these motivations.

Prime members are known for their specific buying behaviors. These customers are typically looking for convenience, speed, and exclusive deals. Prime benefits, such as fast, free shipping, access to exclusive sales, and early access to new releases, heavily influence the purchasing decisions of Prime members. To effectively reach these shoppers, it's important to identify keywords that cater to their need for efficiency, exclusivity, and value. High-intent keywords typically reflect the buyer's stage in the purchasing journey—whether they are actively searching for a product, ready to buy, or seeking something specific. By targeting these high-intent keywords, you are not just driving traffic but attracting shoppers who are more likely to convert.

A great place to begin is by analyzing the keywords that signal a buyer's intent to purchase immediately. Words such as "buy," "purchase," "order," and "shop" are all high-intent keywords that indicate the shopper is ready to make a purchase. However, the specificity of these terms is what truly matters. For example, someone searching for "buy wireless headphones" is further along in the purchasing journey than someone simply searching for "wireless headphones." The addition of "buy" shows that they have already considered their options and are now focused on completing the transaction. Similarly, keywords like "best deal on wireless headphones" or "cheap wireless headphones" indicate a customer who is price-sensitive and actively looking for the most competitive offer.

Another way to identify high-intent keywords relevant to Prime members is by focusing on product-specific terms that indicate a readiness to purchase. For instance, if a customer is searching for "best noise-canceling wireless headphones for travel," they are not just browsing; they are actively looking for a specific solution. This type of keyword is highly targeted and often comes from customers who are well into their decision-making process. By understanding the types of products that Prime members are most likely to be interested in and their purchasing needs, sellers can pinpoint the exact terms these customers are searching for.

To further refine your keyword strategy, it's essential to incorporate long-tail keywords into your research. Long-tail keywords are more specific phrases, typically consisting of three or more words, that help you narrow down the audience and reach individuals who are further along in their buyer journey. Prime members are often looking for products that are highly relevant to their needs, and long-tail keywords can provide a more targeted and cost-effective way of capturing this audience. For instance, instead of targeting the broad keyword "headphones," you could target "best noise-canceling headphones for sleeping," which is far more specific and reflects the buyer's clear intent. While long-tail keywords may have lower search volume, they often come with higher conversion rates because the searchers are more likely to make a purchase.

It is also essential to leverage tools like Amazon Brand Analytics, which provide insights into search terms commonly used by Prime members. Amazon Brand Analytics offers valuable data on the most frequently searched terms within specific categories, allowing you to spot high-intent keywords that have high search volumes and lower competition. By targeting these keywords in your campaigns, you can ensure that you are reaching Prime members who are actively searching for the types of products you offer. This data allows you to make data-driven decisions and ensures that you are targeting keywords with the highest potential for conversion.

Another key to identifying high-intent keywords relevant to Prime members is considering the seasonal and event-driven nature of Amazon Prime. Prime members are often attracted to deals, discounts, and exclusive events such as Prime Day. By understanding the shopping patterns surrounding these events, you can identify high-intent keywords that reflect the urgency and exclusivity of these sales. For example, keywords like "Prime Day deals on electronics" or "Prime Day discounts for Prime members" are highly relevant during the event and can help you attract Prime members looking to capitalize on exclusive offers. Similarly, by analyzing previous sales data and trends, you can predict which keywords will see a spike in demand during certain times of the year and adjust your campaigns accordingly.

The use of modifiers is another powerful strategy for identifying high-intent keywords. Modifiers such as "best," "top," "affordable," and "reviewed" can help you identify consumers who are conducting product research and are actively seeking quality options. Keywords like "best-rated wireless headphones" or "top-rated running shoes" indicate that the shopper is not simply browsing—they are looking for the most reliable and reputable products within a category. These terms are often used by customers who are nearing the final stages of their decision-making process and are looking for reassurance before making their purchase. This is especially relevant for Prime members who expect high-quality products and fast delivery.

Additionally, it is important to monitor and assess the performance of the keywords you are using. Tools like Amazon's search term report can provide insights into which keywords are driving traffic and leading to conversions. By regularly reviewing these reports, you can identify which high-intent keywords are most effective in driving purchases and adjust your strategy as needed. For example, if you find that certain keywords consistently lead to high click-through rates and conversions, you can allocate more of your advertising budget to those terms. Conversely, if a keyword is underperforming, you may need to refine your ad copy or replace it with a more targeted phrase.

Understanding the customer's journey is also key when identifying high-intent keywords. Prime members, in particular, value convenience and speed. Therefore, keywords that emphasize quick delivery, such as "same-day delivery" or "free 2-day shipping," can appeal to this audience. By focusing on terms that highlight the benefits of Prime membership, you are tapping into the specific advantages that Prime members are looking for. Keywords like "Prime eligible" or "Prime exclusive" signal to the customer that they are getting access to exclusive benefits, which can motivate them to complete their purchase.

Competitor analysis can be a highly effective way of identifying high-intent keywords. By reviewing the search terms and ads used by your competitors, you can gain insights into which keywords they are targeting and which are resonating with the Prime audience. Tools like Helium 10, Jungle Scout, and SEMrush allow you to analyze your competitors' advertising strategies and uncover high-intent keywords that you might have missed. By identifying the gaps in your competitors' keyword strategies, you can refine your own approach and stay ahead of the curve.

Identifying high-intent keywords that resonate with Amazon Prime members is a multifaceted process that requires a deep understanding of customer behavior, product relevance, and strategic keyword targeting. By focusing on keywords that reflect a customer's readiness to purchase, using long-tail keywords, and leveraging data from tools like Amazon Brand Analytics and third-party platforms, you can craft an effective advertising strategy that speaks directly to Prime members. The key is to focus on the intent behind the search and ensure that your keywords are aligned with what Prime members are actively looking for, ultimately driving traffic and increasing conversions.

BUILDING COMPREHENSIVE KEYWORD LISTS FOR YOUR CAMPAIGNS

Building comprehensive keyword lists for your advertising campaigns is a crucial aspect of any successful strategy, particularly when advertising on a platform as expansive as Amazon. Keywords are the bridge between your products and potential customers, guiding shoppers to your listings and ensuring that your products appear when they search for items that align with what you offer. However, simply choosing random or generic keywords will not give you the results you need. A well-crafted keyword list is strategically designed, continuously refined, and aligned with the behavior, intent, and expectations of your target audience.

The first step in building a comprehensive keyword list is understanding your target audience and their search behaviors. Customers enter Amazon's search engine with specific intent, and identifying keywords that match that intent is key to driving qualified traffic to your listings. These keywords must be relevant not just to the product you are selling, but also to the way your customers are searching for it. In this process, it's important to think from the customer's perspective—what terms would they use when they are looking for a product like yours? For instance, a seller of running shoes might think about different types of keywords, such as "running shoes for women," "comfortable running shoes," "best running shoes for marathons," or even "affordable running shoes."

Once you have a solid grasp of your target market's language, it's time to begin researching keywords. The next step in building your list involves using various keyword research tools and techniques to identify high-traffic, high-conversion keywords. Tools such as Amazon Brand Analytics, Helium 10, and Jungle Scout can be incredibly useful in this regard. These platforms provide valuable insights into search terms that are most commonly used by customers, including data on search volume, competition, and relevancy. By analyzing this data, you can start to build a list of keywords that have the potential to drive traffic to your product listings.

While using tools like Amazon Brand Analytics, sellers should focus on capturing keywords with high search volume but manageable competition. A highly searched keyword with little competition offers an excellent opportunity for visibility, but it's essential not to ignore keywords with moderate search volume but high conversion potential. These keywords, though less frequently searched, may attract customers who are more likely to make a purchase, especially if they are highly specific or contain a purchasing intent, like "buy," "discount," or "deal." For instance, "buy women's yoga pants" would likely have a higher purchase intent than just "yoga pants," meaning the shopper may be closer to the buying decision.

However, building a successful keyword list is not just about finding high-volume terms; it's also about identifying a variety of keyword types to cater to different stages of the customer journey. The customer journey can be broadly divided into three stages: awareness, consideration, and decision. In the awareness phase, shoppers are gathering information about a product and may search using broad, general keywords such as "running shoes." In the consideration phase, the search becomes more specific, often involving comparisons or additional criteria, such as "best running shoes for flat feet" or "running shoes vs. cross-trainers." The decision phase is the final stage, where shoppers are ready to make a purchase and may search with terms like "buy running shoes online" or "order Nike running shoes."

In addition to targeting these stages of the customer journey, another important aspect of building a comprehensive keyword list is incorporating long-tail keywords. Long-tail keywords are more specific, often consisting of three or more words. While these keywords generally have lower search volume, they tend to attract more qualified traffic and higher conversion rates because they are highly specific to a customer's needs. For example, "best waterproof Bluetooth speaker for hiking" is a long-tail keyword that attracts shoppers looking for a very particular product, making them more likely to purchase. Using long-tail keywords not only helps you stand out from competitors but also allows you to focus on niche markets within your category, ensuring that your ads are reaching the right audience.

The next component of building an effective keyword list involves including both broad and exact match types in your campaigns. Broad match keywords allow your ads to appear for a wide range of related search terms, giving you the opportunity to cast a wider net and attract a broader audience. However, broad match keywords can also lead to less targeted traffic, as they will show your ad for a variety of search queries, some of which may not be highly relevant to your product. On the other hand, exact match keywords ensure that your ad will only be shown to customers who enter the precise search term you've selected. These keywords are highly specific and often result in more conversions because they indicate that the shopper is actively searching for exactly what you offer. A well-rounded keyword list will include a mix of both broad and exact match terms to strike the right balance between reaching new customers and targeting highly relevant ones.

Another crucial aspect of building a comprehensive keyword list is keeping an eye on competitors. Understanding which keywords your competitors are targeting can provide invaluable insights into gaps in the market and potential opportunities for your own campaigns. Using tools like Helium 10, Jungle Scout, or Amazon's search term reports, you can analyze competitor listings and identify which keywords they rank for. This competitive analysis allows you to uncover new keyword ideas and refine your strategy by focusing on terms that may have been overlooked. By differentiating your product through targeted keywords, you can gain a competitive edge in a crowded marketplace.

One of the often-overlooked aspects of building an effective keyword list is continuously optimizing and refining it. The process of keyword research does not end once you've created your list. Regularly monitoring the performance of your chosen keywords is crucial to maintaining a successful advertising campaign. You'll want to keep track of which keywords are driving traffic and conversions and which are underperforming. Amazon's search term report and other analytics tools provide valuable data on keyword performance, allowing you to adjust your strategy in real time. If certain keywords are not delivering the expected results, it's time to replace them with better-performing alternatives or adjust your bid strategy to improve visibility.

Additionally, testing different variations of keywords can help you uncover high-performing terms that you may not have considered initially. For example, you may test singular vs. plural forms, abbreviations, or different word orders. Small changes in keyword phrasing can sometimes yield significant improvements in performance. By constantly testing and optimizing your keyword list, you can ensure that your campaigns remain fresh, relevant, and efficient.

Don't forget about negative keywords. Negative keywords help prevent your ads from showing up for irrelevant or low-converting search terms. For example, if you're selling premium running shoes, you might want to exclude keywords like "cheap running shoes" or "free running shoes" from your campaigns. Negative keywords allow you to maintain better control over where your ads appear and ensure that your advertising budget is being spent effectively.

Building a comprehensive keyword list for your Amazon advertising campaigns requires careful planning, strategic research, and ongoing optimization. By focusing on a variety of keyword types, including both broad and exact match terms, and leveraging tools like Amazon Brand Analytics and competitive analysis, you can develop a targeted, high-performance keyword strategy. Remember that keyword research is not a one-time task but an ongoing process that evolves as customer behavior and market conditions change. By continually refining your keyword list and testing new approaches, you can ensure that your ads consistently reach the right audience and drive meaningful results.

CHAPTER 4
CREATING EFFECTIVE SPONSORED PRODUCTS CAMPAIGNS

CAMPAIGN STRUCTURE: ORGANIZATION FOR OPTIMAL PERFORMANCE

A well-organized campaign structure is the cornerstone of any successful advertising strategy, especially when navigating a complex platform like Amazon. To achieve optimal performance and maximize return on investment, advertisers need to adopt a methodical and strategic approach to how they structure their campaigns. The organization of your campaign influences everything from keyword targeting and bidding strategies to budget allocation and performance tracking. Getting this right not only saves time but also ensures that every dollar spent contributes to your goals efficiently.

At the heart of campaign structure lies the need to make thoughtful decisions regarding campaign organization, ad group setup, targeting, and keyword selection. A clear and logical structure will allow for easier management, tracking, and optimization of your campaigns, while also enabling you to adapt swiftly to changes in customer behavior or marketplace conditions. To begin with, it's essential to define the primary objectives of your campaigns—whether it's boosting visibility, increasing sales, or improving product awareness. These goals will shape the decisions you make throughout the campaign-building process.

One of the first steps to effective campaign organization is deciding how to break down your products into manageable segments. On Amazon, sellers often categorize products into different campaigns based on similarities in type, price, or promotional goals. This segmentation is critical because it allows for more precise targeting and optimization. For example, a retailer selling various types of footwear, such as running shoes, sandals, and boots, might create separate campaigns for each category. This level of organization ensures that each product type gets the attention it deserves and that bids, keywords, and budgets are allocated effectively. Additionally, it ensures that you can track performance and make data-driven decisions for each distinct product category, optimizing your strategies accordingly.

Once the products are segmented into specific campaigns, the next step is structuring ad groups within those campaigns. Ad groups are essentially collections of ads that share similar keywords or targeting criteria. Organizing your ads into distinct ad groups allows for more granular control over targeting, budgets, and bid strategies. It also enables you to track the performance of specific keywords and optimize based on their individual results. For instance, within the "running shoes" campaign, an ad group could focus on keywords related to specific features, such as "waterproof running shoes" or "breathable running shoes." This level of granularity ensures that you are targeting the right customer segments and that your ads are relevant to their specific needs.

An essential part of campaign organization is selecting the right targeting strategies. Amazon offers a variety of targeting options, each suited to different goals and objectives. For example, you can choose automatic targeting, where Amazon uses its algorithms to match your ads with relevant customer searches, or manual targeting, where you select your own keywords and audience segments. Many advertisers choose a combination of both, using automatic targeting to discover new potential keywords and audiences and manual targeting to refine and optimize the most profitable terms. This hybrid approach provides the flexibility to experiment with different strategies while maintaining control over key aspects of the campaign.

When selecting your targeting strategy, it's important to think about how different customer segments will interact with your ads. For example, customers at the beginning of their buying journey might use more general search terms, while customers who are closer to making a purchase will likely use more specific and focused keywords. Structuring campaigns with different audience segments in mind allows for better alignment between your ads and their search intent, which can lead to better performance and higher conversion rates.

At the keyword level, campaign organization takes on even greater importance. Broad, phrase, and exact match types all serve different purposes and should be organized in a way that aligns with your campaign's objectives. Broad match keywords will cast a wider net, bringing in a larger volume of traffic, while exact match keywords are highly targeted and specific, ensuring that your ad appears for only the most relevant search terms. Structuring your keyword targeting by match type allows you to balance reach and precision, ensuring that your ads are shown to customers who are most likely to convert.

Another critical element of campaign organization is setting up your bids and budgets. Once your campaigns and ad groups are structured, it's time to define how much you are willing to spend to achieve your goals. Budgeting and bid management are vital for ensuring that your campaigns operate efficiently. A well-structured campaign should include a budget that aligns with the expected return on investment for each product category. For example, if your running shoes campaign is performing well and driving high conversion rates, you may choose to allocate a larger portion of your budget to it. Conversely, if a particular product category or keyword is underperforming, you might choose to reduce the budget allocated to it or pause the campaign temporarily. This flexibility allows for better resource allocation and ensures that your budget is being spent on campaigns that offer the most value.

Bidding strategies, such as dynamic bidding and fixed bids, should also be considered within the context of campaign structure. Dynamic bidding adjusts your bid in real time based on the likelihood of a conversion, whereas fixed bids maintain a constant bid regardless of performance. Structuring your campaigns with the appropriate bidding strategy can help ensure that you are competitive without overspending. This decision will depend on your objectives, the competitive landscape, and your overall advertising goals.

Effective campaign structure also requires continuous monitoring and optimization. Once your campaigns are live, it's important to analyze performance data and make adjustments as necessary. Amazon provides a range of reporting tools, such as the campaign performance report, that allows you to track metrics like impressions, clicks, and conversions. By reviewing these metrics regularly, you can identify areas that need improvement. For example, if you notice that a particular keyword is driving a lot of clicks but not resulting in conversions, you may need to adjust your bid, refine your targeting, or improve your product listing to enhance its relevance. Similarly, if certain ad groups or campaigns are underperforming, it may be worthwhile to pause them or reallocate the budget to higher-performing areas.

The key to successful campaign management lies in ongoing optimization. Effective use of Amazon's reporting tools allows you to make informed decisions based on data rather than guesswork. Constantly reviewing your campaigns and adjusting your strategy based on performance data ensures that you stay ahead of the competition and continue to meet your business objectives. For example, you might find that one product category consistently generates higher sales at a lower cost per click, while another category underperforms. In this case, adjusting the budget allocation and focusing more on the high-performing category will help maximize your ROI.

Campaign structure also extends beyond the organization of products, ad groups, and keywords. It is essential to integrate your Amazon advertising strategy with other elements of your marketing plan, such as product listings, pricing, and promotions. For instance, running a sale or offering a discount on your product can improve the effectiveness of your ads by making your products more attractive to potential customers. Similarly, ensuring that your product listings are optimized with the right images, descriptions, and reviews will complement your advertising efforts and improve conversion rates.

A well-organized campaign structure is essential for achieving optimal performance in Amazon advertising. By segmenting products into distinct campaigns, creating targeted ad groups, selecting the right match types, and continually monitoring performance, sellers can create a strategic and efficient advertising plan. The ability to track and adjust campaigns based on real-time data ensures that resources are allocated wisely, leading to improved return on investment. A successful campaign structure is dynamic and adaptable, allowing for growth and refinement as the marketplace and customer behavior evolve. By carefully organizing campaigns and regularly optimizing based on performance, sellers can ensure sustained success on the platform.

SETTING BUDGETS AND BIDS: STRATEGIES FOR DIFFERENT GOALS

When it comes to Amazon advertising, setting appropriate budgets and bids is a fundamental aspect of ensuring that campaigns perform optimally. Whether the goal is to increase visibility, drive sales, or build brand awareness, both the budget and bidding strategies need to be tailored to match the specific objectives of each campaign. As Amazon provides a variety of tools and strategies, the key to success lies in understanding how to effectively allocate resources in a way that aligns with business goals and maximizes return on investment (ROI). Properly managing your budget and bid structure enables you to scale your efforts, control costs, and make the most of your advertising budget.

The first step in setting your budget and bids is to define the specific objectives of your campaign. Campaign goals on Amazon vary widely, from generating brand awareness and increasing product visibility to driving direct conversions and sales. Each of these goals will require a different approach to budget allocation and bid management. For example, if your goal is to increase sales, you may want to focus on setting aggressive bids and budgets to ensure your ads appear at the top of search results, driving high-intent customers to your product listings. On the other hand, if your goal is more about awareness and exposure, a more modest budget and lower bids may be appropriate, allowing you to reach a larger audience without overspending on highly competitive keywords.

Once the objective is clear, the next step is determining the overall campaign budget. This figure should be determined by considering the campaign's timeframe, the number of products being promoted, the target audience, and the specific type of ad campaign you are running. The budget is essentially the maximum amount you are willing to spend on a campaign within a given period. This figure should not only account for your goals but also take into consideration your total advertising spend capacity and potential returns.

When setting a budget, it is important to understand that the budget for an Amazon campaign isn't a fixed amount but rather an adjustable figure that may require optimization over time. For campaigns focused on immediate returns, such as generating sales or conversions, allocating a larger budget is generally necessary. Larger budgets will provide you with the flexibility to bid more aggressively on high-performing keywords and reach a larger audience. In contrast, campaigns designed for long-term objectives, such as building brand recognition or gathering customer insights, often work better with smaller budgets distributed over extended periods.

Bidding is another critical component of effective advertising on Amazon, and it requires careful attention to ensure that your campaigns are competitive and cost-effective. The bid amount determines how much you are willing to pay each time a customer clicks on your ad. In the highly competitive Amazon marketplace, setting the right bid is essential for winning auctions and securing valuable ad placements. If your bid is too low, your ad may not be shown as frequently or may not be shown at all, leading to missed opportunities for exposure. Conversely, if your bid is too high, you risk overspending and reducing your ROI.

Different goals require different bidding strategies. For campaigns aimed at increasing sales or driving conversions, using aggressive bidding strategies is often necessary. By setting higher bids, you can ensure that your ads appear at the top of the search results and are more likely to be clicked by potential buyers. This increases your product's visibility and improves the chances of converting clicks into sales. However, while higher bids increase the likelihood of getting clicks, they also come with a higher cost-per-click (CPC), so it's important to balance the increased spending with the expected return. A good practice is to monitor performance data and adjust your bids regularly based on actual results.

For campaigns focused on brand awareness or general visibility, lower bids are often more suitable. Lower bids allow you to reach a broader audience without overspending on clicks. Although the visibility might not be as prominent as with higher bids, the campaign will have the potential to reach many more users over time, which can be valuable for building a brand presence. Lower bids are also appropriate for targeting less competitive keywords or more niche markets, where the level of competition is lower, and impressions can be gained more cost-effectively.

Amazon provides two primary types of bidding strategies—dynamic and fixed. Dynamic bidding allows Amazon to automatically adjust your bid based on the likelihood of a sale. When using dynamic bidding, Amazon increases your bid when it believes there is a higher chance of a conversion and lowers it when the likelihood is lower. This type of bidding can be a useful strategy for campaigns with varying levels of competition or customer intent, as it allows your bid to adapt based on real-time data. On the other hand, fixed bidding gives you more control over your bid amount, as it remains consistent regardless of the auction conditions. This can be advantageous if you have a clear understanding of how much you are willing to spend per click and want to avoid fluctuations.

Additionally, Amazon allows for different targeting strategies such as automatic targeting and manual targeting, which can affect how you set your bids. Automatic targeting uses Amazon's algorithms to display your ads to customers based on search terms, products, and interests that are relevant to your listing. This is a great option for advertisers who are just starting or for those who want to expand their reach with minimal effort. Bids on automatic campaigns may need to be set higher in order to compete with similar ads. However, because automatic targeting is broader and less refined, you may need to adjust bids after evaluating the performance.

Manual targeting, on the other hand, offers more control over which keywords your ads target. This strategy requires more research, as you will need to determine which keywords are most relevant to your product and then bid on those specific terms. For manual campaigns, it is often necessary to set higher bids on keywords with high conversion potential to secure ad placements. In contrast, less competitive, long-tail keywords may warrant lower bids, as they tend to have lower CPCs but may generate fewer clicks.

Another important consideration when setting budgets and bids is the need to monitor and adjust campaigns over time. Amazon's advertising platform provides a range of performance metrics, such as impressions, clicks, click-through rate (CTR), and conversion rate, that allow you to track how well your campaigns are performing. By continuously reviewing these metrics, you can assess whether your bid and budget strategies are delivering the desired results. For example, if a particular keyword is driving a lot of traffic but not converting into sales, you might want to lower your bid for that keyword, adjust the ad copy, or tweak the product listing. Conversely, if a keyword is performing well, increasing your bid can help you secure more impressions and clicks.

In addition to adjusting bids, re-evaluating your budget periodically is crucial. If your campaign is performing well and delivering a positive ROI, you might want to increase your budget to capture more traffic. On the other hand, if your campaign is underperforming, reducing the budget can help you avoid wasting money on ineffective ads.

Setting budgets and bids on Amazon requires a blend of strategy, monitoring, and adjustment. The decisions you make will directly affect how your products are seen by potential customers, and as such, it is important to align your bidding and budget strategies with the overarching goals of your campaign. Whether you are focused on driving immediate sales or expanding your brand's presence on the platform, understanding the relationship between your campaign objectives, budget, and bid strategy is key to maximizing performance and achieving success.

UNDERSTANDING AUTOMATIC VS. MANUAL TARGETING

When it comes to advertising on Amazon, one of the most crucial decisions advertisers face is whether to use automatic or manual targeting for their campaigns. Both approaches offer distinct advantages, and understanding the differences between them is essential for maximizing the effectiveness of your Amazon advertising strategy. Each targeting method has its own set of characteristics that make it suitable for different types of campaigns, objectives, and levels of experience. By understanding these differences and knowing when to use each method, you can optimize your ad spend, reach the right audience, and achieve your advertising goals.

Automatic targeting is often seen as the entry-level option for advertisers who may be new to Amazon's platform or are looking for a more hands-off approach to campaign management. With automatic targeting, Amazon's algorithms take the reins, automatically selecting the keywords and audience segments your ads will target. This means that you do not need to manually choose specific keywords or products for your ads to appear alongside. Instead, Amazon's system uses its vast amounts of data to match your ads to search queries, product listings, and other relevant content that it believes aligns with your product.

One of the biggest advantages of automatic targeting is its simplicity and convenience. Advertisers can launch campaigns without spending significant time researching keywords or manually selecting target audiences. Amazon does the heavy lifting, so you can focus on other aspects of your business. This is particularly helpful for those who are just starting with Amazon advertising or for brands that want to test a broad range of keywords without committing to a specific strategy. Because automatic targeting relies on Amazon's data, it can uncover keywords and audience segments that you might not have considered, revealing new opportunities to reach customers who are actively searching for related products.

Automatic targeting can also be an excellent option for advertisers who want to scale their campaigns quickly without getting bogged down by granular keyword research. For instance, if you're looking to increase product visibility or boost brand awareness, automatic targeting can help you cast a wide net, allowing your ads to appear in front of many potential customers. The broader reach of automatic targeting can be particularly beneficial if you're introducing a new product or trying to expand your customer base across different market segments.

However, while automatic targeting offers convenience and scale, it does come with certain limitations. The most significant drawback is the lack of control over the specific keywords your ads will target. Since Amazon's algorithm handles the targeting, you don't have the ability to fine-tune the exact search terms that trigger your ads. This means your ads might show up for irrelevant or low-converting keywords, which can result in wasted ad spend and lower return on investment (ROI). Additionally, while automatic targeting can drive traffic, it may not always drive the most relevant or high-quality traffic, which can affect your conversion rates. For these reasons, automatic targeting is often best suited for campaigns that focus on broad goals such as raising awareness or testing new products rather than those aimed at driving specific conversions or sales.

On the other hand, manual targeting provides much more control and precision. With manual targeting, advertisers choose the specific keywords, product categories, or customer segments they want to target. This means that you can select search terms that are directly relevant to your products and customer base, allowing you to create highly targeted campaigns that are more likely to result in conversions. Manual targeting also allows you to tailor your bids for each keyword, giving you the ability to allocate more budget to high-performing keywords that drive sales while bidding lower on terms that are less effective.

One of the key benefits of manual targeting is the increased control it gives advertisers over their campaigns. If you already know which keywords are relevant to your products, manual targeting allows you to focus on those terms and exclude any irrelevant or unprofitable keywords. This can significantly improve the relevance of your ads and increase the likelihood of conversion. By targeting specific keywords, you can ensure that your ads appear in front of customers who are actively searching for products similar to yours, which means you're more likely to attract high-intent buyers. Moreover, by monitoring performance over time, you can adjust bids and make data-driven decisions to optimize your campaigns, ensuring that your advertising budget is spent effectively.

Manual targeting is also highly beneficial for advertisers who have a clear understanding of their target audience and want to create highly specific ad campaigns. For example, if you have a well-defined niche product or want to target a particular demographic, manual targeting allows you to create campaigns tailored to those needs. By selecting the most relevant keywords and customer segments, you can ensure that your ads are shown to the right people at the right time, improving the likelihood of making a sale.

However, while manual targeting offers greater control, it also requires more time and effort to manage. Conducting keyword research, choosing the right targeting options, and continually monitoring campaign performance can be time-consuming. This is particularly true for campaigns that involve a large number of products or target audiences. Advertisers must also have a solid understanding of keyword trends and consumer behavior in order to effectively manage manual campaigns. As such, manual targeting is best suited for experienced advertisers who have the resources and expertise to handle the complexities of campaign management.

Both automatic and manual targeting have their place in a comprehensive Amazon advertising strategy, and many advertisers find success using a combination of the two. In fact, using both methods can help you strike a balance between broad visibility and targeted precision. For example, you could start with an automatic targeting campaign to drive broad awareness and gather data on which keywords are generating the most clicks and conversions. Once you have collected enough data, you can use that information to create manual campaigns that focus on the most profitable keywords and refine your targeting for maximum effectiveness.

In some cases, using both targeting methods can also help mitigate the risks associated with relying solely on one approach. For example, if you've been using manual targeting and find that your ads aren't generating as much traffic as you'd like, you could experiment with automatic targeting to reach a larger audience and identify new opportunities. Conversely, if you're seeing that your automatic targeting campaign is generating a lot of clicks but few conversions, switching to manual targeting and refining your keyword selection could help improve the quality of your traffic.

Ultimately, the decision between automatic and manual targeting depends on your advertising goals, resources, and experience level. For advertisers seeking simplicity, scale, and convenience, automatic targeting can be a great starting point. However, for those who want greater control, precision, and optimization, manual targeting is the better option. By understanding the strengths and limitations of both methods, you can make informed decisions about how to structure your campaigns and allocate your budget effectively. Whether you choose one approach or a combination of both, the key to success lies in continuously testing, optimizing, and refining your campaigns to achieve the best possible results.

CRAFTING COMPELLING AD COPY AND PRODUCT LISTINGS

Crafting compelling ad copy and product listings is both an art and a science. It's the bridge between your product and your potential customer's attention, trust, and ultimate decision to purchase. In the intensely competitive Amazon ecosystem, simply having a good product is not enough. How you present that product—how you describe it, what emotions you evoke, what pain points you address, and how well you align with what the customer is already thinking—can make all the difference between being overlooked and being chosen.

To understand how to write copy that sells, you first have to understand the customer mindset when shopping on Amazon. Shoppers are not browsing casually like they might on social media. They come with intent—intent to compare, to evaluate, and often to buy. This means your copy must immediately resonate. It must be precise, benefit-driven, and optimized for both human psychology and Amazon's algorithm. The strongest listings don't just inform; they persuade, reassure, and build trust in the blink of an eye.

At the heart of any high-performing product listing is the product title. This is the first thing the customer sees, and it has to balance clarity, relevance, and keyword integration. A great title doesn't just say what the product is—it says why it matters. It includes relevant attributes like size, quantity, compatibility, or key ingredients. It integrates high-search-volume keywords seamlessly. But most importantly, it communicates value quickly. Titles should never be keyword-stuffed to the point of unreadability; instead, they should read naturally while being rich in terms that resonate with how users search.

Moving beyond the title, the bullet points play a critical role in converting attention into interest. These are not simply a space to list specifications. Instead, they should act like mini sales pitches, each one targeting a different benefit or solving a specific problem. Instead of stating that a phone charger is "durable," great copy would explain how its reinforced braided cable survives thousands of bends—so you won't have to worry about it breaking in the middle of your trip. Bullet points should always speak to the customer's lifestyle and concerns, painting a picture of how life improves with your product in it.

Emotion also plays a vital role. While specifications and features anchor the rational mind, the emotional side of the brain is often what pushes someone to hit the "Buy Now" button. Think about what your product helps people do, avoid, or feel. Does it save time? Make someone feel more confident? Protect their kids? Allow them to relax after a stressful day? These emotional benefits, woven into your bullet points or product description, create resonance and urgency.

Product descriptions, which often get less attention than titles or bullet points, are another opportunity to win over a customer. This is where storytelling comes into play. A great description reinforces key features, offers deeper detail, and expands on how the product fits into a customer's life. It might describe the inspiration behind the product, detail its superior craftsmanship, or explain how it outperforms others on the market. The best descriptions do not read like technical manuals; they read like conversations between brand and buyer—friendly, informative, and focused on what matters to the customer.

Keywords remain the backbone of any successful Amazon listing. But integrating them effectively is where mastery shows. Rather than stuffing keywords unnaturally, the best copywriters incorporate them fluidly throughout titles, bullet points, and descriptions. This helps listings rank higher in search results while still sounding clear and compelling to the reader. Tools like Amazon Brand Analytics and third-party keyword tools can provide insight into what customers are actually searching for. By including these search terms in your copy, you ensure that your product is discoverable and relevant.

Images, while not technically part of ad copy, work in harmony with the written content. The synergy between your words and your visuals can significantly impact conversion. Images should support what the copy claims. If your listing says "easy to use," show it being used by someone effortlessly. If it claims durability, show the product in challenging environments. Every image should tell part of the product's story. Lifestyle photos, infographics, and close-up details can all enhance what the words are already communicating.

When it comes to Amazon ads—whether Sponsored Products, Sponsored Brands, or Sponsored Display—the ad copy must be even more succinct and attention-grabbing. Space is limited, and competition is fierce. Your ad needs to communicate value in seconds. This is where headlines come into play. A strong headline is not vague or generic. It offers a benefit, creates curiosity, or solves a specific problem. For example, instead of "High-Quality Yoga Mat," a more compelling headline might say "No-Slip Yoga Mat That Stays Put, Even in Hot Yoga."

Trust-building elements should also be considered in your copy. Mentioning warranties, guarantees, certifications, or safety features can help customers feel more confident about their purchase. In a space where buyers can't touch or try a product before purchasing, trust is everything. Highlighting customer satisfaction, years in business, or eco-friendly materials can add credibility.

Another often overlooked part of compelling copy is anticipating objections. Great listings neutralize hesitation. If your product is priced higher than the competition, your copy should justify the cost with clear quality claims, unique benefits, or long-term value. If assembly is required, reassure the buyer that setup is simple and instructions are clear. Think about what might hold a customer back and proactively address it.

In a marketplace as crowded as Amazon, uniqueness is an advantage. If you're selling a product similar to many others, your copy needs to clearly differentiate it. What makes yours different? Faster shipping? Better ingredients? Custom design? More inclusive sizing? This unique selling proposition (USP) should be evident throughout your listing, particularly in your first bullet point and your main ad headline. The moment someone clicks your product or sees your ad, they should know why it's the best choice.

One of the best practices in writing persuasive copy is to use language that mirrors the customer's own thoughts and language. Reading customer reviews—both for your products and your competitors'—can reveal the language people use to describe their needs, concerns, and delight. Use those exact words in your copy. If dozens of customers praise how "lightweight" and "easy to carry" your backpack is, reinforce that in your bullet points. If people complain about similar products leaking, emphasize your product's leak-proof technology.

Lastly, A/B testing should never be ignored. Even the most thoughtfully written copy can be improved. By testing different versions of your title, bullet points, or descriptions, you can discover what resonates most with your audience. Sometimes small changes in word choice or benefit emphasis can lead to substantial increases in conversion rates. The Amazon platform supports this kind of experimentation through tools like Manage Your Experiments, giving sellers and advertisers data-driven feedback on what works best.

Effective copywriting is not about pushing products—it's about communicating value, building trust, and helping customers feel understood. It blends persuasive writing with keyword strategy and customer empathy. Whether you're writing an ad that will be seen by millions or refining a single product listing, the goal remains the same: to make the customer see your product not just as an option, but as the answer they were hoping to find.

UTILIZING PRODUCT TARGETING TO REACH RELEVANT AUDIENCES

Reaching the right audience is the bedrock of any successful advertising effort, and within Amazon's expansive advertising ecosystem, product targeting provides one of the most powerful and precise ways to connect with potential customers. Unlike broad keyword targeting that casts a wide net, product targeting allows advertisers to zero in on specific listings, brands, or categories, thereby placing their ads directly in front of people already browsing or considering similar items. This strategic alignment gives sellers the opportunity to position their product as a compelling alternative, enhancement, or superior option exactly when and where the customer is most receptive.

The core idea behind product targeting is to insert your offer into the decision-making process of the shopper at a critical moment—when they're actively researching a product that your offer either complements or competes with. This could mean showing your high-end water bottle next to a lower-rated competitor or surfacing your ergonomic mouse alongside a best-selling keyboard in the same category. The beauty of this approach lies in its specificity: you're not trying to capture random search traffic, but instead engaging people who have already signaled their interests through the types of products they're viewing.

Amazon provides several ways to implement product targeting, including targeting specific ASINs, entire categories, or refining by brand, price range, star rating, and shipping eligibility. Each of these has a distinct strategic use. Targeting individual ASINs is ideal when you have a clear competitive advantage and want to lure customers away from weaker listings. This works particularly well if your product offers better value, higher ratings, or additional features for the same price. By placing your ad on a directly competing product's detail page, you can influence the purchase path without waiting for shoppers to find your product organically.

On the other hand, category targeting enables a broader reach while still retaining contextual relevance. This strategy is useful when you're launching a new product and want to gain visibility across a range of similar items. However, because category targeting covers more ground, it often requires refinement to be truly effective. Amazon's filtering tools allow you to narrow the scope by choosing only products within a specific price bracket, only listings with fewer than a certain number of stars, or only those eligible for Prime shipping. These refinements let you tailor your targeting in a way that puts your product in the best possible light, especially when competing against less desirable listings.

When building a product targeting campaign, research is paramount. It begins with identifying which products your ideal customer is most likely to view before—or instead of—yours. This process can be as simple as browsing Amazon as a shopper would and taking note of the frequently viewed alternatives, related products, and complementary items listed on your competitors' pages. Third-party tools can also help by providing visibility into your competitors' traffic sources, top-ranking ASINs, or buyer behavior within a category. Understanding this landscape enables you to create a targeting list that aligns with real customer browsing habits.

Another layer of strategic product targeting involves leveraging customer psychology. For example, if you're offering a premium version of a common item, targeting budget models may allow you to upsell. Conversely, if your product is a lower-cost alternative to an expensive or over-engineered option, you can use product targeting to siphon off value-conscious shoppers from more expensive listings. Similarly, if your product works as an add-on or accessory, targeting complementary ASINs can position your offer right when a customer is preparing to buy something it enhances. Think of screen protectors placed on smartphone listings, or compatible ink cartridges advertised alongside popular printers.

What makes product targeting especially valuable is its position in the shopper's journey. Unlike search ads that appear based on keywords, product targeting ads surface while the shopper is deeply immersed in consideration. They're already reading specs, scanning reviews, and weighing choices. At this point, attention is high, intent is strong, and the opportunity to sway the buyer's decision is at its peak. By placing your product in this window, you tap directly into that high-conversion moment.

It's also important to consider ad creative when deploying product targeting campaigns. Your headline, image, and price all play a significant role in whether your ad captures attention. In a product detail page environment, your ad is not competing for space in isolation—it's literally side-by-side with another product the shopper is already interested in. This means your presentation must stand out. Crisp, clear imagery, a compelling value proposition, and strong social proof (such as high ratings or a large number of reviews) are crucial. Even something as simple as including a star rating and price point in the ad creative can dramatically affect performance.

Another advantage of product targeting is its usefulness for brand defense. By targeting your own ASINs, you can keep competitors from stealing traffic on your own product detail pages. This tactic, often called defensive targeting, ensures that your other products are showcased in the "sponsored products related to this item" section. For brands with a wide catalog, this creates a cross-sell ecosystem that keeps customers within your offerings, potentially increasing average order value and strengthening brand loyalty. For example, a customer browsing your running shoes might also discover your line of performance socks or hydration belts—items they may not have sought out initially but now see as part of a cohesive brand experience.

From a budget and performance standpoint, product targeting can often yield better returns than keyword targeting. Because you're reaching customers who are already deep in the purchase funnel, conversion rates tend to be higher. At the same time, because these placements may be less competitive than popular search terms, cost-per-click can be lower. This combination of lower cost and higher intent makes product targeting one of the most efficient strategies for scaling advertising without inflating your ad spend.

However, success with product targeting is not a set-it-and-forget-it affair. Continual refinement is essential. As data rolls in, you'll need to monitor which ASINs are driving conversions and which are wasting budget. Negative targeting can help by excluding underperforming placements. Likewise, doubling down on high-converting ASINs with higher bids or expanded presence can optimize return on ad spend. Amazon's reporting tools, particularly the product targeting placement report, offer valuable insights into what's working. Over time, this data-driven approach lets you create a finely tuned campaign that consistently outperforms.

Product targeting also complements other types of Amazon ads beautifully. It fills in the gaps left by keyword targeting and allows you to saturate the customer's experience at every stage. When combined with a smart keyword campaign and a well-structured Sponsored Brands effort, product targeting creates multiple touchpoints that reinforce your product's visibility and trustworthiness. It ensures that whether a shopper is searching, browsing, or comparing, your product is always part of the conversation.

As Amazon continues to grow and evolve, the advertisers who will win are those who know how to meet customers exactly where they are—both in behavior and mindset. Product targeting is one of the sharpest tools available to make this possible. It respects the intelligence of the modern consumer by providing relevant, timely alternatives, and when used effectively, it doesn't just interrupt the buying process—it enhances it. By inserting your product as a natural, valuable alternative at the perfect moment, product targeting helps transform awareness into consideration, and consideration into conversion.

CHAPTER 5
OPTIMIZING AND SCALING SPONSORED PRODUCTS CAMPAIGNS

ANALYZING KEY PERFORMANCE METRICS: ACOS, CTR, CONVERSION RATE, IMPRESSIONS

Success in advertising is never accidental. It is born from intentional, strategic choices backed by data and refined through continuous measurement. In Amazon's advertising ecosystem, data is abundant, but knowing which metrics to focus on and how to interpret them separates high-performing campaigns from mediocre ones. For advertisers who want to consistently optimize performance and stretch every advertising dollar, mastering key performance indicators like ACoS, CTR, conversion rate, and impressions is not just valuable—it's essential.

One of the most watched metrics in Amazon advertising is ACoS, or Advertising Cost of Sales. It measures how much you're spending on ads to generate a dollar of revenue. The calculation is straightforward: divide your ad spend by your attributed sales and multiply by 100 to get a percentage. But interpreting that number is where the real skill lies. A low ACoS typically means you're getting more sales for less money, which might seem like the ultimate goal. However, context matters. A very low ACoS might also indicate that you're underbidding and not capturing as much visibility as you could. On the flip side, a high ACoS might be acceptable—or even desirable—if you're running an aggressive brand awareness campaign or pushing a product with strong lifetime value. In these cases, the initial cost may be justified by long-term profit or increased market share.

ACoS should never be viewed in isolation. Click-through rate, or CTR, is another vital indicator that speaks directly to how engaging and relevant your ad is to your target audience. It is calculated by dividing the number of clicks by the number of impressions and is expressed as a percentage. A high CTR means your ad is compelling and resonates with the shopper, while a low CTR might signal that your creative, keywords, or targeting need refinement. It's an early signpost in the customer journey—a way to measure the effectiveness of your ad in capturing interest. If people see your ad but don't click it, they're not even entering the conversion funnel. So CTR often acts as an early warning system, flagging issues before they escalate into poor sales performance.

Conversion rate takes the baton from CTR and carries it to the next crucial phase: turning clicks into purchases. This metric reveals how persuasive your product detail page is once a customer arrives. It is calculated by dividing the number of orders by the number of clicks and is also shown as a percentage. A strong conversion rate suggests your listing is doing its job—it's convincing, informative, well-reviewed, and priced competitively. But a poor conversion rate, especially when paired with a high CTR, can reveal a major disconnect. It could mean that your ad is attracting clicks from the wrong audience, that your product page doesn't match the expectations set by the ad, or that there are barriers to purchase such as lack of social proof or subpar imagery. A successful advertiser treats conversion rate as a diagnostic tool. It doesn't just reflect outcomes; it points to the root of the issue when results fall short.

While CTR and conversion rate evaluate engagement and performance once your ad is served, impressions reveal how often your ad is actually being seen. This metric refers to the number of times your ad appears on Amazon, whether or not it is clicked. High impressions indicate that your targeting and bids are competitive enough to secure placements. But without corresponding increases in CTR and conversions, impressions alone don't deliver value. In fact, a campaign with sky-high impressions and minimal clicks or sales might be hemorrhaging budget. Conversely, if impressions are too low, your bids might be too conservative or your targeting too narrow. Evaluating impressions in tandem with CTR and ACoS helps clarify whether your ads are reaching enough people, and whether those people are engaging with your content as intended.

These four metrics—ACoS, CTR, conversion rate, and impressions—are interrelated and must be examined collectively. If you think of a customer's journey as a funnel, impressions sit at the top. They represent reach and visibility. CTR shows how well you're pulling people into the funnel. Conversion rate tracks how efficiently you guide them through to purchase. And ACoS evaluates the cost-effectiveness of the entire process. Small changes in any of these metrics can ripple through the entire advertising campaign. A slight improvement in CTR, for instance, not only increases engagement but also can improve your ad rank, leading to more impressions at a lower cost per click. Similarly, increasing your conversion rate can lower your ACoS, making every dollar of ad spend go further.

Interpreting these metrics also requires an understanding of goals and product lifecycle stages. During a product launch, a higher ACoS and lower conversion rate may be acceptable as you build reviews and establish a foothold. In this phase, impressions and CTR become more critical—they indicate whether your product is gaining exposure and piquing interest. Over time, as your product matures and your listing is optimized, conversion rate becomes a bigger focus, and ACoS should stabilize or decrease. There is no one-size-fits-all performance benchmark; success is always relative to objective. A luxury product may always convert at a lower rate but have a higher average order value, justifying a higher ACoS.

A consumable with repeat purchase potential might support aggressive spend in the early days because of the potential lifetime value.

To act on these insights, advertisers must adopt a mindset of continual refinement. High CTR but low conversions? Revisit your product listing. Poor impressions but high CTR when visible? Adjust bids or broaden targeting. Good conversion rate but weak ACoS? You may be overpaying for traffic and need to trim poor-performing keywords. No matter the situation, the key is responsiveness. Amazon's marketplace moves quickly, and stale campaigns can become inefficient in a matter of weeks.

Advanced advertisers often take this analysis further by slicing metrics by ad type, time frame, and targeting method. For instance, Sponsored Products may show strong ACoS but lower impressions compared to Sponsored Brands, which might deliver higher visibility but weaker conversion rates. Analyzing performance by device type or even day of the week can reveal subtle but important trends. Amazon provides detailed reporting dashboards that allow for deep dives into every corner of campaign performance, and third-party platforms can add layers of visualization and automated insight.

What ultimately empowers an advertiser to succeed is not the sheer volume of data, but the skill to extract meaningful patterns and respond in kind. These metrics are not just numbers—they are signals from your audience, indicating what's working, what's being ignored, and where you need to pivot. Learning to listen to these signals and translate them into action is what transforms campaigns from average to exceptional.

Understanding and applying performance data in real-time also supports smarter budget allocation. Instead of evenly distributing spend, you can direct funds to the most efficient campaigns, scale winners, pause underperformers, and experiment more freely without fear of waste. You move from reactive to proactive, from gut feeling to data-backed decisions. Over time, this approach compounds into a competitive edge, one that separates high-volume sellers from those who plateau.

In the ever-evolving landscape of digital advertising, adaptability is power. The ability to read and act on key metrics—ACoS, CTR, conversion rate, and impressions—is not just about improving performance today. It's about building the strategic muscle to thrive through marketplace changes, seasonal trends, and shifting customer behavior. Data, when interpreted with skill and intention, becomes not just a measurement tool, but a roadmap to scalable growth.

IMPLEMENTING NEGATIVE KEYWORDS TO REFINE TARGETING

In the world of digital advertising, success often depends not only on what you target but also on what you choose not to target. The ability to refine who sees your ads, and under what search conditions, is just as important as selecting the right keywords. This is where negative keywords come into play—an essential but often underutilized tool that can significantly sharpen your advertising strategy and boost profitability.

Negative keywords are the terms and phrases for which you specifically do *not* want your ad to appear. They serve as a filter, allowing you to avoid wasting impressions and ad spend on irrelevant traffic. When used thoughtfully, they help reduce unqualified clicks, lower Advertising Cost of Sales (ACoS), and increase overall campaign efficiency by ensuring your ad only appears in contexts where it's truly relevant. This level of control is especially important in a highly competitive marketplace where a single misalignment in targeting can cost more than just a few wasted dollars—it can cost visibility, credibility, and momentum.

Understanding why negative keywords matter begins with understanding how search behavior works on the platform. Shoppers frequently search using broad or ambiguous terms, especially in the early stages of their buying journey. They may use general phrases like "best gift for mom," "cheap phone accessories," or "how to fix a leaky faucet." While these searches may contain some keywords related to your product, they don't necessarily indicate strong buying intent or match your offer. If your ad appears for these terms and gets clicked, you pay for that interaction—regardless of whether it results in a sale. Multiply this scenario across hundreds of irrelevant impressions and clicks, and the inefficiency becomes clear. Without negative keywords, your campaign risks bleeding budget with little return.

The power of negative keywords lies in their ability to fine-tune your visibility. For example, if you sell premium stainless steel water bottles, you may want to exclude terms like "cheap," "plastic," or "budget" from your campaigns. Not because those searches are inherently bad, but because they attract a different kind of customer—one who is likely to bounce or abandon the cart when they see your higher price point. Similarly, if you offer a product for adults, you might want to exclude terms like "kids," "children," or "toddler." The more precisely you define who your product is *not* for, the more you ensure that your ad is served to the people most likely to convert.

Another important aspect of using negative keywords is how they interact with different match types. Just as regular keywords can be broad, phrase, or exact match, negative keywords also follow this logic. A negative broad match keyword prevents your ad from appearing for searches that contain all the words in any order. A negative phrase match blocks searches that contain the exact keyword phrase in the same sequence. Negative exact match only prevents your ad from appearing for that specific search query with no variations. The match type you choose should be determined by how narrowly or broadly you want to block certain terms. Too narrow, and you may miss the chance to eliminate unqualified clicks. Too broad, and you might unintentionally suppress relevant traffic. Finding the balance requires regular review, testing, and iteration.

The process of identifying effective negative keywords starts with analysis. The most valuable source for this insight is Amazon's search term reports. These reports provide a granular view of which customer queries are triggering your ads, which are getting clicked, and which are leading to conversions. By studying these reports, you can quickly identify terms that generate clicks without conversions—a strong indicator of mismatched intent. Perhaps people are clicking on your yoga mat ads when they search "yoga mat for hot yoga," but your product isn't optimized for that activity. That phrase becomes a candidate for negative keywording, saving you money and refining your audience targeting.

Beyond search term reports, other sources can also help build your negative keyword list. Customer reviews and questions can reveal misconceptions about your product. Competitor listings can uncover adjacent categories or use cases that might overlap but aren't aligned with your offer. Even your internal customer service data can be useful—look for patterns in returns, complaints, or confusion about product features. These pain points often point to disconnects between what people expected and what they received, and eliminating those mismatched search terms can reduce friction in the buying process.

Timing is also a critical factor. Negative keywords are not a one-and-done setup. As your campaign matures, shopper behavior evolves, and your product gains exposure, the landscape of search changes. A term that was irrelevant in the early stages might become valuable after a product update, seasonal shift, or strategic repositioning. Regular audits of your search term performance help ensure your negative keyword strategy remains aligned with your goals. Some advertisers implement a weekly or bi-weekly review cycle, using automation tools to highlight anomalies in CTR or conversion rate and flag potential keyword mismatches.

There's also a strategic layer to applying negative keywords across multiple campaigns. For advertisers running both automatic and manual targeting campaigns, negative keywords can help avoid internal competition. For instance, if you're using an automatic campaign to discover new high-performing terms but also running a manual campaign for your best keywords, you can apply negative keywords in the automatic campaign to prevent overlap. This way, your manual campaign retains control over the most important terms, while your automatic campaign explores new ground without cannibalizing performance.

Moreover, negative keyword segmentation helps tailor your messaging more effectively. By excluding certain terms, you can create more customized campaigns that speak directly to niche audiences. If you sell a variety of fitness products, for instance, you might have separate campaigns for yoga, weightlifting, and cardio gear. By excluding keywords related to yoga in your weightlifting campaign and vice versa, you ensure that each campaign delivers hyper-relevant ads, leading to better engagement and stronger conversion rates.

It's also worth noting that negative keywords play a critical role in protecting brand integrity. If your brand is premium, specialized, or niche, you don't want to appear alongside mass-market or irrelevant searches. That dilutes your brand value and wastes your marketing efforts. Negative keywords act as a brand safeguard, ensuring your product shows up only where it aligns with your positioning.

For large catalogs or brands managing multiple SKUs, negative keywords can help maintain clarity between product lines. If you have two similar products aimed at different customer segments, negative keywording can prevent confusion and ensure each ad is shown to the correct audience. This level of segmentation not only improves conversion but can also provide clearer performance insights by isolating which products are resonating with which audiences.

In the end, the goal of negative keywords is simple: protect your budget, preserve your brand, and ensure your ads speak only to the most relevant shoppers. They are not just a tool to block traffic—they are a tool to elevate it. Every dollar you save by excluding irrelevant clicks can be reinvested in scaling high-converting campaigns. Every impression you avoid wasting becomes an opportunity to deliver a better, more accurate customer experience elsewhere.

Mastering the use of negative keywords requires discipline, curiosity, and a deep understanding of your customer's intent. It's a practice that evolves over time, growing more powerful as you accumulate data and refine your strategy. When used correctly, negative keywords don't limit your reach—they sharpen it. They make every click count and every dollar work harder. And in a world where every detail of a campaign can mean the difference between scaling profitably and falling behind, that precision can be your greatest advantage.

A/B TESTING AD COPY AND BIDS FOR CONTINUOUS IMPROVEMENT

The cornerstone of high-performing digital advertising campaigns lies in constant iteration. Success on Amazon's advertising platform isn't a one-time setup or a fixed formula. It is a fluid process, grounded in testing, observation, and refinement. Among the most effective strategies for improving campaign performance over time is A/B testing—a disciplined approach that pits one variable against another to identify what drives better outcomes. When it comes to optimizing your campaigns, A/B testing ad copy and bids is one of the most impactful ways to achieve consistent, measurable growth.

At its core, A/B testing involves creating two or more versions of a specific ad component—such as the headline, image, product description, or bid amount—and serving them to different segments of your audience under similar conditions. The goal is to isolate the effect of a single variable on performance metrics like click-through rate (CTR), conversion rate, or return on ad spend (ROAS). It's a method that transforms guesswork into evidence-based decision-making, allowing advertisers to make confident choices based on real user behavior rather than assumptions or intuition.

Effective A/B testing begins with a clear hypothesis. This means defining what you want to test, why you want to test it, and what metric will determine the winner. For instance, if you suspect that emphasizing free shipping in your ad copy will increase conversions, your test might involve creating two nearly identical ads—one that includes the phrase "Free Shipping on All Orders" and one that doesn't. Over time, by monitoring the performance of both versions, you can see whether the inclusion of that phrase actually influences buying behavior. This clarity of intention is what separates successful testing from random tinkering.

When testing ad copy, there are several levers you can pull. The title of your product listing is often the first touchpoint for potential buyers and can significantly influence CTR. Small changes in word choice—like "lightweight" versus "portable," or "luxury" versus "premium"—can shift perception and engagement. Bullet points and product descriptions are another valuable test area. Here, the structure, tone, and featured benefits can all be varied to determine what resonates most with different segments of your audience. Visuals play a powerful role as well. If your product images are static or generic, try testing lifestyle photos, close-ups of features, or before-and-after scenarios to see which drives more clicks or purchases.

In addition to creative elements, A/B testing bids is essential for maximizing the efficiency of your ad spend. Bid testing allows you to understand how different cost-per-click (CPC) levels impact your ad visibility and profitability. For instance, increasing a bid might raise your impressions and place your product higher in search results, but it may not always yield better ROI if the added exposure doesn't lead to proportionally more conversions. Conversely, lowering bids might reduce impressions but increase profitability if it results in more efficient clicks. A/B testing these scenarios can help uncover your bid sweet spot—the point at which you gain optimal traffic at a sustainable cost.

Running bid tests requires an understanding of Amazon's auction-based ad environment. Bids are not just about placement but about value alignment. Amazon's algorithm considers both the bid amount and the relevancy of the ad when determining where it shows up in search results. Therefore, when testing bids, it's crucial to keep other variables consistent—like keywords and targeting—to ensure that any performance differences are truly due to the bid change and not some other fluctuation in campaign conditions.

One of the most important principles in A/B testing is ensuring that your tests are statistically sound. This means letting tests run long enough to gather meaningful data before drawing conclusions. Premature decisions based on insufficient data can lead to incorrect assumptions and suboptimal changes. Ideally, you want to let your test gather a significant number of impressions and clicks—often in the thousands—before you evaluate results. It's also crucial to isolate variables. Testing multiple changes at once may speed things up, but it muddies the water and makes it impossible to attribute success or failure to a specific factor. If you change the ad title and the image simultaneously, how will you know which one made the difference?

Beyond individual ad performance, A/B testing also supports long-term strategic learning. As you accumulate results from multiple tests over time, you build a deeper understanding of your audience. You begin to notice patterns in what types of messaging appeal to different segments. Maybe budget-conscious customers respond best to price-focused language, while quality-driven shoppers engage more with detailed descriptions of materials and construction. These insights not only help you optimize current campaigns but also guide your broader marketing and branding strategies.

Another often overlooked benefit of A/B testing is its role in reducing risk. When launching a new product, entering a new market, or scaling a campaign, there's always a level of uncertainty. A/B testing allows you to test the waters with minimal investment, identifying what works before going all-in. Instead of launching one expensive campaign based on a hunch, you launch two lean versions and let the data point the way. This controlled experimentation builds confidence and protects your budget.

It's also worth considering how automation tools and Amazon's own features can aid your testing efforts. Sponsored Products and Sponsored Brands campaigns allow for some degree of split testing, especially when you structure campaigns with mirrored setups and adjust only one element between them. Third-party tools and ad tech platforms often offer more robust A/B testing capabilities, such as multivariate testing or automated performance analysis. Leveraging these tools can save time, reduce errors, and help scale your testing strategy across large catalogs or multi-market campaigns.

Yet even the most sophisticated testing setup won't be effective without a commitment to ongoing refinement. A/B testing is not a one-time event—it's a continuous loop of hypothesis, execution, observation, and adjustment. Markets shift, customer preferences evolve, and new competitors emerge. What works today may not work next quarter. That's why the mindset behind A/B testing is just as important as the mechanics. It requires curiosity, humility, and a willingness to challenge assumptions regularly.

Transparency and documentation are also vital components of a robust A/B testing framework. Keeping a detailed log of your tests—what you changed, why you changed it, when the test ran, and what the results were—allows you to avoid redundant efforts and build institutional knowledge over time. These records become invaluable when scaling teams, transitioning campaigns, or revisiting past decisions in light of new data.

In the fast-paced, data-driven ecosystem of online advertising, standing still is the fastest path to irrelevance. A/B testing empowers you to stay agile, competitive, and continually aligned with what your customers care about most. It transforms marketing from an art of persuasion into a science of performance. It takes what is subjective and turns it into something measurable. And most importantly, it ensures that every decision you make is grounded not in speculation but in truth, drawn directly from the behavior of your real audience in real time.

Done well, A/B testing doesn't just improve individual ads—it transforms entire campaigns. It creates a culture of learning where experimentation leads to excellence. It replaces guesswork with clarity. And in a marketplace as dynamic and crowded as Amazon's, that edge can be the difference between running ads that merely show up—and running ads that actually sell.

STRATEGIES FOR SCALING SUCCESSFUL CAMPAIGNS

Scaling a successful advertising campaign on Amazon is not simply about increasing your budget or duplicating your current efforts. It's a strategic, data-informed process that blends expansion with control. Campaigns that perform well in their early stages often show signs of promise—strong click-through rates, healthy conversion rates, and efficient cost-per-click metrics. But scaling that success without losing profitability or control requires a disciplined approach that considers timing, audience segmentation, creative variation, and an evolving bidding strategy.

The first essential mindset to adopt when scaling is to treat your current performance data as your foundation. Before expanding, a campaign needs to demonstrate consistent, repeatable success over a meaningful period. A few days of strong performance don't necessarily indicate long-term viability. Look for stability in performance metrics such as return on ad spend (ROAS), advertising cost of sales (ACoS), and customer acquisition cost. Trends across these indicators should signal that your ad is not just riding a temporary high from seasonality or one-time search behavior, but that it is connecting deeply and consistently with the right audience.

Once this performance baseline is verified, the next step involves increasing budget incrementally. Rather than pouring a massive increase into the campaign all at once, successful advertisers often raise their daily budget or bid caps gradually. This cautious approach allows the Amazon algorithm to adapt without shocking the campaign system. It helps maintain performance by giving the platform time to test and understand the new level of spend and the resulting shifts in competition, placement, and traffic volume. As spend increases, keep a close watch on efficiency metrics. Scaling is only successful if those metrics remain stable or improve.

Audience segmentation becomes a powerful lever in the scaling process. As your campaign grows, your audience often becomes more diverse. Initially, you may have focused on a narrow, high-intent group. But with scaling comes reach into broader or colder segments. Instead of running the same ad to everyone, consider breaking your campaign into separate ad groups that target different customer profiles, each with its own tailored messaging and bid strategy. For example, one group could target loyal repeat buyers, while another could focus on first-time shoppers who are unfamiliar with your brand. This segmentation allows for more personalized communication and better budget control across different levels of the sales funnel.

Expanding keyword coverage is another powerful tactic when scaling. While your initial campaign may have been limited to a few high-performing keywords, scaling requires casting a wider net. This doesn't mean abandoning your top performers but augmenting them with related search terms that reach adjacent customer interests or product categories. Tools like Amazon Brand Analytics, Helium 10, and Jungle Scout can uncover long-tail keywords and rising search terms within your niche. These lower-competition, high-intent phrases often yield strong performance at a lower cost, helping to balance the campaign as it scales.

Another key strategy in scaling is diversifying your ad formats. If you've seen early success with Sponsored Products, it may be time to explore Sponsored Brands or Sponsored Display. Sponsored Brands allow you to promote multiple products and integrate brand messaging, which can increase average order value and support long-term brand equity. Sponsored Display ads enable retargeting, so you can re-engage shoppers who viewed your products but didn't convert. Each of these formats offers different placement opportunities and behavior triggers, which expands your visibility across the platform while reinforcing your messaging at different stages of the customer journey.

Campaign scaling should also involve creative refreshes. What captures attention and drives action at a smaller scale may begin to lose its edge when exposed to a broader audience. This is where iterative testing becomes invaluable. A/B testing different product images, headlines, bullet points, and ad copy ensures that your creative remains compelling as your audience grows. Additionally, rotating creatives can reduce ad fatigue, especially for users who are repeatedly exposed to your content without converting.

Geographic expansion is another dimension of scaling worth exploring. If your campaign is performing well in one region or marketplace, it may be time to test performance in other Amazon marketplaces. This kind of international scaling comes with its own complexities—logistics, language localization, and pricing strategies—but it also offers a massive opportunity to tap into new pools of demand. The core campaign structure can often remain the same, but must be localized in terms of language, cultural relevance, and buyer preferences.

Automated rules and bid management systems can become crucial allies in scaling as campaign complexity increases. As you expand into more ad groups, more keywords, and more formats, managing everything manually becomes less feasible. Amazon provides automation tools that allow for rule-based bidding adjustments, budget reallocation, and keyword pausing based on performance thresholds. Third-party platforms can offer even deeper automation with AI-driven optimization. These systems help ensure that campaigns remain efficient and responsive to real-time data, even at scale.

A frequently overlooked aspect of scaling is inventory readiness. As your advertising efforts drive more visibility and conversions, your supply chain must be prepared to meet increased demand. There's little point in scaling a campaign if it results in stockouts or shipping delays. Advertising success on Amazon is closely linked to the health of your product listings, including availability, fulfillment speed, and customer satisfaction. Before turning up the volume on your campaign, ensure that your inventory, logistics, and customer service systems are aligned to support that growth without disruption.

It's also vital to remain strategic about attribution and lifecycle tracking during scaling. Some sales may occur days after the initial ad impression or click, especially for higher-priced items or considered purchases. Amazon's attribution models and reporting tools can help track delayed conversions and multi-touch journeys. Understanding how different touchpoints contribute to sales over time will allow you to scale the channels and campaigns that actually influence purchase decisions—not just those that drive immediate action.

Long-term success in scaling campaigns lies in balancing aggressiveness with discipline. The temptation to scale quickly can lead to inefficiencies, overbidding, or overspending if not carefully monitored. Conversely, overly cautious scaling may result in missed opportunities or stagnant growth. The most successful advertisers operate in a cycle of proactive experimentation, rapid learning, and incremental scaling. They remain agile, allowing performance data to inform next steps, while staying anchored in a clear vision of profitability and customer relevance.

Ultimately, scaling isn't just about more—it's about better. It's about taking what works, understanding why it works, and replicating that success across a broader canvas without compromising the core strategy. It's a process of continuous adaptation, where each stage of growth informs the next. The goal isn't merely to spend more or appear more frequently but to maintain the same, or improved, level of efficiency while reaching more of the right customers. When done well, scaling transforms a promising campaign into a cornerstone of sustainable, long-term brand growth on one of the world's most competitive and rewarding digital marketplaces.

TROUBLESHOOTING COMMON SPONSORED PRODUCTS ISSUES

Sponsored Products campaigns are among the most powerful tools available on Amazon, offering direct visibility to shoppers already deep in the purchasing funnel. However, running these campaigns successfully is rarely a "set it and forget it" endeavor. Despite careful planning and strategic execution, advertisers frequently encounter challenges that interfere with performance and profitability. These problems range from technical hiccups to poor campaign structure, underwhelming creative elements, and misaligned bidding strategies. Effectively troubleshooting these issues is crucial to maintaining momentum, regaining lost performance, and ensuring long-term advertising success.

One of the most common and frustrating problems advertisers face is the lack of impressions. When an ad receives little to no visibility, it usually means the campaign is not competing effectively in the auction process. This can be a result of multiple factors, but the most frequent culprits are overly restrictive targeting, low bids, or insufficient budget. Low impressions signal that your ads are simply not being shown often enough to gather meaningful data or drive traffic. In many cases, raising bids slightly can help the ad become more competitive. However, it's not just about bidding more—it's about understanding the ecosystem you're participating in. If your keywords are highly competitive, especially in popular categories, you may need to adjust your strategy by targeting more specific long-tail keywords or testing different match types to access more affordable traffic segments.

Another issue closely tied to poor impressions is keyword irrelevance. Amazon's algorithm is designed to reward relevance. If the keywords you are bidding on have little semantic or contextual relationship to your product listing, the system deprioritizes your ad, even if you offer a high bid. This often happens when advertisers attempt to target broad, trendy search terms that don't align with the product's actual features or benefits. Ensuring keyword alignment with your product's title, bullet points, backend search terms, and description is essential. Amazon crawls these areas to determine relevance, and the closer the match between the ad's keywords and the product's content, the greater the chance of ad delivery and strong performance.

Low click-through rates (CTR) present a different challenge altogether. If your ad is being displayed but failing to attract clicks, the problem may lie in your product image, title, or price competitiveness. Amazon is a visually-driven platform. Shoppers often make split-second decisions based on thumbnails and short titles. If your product image lacks clarity, brightness, or visual appeal compared to competitors, CTR suffers. Titles that are either too vague or too cluttered with keywords also tend to repel clicks. Price also plays a critical role—if you are not priced competitively or lack visible social proof (like strong star ratings or review volume), your ad may be overlooked in favor of better-positioned alternatives. A/B testing your creative elements is one of the most effective ways to identify the optimal combination that generates interest and interaction.

Conversion rate issues often surface after you've managed to attract clicks but notice that shoppers aren't completing their purchase. This is a red flag indicating a disconnect between the shopper's expectations and the product detail page. Poor conversion rates can stem from a range of issues including misleading ad copy, lackluster product descriptions, unconvincing bullet points, low review count, or shipping and fulfillment concerns. If the product detail page doesn't reinforce the value promised by the ad, customers will abandon the purchase. Improving your product listing's persuasive power through better storytelling, clearer benefits, and enhanced imagery can help bridge this gap and boost conversion.

Campaigns that spend too quickly without producing returns typically point to overly broad targeting or unqualified traffic. This is often seen in automatic targeting campaigns that lack negative keywords or manual campaigns using broad match keywords without oversight. When your targeting lacks specificity, your ad may be displayed for irrelevant searches that burn through your budget without converting. Regularly reviewing your search term reports helps identify wasteful clicks and offers the opportunity to refine targeting by adding negative keywords or switching to more precise match types. Keeping a tight rein on your targeting parameters ensures that your budget is allocated toward audiences most likely to convert.

Another subtle yet impactful issue is campaign cannibalization. This happens when multiple campaigns or ad groups compete against each other for the same search terms, often bidding against one another and driving up costs unnecessarily. It also makes performance analysis more difficult, as conversions can be split across multiple campaigns, masking the true efficiency of any single effort. To avoid this, structure your campaigns clearly by separating branded terms from non-branded terms, segmenting by match type, and organizing by product line or goal. A well-structured account is easier to manage, measure, and scale.

Ad disapprovals and delivery issues can also stall performance. Sometimes, an ad doesn't go live at all due to policy violations, missing content, or incompatible targeting. These problems can often be traced back to the product detail page. Amazon's advertising policies require a baseline level of listing quality before an ad can be promoted. Ensure your listings include clear titles, images, product features, and comply with all content guidelines. If an ad is repeatedly not delivering without a clear reason, reaching out to Amazon's advertising support team may reveal underlying issues such as suppressed listings or incomplete category information.

Underperformance across a previously successful campaign is another challenge many advertisers face. If performance begins to dip after a period of stability, it may be due to increased competition, market saturation, seasonal shifts in demand, or changes in customer behavior. Amazon's marketplace is dynamic, and what works well today may become outdated in a few months. Regular optimization is key—reviewing your bids, creatives, keywords, and segmentation should be part of an ongoing routine. Staying informed about competitive activity through Amazon Brand Analytics can also help you adjust quickly when market conditions change.

In some cases, the issue lies in budget pacing. Campaigns with small daily budgets often run out of funds early in the day, leading to missed opportunities during high-conversion hours later. This limits exposure and distorts performance metrics, giving you an incomplete picture of how your ads might perform with a more balanced pacing. Setting a higher daily budget or implementing budget rules that adjust spending based on real-time results allows for more even distribution of impressions across the day.

Misaligned performance expectations can create the perception of a problem when, in fact, the campaign is operating within normal parameters. It's important to match your advertising goals with the correct performance benchmarks. A campaign focused on brand visibility will have different KPIs than one focused on direct sales. A product launch may experience lower initial ROAS while building momentum. Understanding what success looks like for each campaign and adjusting your expectations accordingly prevents premature changes that can disrupt promising campaigns.

The reality is that even the most carefully designed Sponsored Products campaigns will encounter obstacles. The key to sustainable success lies in diagnosing problems quickly, implementing data-informed solutions, and maintaining flexibility. Amazon's advertising environment is fast-moving, and those who thrive are the ones who treat every challenge as a signal—a chance to refine, iterate, and improve. Whether it's low impressions, high spend, or sluggish conversions, each issue offers insight into how your campaign is performing in the real world and what steps can be taken to sharpen its edge.

PART 3

Building Your Brand with Amazon Sponsored Brands Ads

CHAPTER 6

UNDERSTANDING THE POWER OF SPONSORED BRANDS

SHOWCASING YOUR BRAND AND PRODUCT PORTFOLIO

Building a recognizable brand on Amazon goes far beyond having a great product. The competitive edge lies in how effectively your brand and product portfolio are showcased. With millions of listings vying for shopper attention, your ability to stand out relies on crafting an immersive, trust-building experience that makes customers not only want to buy from you once but continue coming back. Showcasing your brand on Amazon isn't just about presentation—it's about creating connection, building credibility, and telling a story that resonates.

To begin with, it's essential to understand that Amazon shoppers often interact with products in a siloed, transactional way. They come with a purpose: find a solution, compare prices, and make a quick decision. This transactional nature can work against brands unless a deliberate effort is made to transform a simple product listing into a brand destination. One of the most powerful tools for this transformation is Amazon's Brand Registry. By enrolling, you gain access to enhanced brand content, or A+ Content, as well as Brand Stores, Sponsored Brands ads, and access to analytics that help you understand how customers are interacting with your brand across the platform.

A+ Content is one of the most direct ways to elevate your product listings. It allows you to replace the plain text product descriptions with rich visuals, comparison charts, and modular layouts that highlight unique selling points. When done well, this content creates a visual narrative that increases buyer confidence. Imagine a shopper comparing two identical products—one with generic bullet points and another with high-resolution images, a brand story, feature breakdowns, and lifestyle shots. The latter creates a compelling emotional appeal, helping the shopper see the product in their life, solving their problem. That's the power of A+ Content—it doesn't just describe a product; it sells a lifestyle, a purpose, a brand promise.

Beyond individual product listings, your Brand Store becomes the digital equivalent of your own branded website within Amazon. It offers a curated environment where shoppers can explore your full portfolio, learn about your mission, and navigate seamlessly between product lines. This is crucial for cross-selling, upselling, and building brand affinity. A well-designed Brand Store doesn't feel like just another Amazon page—it feels like a unique shopping experience. It allows you to create customized navigation, highlight best sellers, showcase seasonal promotions, and tell your brand's story through visuals and content that mirror your external branding.

Your Brand Store also plays an essential role in reinforcing the breadth and depth of your product portfolio. It's where you can show how your products complement each other. A single customer may arrive looking for one item, but through strategic layout and messaging, you can guide them to explore companion products. For example, a customer looking for a fitness tracker might also discover your workout gear, nutritional supplements, or wellness journals—all because the store was designed to encourage discovery. These internal product relationships, presented organically and visually, can significantly increase the average order value.

Another critical component of brand showcasing is how your product portfolio is structured across categories. Too often, sellers treat each product as an isolated listing, failing to build cohesion across the portfolio. But brand equity grows when there is a visible and thematic link between products. Naming conventions, imagery style, tone of copy, and even color schemes can all be harmonized to present a unified identity. When a shopper sees consistency across your offerings, it reinforces trust. It signals professionalism, reliability, and quality.

High-quality photography and video content are also indispensable when showcasing your brand. On Amazon, customers can't touch, try, or test the product. Their entire decision is based on what they see and read. Investing in professional images that show your product from multiple angles, demonstrate scale, and capture it in real-life usage scenarios builds credibility. Video takes this even further. A short, engaging product video that walks customers through features, demonstrates real-world benefits, or highlights your brand's ethos can be a powerful differentiator. Videos can turn uncertain browsers into confident buyers by reducing doubt and elevating perceived value.

Your customer reviews and ratings are another silent but powerful showcase of your brand. They reflect public perception and directly influence conversion. Actively managing your customer feedback loop— requesting reviews post-purchase, addressing complaints, and using insights to refine your offerings—helps shape a positive brand reputation. Additionally, responding to reviews publicly, especially the negative ones, shows accountability and commitment to customer satisfaction. When shoppers see a brand actively engaged with its customers, it builds emotional capital and encourages loyalty.

Advertising plays a complementary role in showcasing your brand by directing traffic strategically. Sponsored Brands campaigns, in particular, allow you to promote your logo, a custom headline, and multiple products within a single ad that links directly to your Brand Store or curated landing page. These campaigns are invaluable for top-of-funnel visibility. They not only attract shoppers but guide them into your ecosystem, where the full breadth of your brand is on display. Unlike Sponsored Products ads, which drive clicks to individual listings, Sponsored Brands serve as digital billboards—brand builders designed to make a lasting impression.

Equally important is how you manage the customer journey post-click. If a shopper lands on a beautifully branded page but finds that your listings are inconsistent, inventory is frequently out of stock, or your pricing feels erratic, it erodes trust. Operational excellence is as much a part of your brand showcase as the creative elements. Ensure your listings are regularly updated, pricing is competitive and stable, and availability is consistent. Logistics might not be glamorous, but they are a core part of your brand experience.

Another often-overlooked dimension of showcasing your brand is leveraging customer data for personalization and strategic positioning. Amazon's Brand Analytics gives you access to demographic reports, repeat purchase behavior, and market basket insights. These tools allow you to understand who your buyers are, what they purchase alongside your products, and how often they return. With this knowledge, you can tailor your messaging, group complementary products, and even adjust your branding to better appeal to your core audience. Knowing your customers in depth is what separates generic brands from resonant ones.

In the end, showcasing your brand and product portfolio on Amazon is about creating a complete, unified experience. It's about aligning every element—from visuals and copy to pricing and fulfillment—with your core values and customer promise. It's a continuous process of refinement and storytelling, where every touchpoint adds another layer of trust and connection. When done correctly, your brand becomes more than just a seller on Amazon. It becomes a destination, a reliable source, a familiar name customers recognize and return to. And that, in a marketplace defined by endless choice, is the most powerful position to hold.

UTILIZING DIFFERENT SPONSORED BRANDS FORMATS

Sponsored Brands ads provide a unique and potent avenue for elevating brand awareness on Amazon by not only promoting individual products but creating branded experiences that resonate with customers beyond a single transaction. These ads, appearing prominently in search results, offer a variety of creative formats designed to tell a richer story. They don't just highlight a product—they showcase a brand's personality, philosophy, and product ecosystem in a way that is engaging and highly visible. Leveraging each format strategically—Product Collection, Store Spotlight, and Video Ads—requires an understanding of their strengths and optimal use cases. Done right, they can be the cornerstone of a scalable brand-building strategy that drives both awareness and conversion.

The Product Collection format is often the starting point for many advertisers. It's the most familiar version of Sponsored Brands and provides a flexible but structured way to showcase multiple items together under one brand umbrella. These ads allow for a custom headline, brand logo, and a selection of up to three products. The goal is to capture user attention early in the search journey and direct that attention toward a cohesive product presentation. When someone searches for a relevant keyword, the Product Collection ad appears at the top of the results, often before any organic listings or Sponsored Products. This prime real estate ensures visibility, but more importantly, it offers an invitation to explore your offerings in a branded context.

The effectiveness of Product Collection ads lies in their ability to group complementary items. Whether it's different variants of the same product, accessories that go with a main item, or an assortment from the same category, this format encourages bundling and increases the likelihood of multi-item purchases. For instance, a fitness brand might display a yoga mat, a foam roller, and a resistance band—items that naturally go together. Customers seeing such ads don't just think about the product they searched for—they start imagining the broader solution you're offering. The headline and logo serve as trust signals, especially when they reflect a clear and consistent brand voice. It's this combination of utility and branding that makes the Product Collection format so powerful for growing not just sales, but customer loyalty.

Store Spotlight takes the strategy a step further by focusing not just on individual products but on the overall brand experience. Instead of directing shoppers to a single product detail page, these ads drive them to your Brand Store, specifically to different pages within that store based on what you choose to feature. This format is ideal for brands with multiple product lines or subcategories, allowing them to showcase breadth while offering tailored pathways. A beauty brand, for example, might use a Store Spotlight ad to highlight skincare, makeup, and haircare sections of their Brand Store, giving each category equal prominence and inviting shoppers to explore based on their specific interests.

The true advantage of Store Spotlight lies in its ability to increase time spent within your branded environment. When users land in your store rather than on a product page, they're more likely to browse additional items, read your brand story, and interact with your content. This extended engagement helps build emotional connection and brand affinity. It's especially effective for businesses looking to grow customer lifetime value and encourage repeat purchases. The Brand Store acts like a mini-website within Amazon, and Store Spotlight is the entry point that brings users into that curated world. It's a format best utilized when your catalog is diverse and your brand story is strong.

Then there's the Sponsored Brands Video format—a game-changing addition to Amazon's advertising suite. These ads consist of autoplay video content that appears directly in the search results, typically mid-page. The motion, sound, and visual storytelling elements create a natural disruption in a sea of static listings. Shoppers are naturally drawn to moving content, especially when it's concise, well-produced, and informative. Unlike other platforms where video ads might be ignored or skipped, Amazon video ads capture attention precisely at the moment of purchase intent. They meet the customer where they're actively researching and making decisions.

Sponsored Brands Video ads are particularly effective for highlighting product features, demonstrating usage, or addressing common questions in a visual format. A kitchen appliance, for example, can be shown in action, illustrating its benefits in a way that bullet points never could. A skincare product can show application methods, textures, and before-and-after effects. The key is to deliver value in the first few seconds—whether that's through stunning visuals, a powerful opening line, or a compelling use case. Since the ad links directly to a product detail page, it allows for a smooth transition from interest to purchase.

The production quality of Sponsored Brands Video ads matters deeply. This is not the place for generic footage or unpolished messaging. The video must reflect the quality and credibility of the brand it represents. Crisp visuals, clear voiceovers or captions, and a fast-paced edit are essential. The video should answer the customer's silent questions: Why this product? What makes it different? How will it fit into my life? The closer your video comes to mirroring the decision-making process of the shopper, the higher the engagement and conversion.

While each Sponsored Brands format serves a distinct purpose, the real power comes from integrating them into a unified advertising strategy. Product Collection ads build front-line visibility and drive conversions for key products. Store Spotlight promotes broader brand discovery and product exploration. Sponsored Brands Video educates and convinces with emotional appeal and practical demonstrations. Using all three in concert creates multiple entry points into your brand ecosystem, each tailored to a specific stage of the customer journey.

Strategic implementation also involves targeting the right keywords for each format. Product Collection may benefit from broader keywords with high search volume, ensuring visibility among shoppers still exploring their options. Store Spotlight can be paired with branded keywords or category-specific terms to attract users already inclined to trust a known name or category leader. Video ads, because of their disruptive power, can target more competitive or niche keywords to help you stand out among similar listings. Refining your targeting based on performance data ensures that each ad format reaches the audience most likely to convert through that specific engagement style.

It's also important to continually optimize creative assets across formats. Swap out products in your Product Collection ad to reflect seasonal trends or inventory priorities. Update your Brand Store layout and landing pages to align with Store Spotlight ads for continuity. Refresh video content to test different messaging angles, styles, or featured benefits. Each format should evolve based on performance metrics, customer feedback, and shifts in your catalog or marketing goals. An adaptive strategy ensures longevity and effectiveness.

Ultimately, Sponsored Brands formats offer more than just a means of driving clicks—they provide a platform for storytelling, brand building, and customer engagement that transcends the limitations of traditional product ads. By mastering how and when to use Product Collection, Store Spotlight, and Video Ads, advertisers can build campaigns that not only sell more, but create lasting impressions that drive brand equity and future growth.

CREATING ENGAGING HEADLINES AND BRAND LOGOS

In the world of digital advertising, the power of a compelling headline and a memorable brand logo cannot be overstated, especially when it comes to advertising on Amazon Prime. These elements are the first things a potential customer notices when they come across your ad. They serve as the initial touchpoint in what could be the beginning of a customer's journey with your brand. A carefully crafted headline grabs attention and piques curiosity, while a strong brand logo builds trust and reinforces recognition. Together, they are the foundation of a successful ad that not only attracts clicks but converts them into sales. Understanding how to create engaging headlines and impactful brand logos is crucial for any advertiser looking to stand out in the crowded Amazon marketplace.

Headlines are the first thing consumers see when they encounter your ad, and this makes them incredibly important. A headline's primary role is to capture attention immediately. In an environment as competitive as Amazon, where multiple products and brands compete for visibility, you have a split second to make an impression. To achieve this, your headline must be concise, clear, and direct while also evoking curiosity. It should give potential customers just enough information to entice them to click but not so much that they feel they have already learned everything they need to know. It's about striking the right balance between intriguing and informative.

Effective headlines often focus on the benefits of the product rather than just its features. While features are important, consumers are more interested in how the product will solve a problem or improve their lives. For example, a headline for a kitchen appliance might not focus on the fact that the appliance has a stainless-steel body, but instead, it could highlight how it saves time or enhances the cooking experience. This type of language speaks directly to the consumer's desires and needs, which is far more likely to grab their attention.

Additionally, using power words and emotional triggers in your headline can significantly increase its effectiveness. Words like "exclusive," "limited-time," "premium," or "best-selling" evoke a sense of urgency or superiority, which can encourage consumers to take action. Similarly, emphasizing how your product can improve a customer's life or solve a particular problem can tap into the consumer's emotions. A headline like "Achieve Your Fitness Goals Faster with Our Revolutionary Resistance Bands" appeals directly to the consumer's aspirations, making it not only attention-grabbing but also motivating.

The tone and style of the headline are also important. Depending on your brand identity, your headline should reflect your brand's voice. A playful, witty headline might work well for a younger, more casual audience, while a more formal and straightforward headline might be better suited for a professional or high-end market. It's important that the tone aligns with the overall messaging of your brand to maintain consistency. Inconsistencies in tone can lead to confusion or mistrust among consumers, so keeping your messaging coherent is vital.

Equally important as the headline is the brand logo. A logo is the visual representation of your business, and it's a critical element in creating brand recognition. When your logo appears alongside your products, it reinforces your brand's identity and can help build trust with consumers. The Amazon platform, with its vast array of sellers, can sometimes make it difficult for customers to differentiate one seller from another. Your logo helps create that distinction, making your products stand out in a sea of options. Over time, a recognizable logo can be a significant asset in establishing brand loyalty.

A good logo is simple yet distinctive. It should be memorable and easily recognizable, even at a glance. A complex logo with too many details can be overwhelming and hard to recall, especially when viewed on smaller devices like smartphones, which are commonly used to shop on Amazon. A clean and minimalistic design is often more effective because it allows your brand to be easily identifiable in a crowded marketplace.

When designing a logo, it's essential to consider the color scheme. Colors play a huge role in conveying emotions and setting the tone for your brand. For example, blue is often associated with trust and reliability, while red can evoke excitement and urgency. Green is commonly used in eco-friendly or health-related products, as it symbolizes nature and wellness. Choose colors that align with the values and personality of your brand. This will help convey your message visually and ensure that the logo resonates with the target audience.

Another key consideration in logo design is scalability. Your logo will appear in various sizes across different platforms, from large banners on your Brand Store to small icons in Sponsored Brands ads. It's important that your logo remains clear and legible, regardless of the size or format. Avoid overly intricate fonts or designs that might become blurry or difficult to interpret when scaled down. A simple logo with a strong, clear design will maintain its effectiveness across all platforms and device types.

While creating the logo and headline are crucial for an ad's initial success, the alignment of these elements with the product and customer needs is just as important. A headline that promises benefits must be backed by a logo that instills confidence and trust. A beautifully designed logo will fall short if the headline doesn't resonate with the audience or if the product itself fails to deliver. Similarly, a compelling headline can lose its impact if it leads to a product page that lacks clarity, poor images, or subpar descriptions.

To create a successful brand experience, both the headline and logo must speak to the same narrative. For example, if you are advertising a high-tech gadget, the headline should reflect innovation and efficiency, while the logo should convey cutting-edge technology. The synergy between these two elements ensures that the consumer's expectations are set correctly and reinforces your brand's promise.

As you work to create engaging headlines and impactful logos, don't forget to continuously test and optimize. A/B testing headlines is a common practice that can provide valuable insights into what resonates most with your target audience. Similarly, testing different logo designs or iterations can help you refine your brand's visual identity to maximize its effectiveness. These testing practices allow you to gather data on consumer preferences and adjust your approach accordingly.

In the fast-paced world of Amazon advertising, success hinges on your ability to capture attention quickly and make a lasting impression. A well-crafted headline does just that, and when paired with a strong, recognizable logo, it can elevate your advertising efforts and drive both awareness and sales. By understanding the importance of these two elements, advertisers can build campaigns that not only stand out but also connect meaningfully with their audience. This connection, once made, can lead to brand loyalty, increased sales, and long-term success.

DRIVING TRAFFIC TO YOUR AMAZON STORE AND PRODUCT DETAIL PAGES

Driving traffic to your Amazon Store and product detail pages is one of the most crucial aspects of achieving success on the platform. With millions of sellers and an even larger number of products available, standing out in Amazon's marketplace can seem like a daunting task. However, strategically driving traffic to your product listings and store can significantly boost your visibility, increase your sales, and improve your overall brand presence. To achieve this, a combination of effective advertising strategies, optimization techniques, and engaging content is necessary. By mastering these techniques, you can create a steady stream of potential customers to your Amazon storefront.

One of the most straightforward methods of driving traffic to your Amazon Store and product detail pages is through Amazon's internal advertising tools. Amazon offers a variety of advertising solutions designed to help sellers increase their visibility and direct traffic to their listings. The most commonly used tools are Sponsored Products, Sponsored Brands, and Sponsored Display Ads. These tools allow sellers to target customers who are actively searching for products like theirs, which increases the likelihood of conversions.

Sponsored Products ads are an effective way to promote individual products and drive traffic directly to the product detail page. These ads appear in the search results and on product detail pages, ensuring that your product gets noticed by customers who are already interested in similar items. With Sponsored Products, you can target keywords or product categories relevant to your product, ensuring that your ad is seen by customers who are most likely to convert. Bidding on keywords that are closely related to your product ensures that your ad appears in front of the right audience at the right time.

Sponsored Brands, on the other hand, go a step further by showcasing your entire brand or a selection of your products. These ads appear at the top of Amazon search results, making them highly visible to shoppers. Sponsored Brands are an excellent tool for driving traffic to your Amazon Store, as they allow you to showcase a variety of products in a single ad. This is particularly useful for brands that offer a range of related products, as it encourages customers to explore more of what your brand has to offer. By creating a Sponsored Brands campaign that links to your Amazon Store, you can increase traffic to both your individual product pages and your storefront.

Another highly effective method of driving traffic to your Amazon Store is by utilizing Amazon's Display Ads. Sponsored Display Ads appear both on and off Amazon, targeting potential customers based on their shopping behavior. These ads are designed to capture the attention of shoppers who have already shown interest in similar products, either through recent searches or product views. Sponsored Display Ads can be customized to direct traffic to your product detail pages or your Amazon Store. By using these ads strategically, you can re-engage customers who have shown interest in your products but may not have completed their purchase.

In addition to Amazon's own advertising tools, it's essential to optimize your product listings for organic traffic. When potential customers search for products on Amazon, the search results are primarily driven by relevancy, so having an optimized product detail page is crucial. One of the most important elements of optimization is the product title. The title should clearly describe the product while incorporating relevant keywords that customers are likely to use when searching for products like yours. A well-crafted product title helps your listing appear in search results and immediately conveys to the customer what the product is.

Beyond the title, your product description and bullet points are essential for converting traffic into sales. Product descriptions should clearly highlight the key benefits and features of the product, answering any potential questions a customer might have. It's important to include relevant keywords throughout the description, but they should be used naturally to avoid sounding like keyword stuffing. Bullet points, on the other hand, should focus on the product's unique selling points, emphasizing what sets your product apart from the competition. By clearly outlining the product's benefits, you help customers make an informed purchasing decision, increasing the likelihood that they will click the "Buy Now" button.

Product images are another crucial element in driving traffic and encouraging conversions. High-quality images that show the product from different angles, in use, and in a well-lit environment can significantly improve a customer's experience. Images should not only be clear and professional but should also showcase the product's features. For example, if you are selling a kitchen appliance, showing the appliance in use can help customers visualize how it will fit into their lives. The more engaging and informative your product images are, the more likely they are to convert traffic into sales.

One of the most powerful ways to drive traffic to your Amazon Store is by creating a branded Amazon Storefront. An Amazon Storefront allows you to create a customized, immersive shopping experience for your customers. By featuring a variety of your products in an easy-to-navigate layout, you can entice customers to explore more of what your brand has to offer. Your Storefront should reflect your brand identity, with cohesive design elements, including your logo, color scheme, and product categories. It should be optimized for mobile, as a significant percentage of Amazon shoppers browse and shop from their smartphones.

Once you've set up your Amazon Store, it's important to drive traffic to it using the various advertising methods available. Sponsored Brands are an excellent way to promote your Storefront, as they allow you to showcase your brand and products in one cohesive ad. You can also use social media, email marketing, and other external channels to drive traffic to your Amazon Store. Promoting your Storefront outside of Amazon increases your visibility and helps attract customers who may not have found your products through Amazon's search results.

In addition to paid ads, organic strategies can also help drive traffic to your Amazon Store. One such strategy is leveraging reviews and ratings. Products with higher ratings and positive reviews are more likely to rank higher in search results, which can lead to more visibility and increased traffic. Encourage satisfied customers to leave reviews and ensure that your products meet or exceed customer expectations to maintain a strong reputation on the platform.

Another organic method for driving traffic is participating in Amazon's Lightning Deals or other promotional events. These time-sensitive promotions can significantly increase traffic to your listings by offering limited-time discounts to customers. When participating in these events, make sure that your product listings are optimized and ready to convert, as the increased visibility can result in a surge of traffic and potential sales.

Lastly, consider utilizing Amazon's Affiliate Program to drive traffic to your product listings and Storefront. By partnering with bloggers, influencers, and content creators, you can tap into a wider audience who can help promote your products. Affiliates can earn a commission for driving sales, which incentivizes them to share your products with their followers. This strategy can help you expand your reach and drive targeted traffic to your listings, leading to increased visibility and higher sales.

Driving traffic to your Amazon Store and product detail pages is not a one-time effort; it requires ongoing optimization, experimentation, and adaptation to changes in customer behavior and platform trends. By combining effective advertising strategies with a well-optimized product listing, engaging content, and external traffic-driving methods, you can build a sustainable flow of traffic to your Amazon presence. Over time, this increased visibility can lead to higher conversions, improved sales, and long-term success in the competitive Amazon marketplace.

MEASURING THE IMPACT OF SPONSORED BRANDS ON BRAND AWARENESS

Measuring the impact of Sponsored Brands on brand awareness is a vital aspect of evaluating the effectiveness of your advertising campaigns on Amazon. Sponsored Brands are an essential advertising tool that allows businesses to showcase their brand and products to a targeted audience, helping to increase visibility and drive more traffic to their Amazon stores or product listings. Understanding how these ads influence brand awareness can provide valuable insights into the success of your campaigns and help you refine your strategies for better results.

Brand awareness refers to how well customers recognize and recall your brand, and it plays a significant role in influencing purchasing decisions. For any brand looking to expand its reach, Sponsored Brands are an effective tool to create long-term visibility. These ads not only display your products in Amazon's search results but also highlight your brand as a whole, giving you the opportunity to introduce your entire catalog or a specific product line. This holistic view increases the chances of your brand becoming familiar to consumers over time, which can lead to repeat purchases and improved customer loyalty.

To measure the impact of Sponsored Brands on brand awareness, it's crucial to first understand the key metrics and tools that can be used to track and assess the effectiveness of these campaigns. Amazon provides several built-in features and reports that can help advertisers gauge the success of their Sponsored Brands ads, including performance metrics such as impressions, click-through rates (CTR), conversion rates, and brand lift data. While traditional metrics like sales and ACoS (Advertising Cost of Sales) are useful for tracking direct ROI, assessing brand awareness requires a more nuanced approach, which often involves analyzing softer indicators like impressions, engagement, and customer sentiment.

One of the most significant metrics to consider when measuring brand awareness is impressions. Impressions refer to the number of times your Sponsored Brands ad is displayed to potential customers, regardless of whether they click on it. While impressions alone don't guarantee a sale, they are a key indicator of visibility. A high number of impressions means that your brand is reaching a wide audience, which is essential for building brand awareness. However, it's important to pair impressions with other metrics to get a more comprehensive view of your ad's effectiveness.

Click-through rate (CTR) is another critical metric when measuring brand awareness. CTR represents the percentage of people who clicked on your ad after seeing it, and it serves as a strong indicator of how engaging your ad is. A high CTR suggests that your ad is capturing the attention of customers and motivating them to learn more about your brand. This is particularly important for brand awareness, as it shows that your ad is not only being seen but is also compelling enough to drive engagement. However, CTR should not be viewed in isolation; it must be evaluated in conjunction with impressions to get a complete understanding of how well your Sponsored Brands ads are increasing brand recognition.

While impressions and CTR provide valuable data on visibility and engagement, measuring the overall impact on brand awareness goes beyond immediate interactions. To truly understand how Sponsored Brands affect brand awareness, you need to analyze longer-term customer behavior. This can be done by tracking customer search behavior, repeat visits to your product listings or Amazon Storefront, and the growth of branded search terms over time. For example, if you notice an increase in the number of customers searching for your brand name or specific branded keywords after running a Sponsored Brands campaign, this can be an indicator that your ad is having a lasting impact on brand recognition.

Another important aspect of measuring brand awareness is the use of brand lift studies. These studies are designed to measure how exposure to an ad influences consumer perception and awareness. Amazon provides brand lift measurement tools that allow you to assess the effectiveness of your Sponsored Brands campaigns in terms of how they impact customer recall and awareness of your brand. These tools collect data from customers who have been exposed to your ads and compare it to a control group who has not seen the ads, offering insights into how much your ad campaign has contributed to increasing brand recognition.

Sales data, while not a direct measure of brand awareness, also plays an important role in evaluating the effectiveness of Sponsored Brands ads. Even though brand awareness is typically associated with soft metrics like impressions and engagement, a well-executed campaign can eventually lead to an increase in sales. If your campaign drives higher sales over time, it may be a sign that your brand has become more recognizable to consumers, leading to more confident purchasing decisions. This, in turn, strengthens the relationship between brand awareness and brand loyalty. Consistently high sales figures, especially from customers who have previously interacted with your brand, can indicate that your Sponsored Brands efforts are successfully elevating brand awareness in the long run.

The correlation between Sponsored Brands ads and customer retention is another significant consideration. While the primary goal of these ads is often to increase visibility and drive traffic, successful campaigns can also help reinforce brand loyalty. Customers who are familiar with your brand are more likely to make repeat purchases, and this behavior can be measured through tools like Amazon's Repeat Purchase Rate (RPR) or by tracking customer reviews and feedback. If Sponsored Brands ads contribute to higher customer retention rates, this could signify that your brand is being recognized and valued by a growing audience.

Additionally, sentiment analysis can provide valuable insights into how your brand is perceived in the market. Sentiment analysis involves evaluating customer reviews, social media mentions, and other forms of customer feedback to gauge how your brand is being discussed and perceived. Positive sentiment indicates that customers not only recognize your brand but have a favorable impression of it. Sponsored Brands ads that lead to increased positive sentiment can be seen as highly effective in raising awareness and shaping a positive brand image.

To maximize the effectiveness of Sponsored Brands ads in boosting brand awareness, it's essential to ensure that the ad creatives align with your brand's identity. This includes the visual elements, messaging, and overall tone of the ad. Consistency in branding is crucial for fostering recognition, as customers are more likely to remember a brand that presents a cohesive and professional image. The use of strong, clear headlines, engaging visuals, and compelling product descriptions can enhance the likelihood of generating interest and increasing awareness.

It's also important to continuously refine and optimize your Sponsored Brands campaigns based on the data collected. Testing different ad formats, adjusting targeting strategies, and experimenting with different bidding approaches can all contribute to more effective campaigns. By regularly monitoring your campaign's performance and making necessary adjustments, you ensure that your ads remain impactful and continue to drive brand awareness over time.

Measuring the impact of Sponsored Brands on brand awareness involves tracking a variety of metrics, from impressions and CTR to long-term customer behavior and brand lift data. By analyzing these factors, you can gain a clearer understanding of how your campaigns are influencing customer recognition and perception of your brand. The insights gained from these measurements will allow you to refine your strategies, optimize your ads, and ultimately enhance your brand's presence in the Amazon marketplace.

CHAPTER 7
DESIGNING EFFECTIVE SPONSORED BRANDS CAMPAIGNS

STRATEGIC SELECTION OF PRODUCTS TO FEATURE

Selecting the right products to feature in advertising campaigns is one of the most critical decisions for any business aiming to maximize its success on Amazon. The products you choose to promote not only represent your brand's identity but also significantly impact the efficiency and profitability of your campaigns. A strategic approach to selecting the right products to feature can help you optimize your advertising efforts, increase visibility, and drive greater sales. However, this decision is not one to be made lightly, as it requires an in-depth understanding of your products, market trends, and consumer behavior.

One of the first steps in making a strategic product selection is to assess your product catalog comprehensively. You may have a wide range of products, each with its own set of strengths and challenges. The key to selecting which ones to feature lies in understanding what each product brings to the table. Products that already have strong customer ratings and a solid track record of sales performance are natural candidates for featuring in advertising campaigns. These products are likely to have the best chance of delivering positive results because they have already gained the trust of customers. On the other hand, if a product has not been performing well, it could be a sign that it needs further optimization before it's promoted on a larger scale. For example, this could involve improving the product listing with better images, more engaging descriptions, or higher-quality keywords to ensure that it stands out when advertised.

A key consideration when selecting products to feature is understanding their profit margins. Some products may have a higher price point and consequently, offer higher profit margins, but they may also come with more competition. Others may be lower-priced items but offer steady sales due to their demand. It's essential to assess the potential return on investment (ROI) for each product. An item with a lower profit margin but high demand can still be a profitable choice if it generates significant volume in sales, particularly when leveraging the power of Amazon's advertising platform. By focusing on products that strike the right balance between profitability and demand, you can maximize your advertising budget and drive the best results for your business.

In addition to profitability, understanding the seasonality of your products is crucial. Some products may only be in demand during specific seasons or around particular events, such as holidays or annual sales. This requires a level of foresight and planning when selecting products to feature in ads. For example, if you're selling winter clothing, you'll want to focus your advertising efforts during the colder months when demand is highest. Conversely, promoting summer items in the winter might not yield the same results. Additionally, monitoring sales trends and keeping an eye on upcoming events can help you identify products that are likely to experience increased demand, allowing you to tailor your advertising strategy accordingly.

Another important aspect of product selection is the level of competition. It's essential to evaluate how competitive the market is for a specific product or product category. If a product is in a highly saturated market, you may face a higher cost-per-click (CPC) for advertising, making it harder to achieve a positive return on investment. In such cases, it may be more beneficial to focus on products that face less competition, where you can establish a foothold more easily. This might include unique or niche products that cater to specific customer segments. By selecting products with less competition, you can often find more cost-effective advertising opportunities and achieve better results with your campaigns.

To further refine your product selection, it's also essential to evaluate the customer's journey and how your products fit into their purchasing decisions. Amazon's advertising platform is designed to meet customers where they are in the buying process, from initial product discovery to final purchase. Featuring products that align with the intent and interests of potential customers is essential for successful advertising campaigns. For instance, products that are commonly bought together or those that complement other high-demand items should be highlighted. This strategy can increase your chances of appearing in relevant customer searches, thereby improving the effectiveness of your advertising and boosting the likelihood of making a sale.

Utilizing data insights from Amazon's analytics tools can help in making these strategic decisions. Amazon provides valuable metrics and reports that give you a deep dive into how your products are performing. Understanding these analytics is essential when selecting products for advertising. Tools like Amazon Brand Analytics or the Campaign Manager provide data on which products are generating the most clicks, conversions, and impressions. These insights can reveal trends and highlight which products are gaining traction with customers. By continuously monitoring these metrics, you can identify top performers and products that show promising growth potential. Selecting these high-performing products can increase the likelihood of success, as you're already capitalizing on what customers are actively seeking.

For businesses with a broad product range, segmentation can be an effective strategy when selecting products to feature. Instead of trying to promote all your products at once, consider grouping your products into categories based on factors such as customer demographics, purchasing habits, and product usage. You may choose to focus on products for specific customer segments, such as new parents or pet owners. By tailoring your advertising campaigns to particular groups, you can ensure that your ads are highly relevant, which often leads to higher engagement and better conversion rates. This segmentation strategy allows you to tap into the unique needs of different customer groups while optimizing your advertising spend.

When considering which products to feature, it's also important to evaluate the overall customer experience associated with each product. Offering exceptional customer service, fast shipping, and high-quality products is essential to maintaining a positive reputation on Amazon. Products that come with excellent reviews and positive customer feedback are more likely to perform well in ads because they create trust and credibility with potential buyers. Conversely, if a product has frequent customer complaints or negative reviews, it could undermine your advertising efforts. Before promoting a product through Amazon's advertising platform, ensure that it has met the standard for quality and customer satisfaction, as this will significantly affect its ability to perform well in campaigns.

Another consideration for product selection is how well your products align with current trends. Consumer preferences are constantly evolving, and staying up-to-date with market trends can give you an edge in selecting the right products to feature. For example, if there's a growing interest in sustainable or eco-friendly products, featuring items that align with this trend can position your brand as a leader in that space. Identifying emerging trends and tapping into them early can provide a significant boost to your advertising campaigns, increasing your visibility and helping you reach customers who are actively seeking these products.

Lastly, it's essential to consider the overall goals of your advertising campaigns. If your goal is to increase brand awareness, featuring a mix of your best-selling products and new, innovative products can help capture attention and drive recognition. On the other hand, if your goal is to increase sales for specific products, focusing on high-converting, in-demand items may be more effective. Aligning your product selection with your campaign objectives is crucial to ensuring that your ads are optimized for success and that you're achieving the desired outcomes from your efforts.

The strategic selection of products to feature in your Amazon advertising campaigns is a multifaceted process that involves evaluating profitability, competition, seasonality, customer demand, and performance data. By understanding your product catalog in depth and using insights from Amazon's analytics tools, you can make more informed decisions that maximize the effectiveness of your campaigns.

Selecting the right products not only improves your chances of success but also ensures that your advertising budget is being spent efficiently, leading to higher returns and greater visibility on the platform.

CRAFTING COMPELLING CREATIVE ASSETS: IMAGES AND VIDEOS OPTIMIZED FOR PRIME VIEWERS

Creating visually compelling and engaging creative assets is crucial to capturing the attention of potential customers on Amazon Prime, where competition for consumer attention is fierce. Whether through images or videos, your product's visual presentation plays a significant role in convincing shoppers to click on your ad and ultimately make a purchase. Optimizing your creative assets for Prime viewers requires a nuanced approach that balances creativity, functionality, and user experience. In this highly visual digital marketplace, the power of high-quality images and videos cannot be overstated.

Images serve as the first point of contact between your product and potential customers. They must not only show the product but also highlight its key features and benefits in a way that appeals to the viewer's emotions and needs. The importance of clear, high-resolution images cannot be overemphasized. Blurry, poorly lit, or cluttered images may deter potential customers, causing them to overlook your product in favor of one with better visual appeal. For Prime viewers who are accustomed to a premium experience, the expectation for high-quality visuals is even more pronounced. To stand out in such an environment, it's vital to ensure that all images are crisp, well-lit, and professionally composed.

Furthermore, optimizing images involves showcasing the product from multiple angles to give customers a full view of what they are considering purchasing. While the main image should focus on the product in its entirety, additional images should capture close-ups of important details or features that set your product apart. For example, if you're selling a kitchen gadget, a close-up image of the product in action— chopping vegetables or mixing ingredients—can help customers envision how it will fit into their own lives. Demonstrating practical use cases through images not only highlights functionality but also helps potential buyers visualize how they would use the product, which in turn can improve conversion rates.

Another powerful technique in image optimization is the use of lifestyle images. These images show the product in real-life scenarios and can evoke an emotional connection with customers. For instance, if you're advertising outdoor gear, images showing the product in use during a camping trip or on a mountain hike can help customers imagine themselves in those same scenarios. Lifestyle images are particularly effective for products that offer a lifestyle benefit or cater to specific hobbies and interests. These images don't just sell the product—they sell the experience and the benefits of ownership, making them a critical part of your visual strategy.

To further elevate the quality of your images, consider using advanced photo editing techniques that enhance product colors, make backgrounds more minimal, or adjust lighting to showcase the product in the best possible way. However, it's important to avoid over-editing, as this can create a false representation of your product. Consumers are increasingly savvy, and they can spot overly manipulated images, which can lead to distrust or disappointment when they receive the product in person. Transparency in product presentation is key to building trust with Prime viewers.

Equally important are video ads, which have become an essential tool for promoting products on Amazon. Video is an inherently engaging medium, as it combines both visual and auditory elements to create a dynamic experience for the viewer. Videos provide an opportunity to bring the product to life in ways that static images cannot, allowing you to show it in action, demonstrate its features, and tell a compelling story that connects emotionally with the audience. For Prime viewers, who expect a more interactive and immersive shopping experience, video content can help your brand stand out and capture attention.

The key to an effective video ad lies in keeping it concise while still delivering a clear message. Prime viewers have limited attention spans, so the first few seconds of a video are crucial in hooking them. Start with a compelling hook—whether it's a provocative question, an eye-catching visual, or a bold statement—that draws the viewer in right away. The video should clearly introduce the product and its key benefits within the first few moments, ensuring that even if the viewer doesn't watch the entire video, they still walk away with a solid understanding of what the product is and why it's worth their attention.

In addition to the initial hook, it's important to provide demonstrations of the product in action. While images can show the product's features, videos can show how those features work in real life. If you're advertising a piece of tech, for instance, showing how the product functions in real-world scenarios—whether it's setting it up or demonstrating its key functions—helps viewers connect with it on a practical level. Videos also allow you to address common questions or pain points directly, providing a fuller, more complete representation of your product. If you're advertising a kitchen tool, for example, showing it in use while preparing a meal not only demonstrates its effectiveness but also helps the viewer imagine themselves using it in their own kitchen.

When creating video ads, it's crucial to ensure that the production quality matches the expectations of Prime viewers. Videos should have clear audio, high-definition visuals, and professional editing. The production quality of your video reflects the quality of your brand and product, so it's worth investing in skilled video editors or professional services to ensure that your video stands out for all the right reasons. Remember, the goal is not just to capture attention but to instill a sense of trust and professionalism that aligns with the Amazon Prime experience.

Another important aspect of optimizing your creative assets for Prime viewers is tailoring your images and videos to different ad formats. On Amazon, you may choose from several ad formats—such as Sponsored Products, Sponsored Brands, or Sponsored Display—which each have their own unique requirements for creative assets. Sponsored Brands ads, for example, feature your product alongside your logo and a custom headline, which means that you need to craft not only visually compelling images and videos but also strong messaging that highlights your brand identity. Sponsored Display ads may feature lifestyle images, and you'll need to ensure that they are optimized for a more casual, less transactional shopping environment.

The aspect ratio and resolution of your images and videos must also be in line with Amazon's specifications. For video, the recommended resolution is 1080p with a 16:9 aspect ratio, and for images, high-quality, high-resolution photos are essential. Subpar resolution can make your ads appear unprofessional and can hinder their performance.

Testing and optimizing your images and videos is key to achieving success. What works for one product may not work for another, so it's crucial to continually monitor how your creative assets are performing and make adjustments as necessary. If a particular video or image isn't performing well, consider testing different variations—adjusting the messaging, visuals, or call-to-action—and seeing if those changes improve results. A/B testing can help you identify which types of images or videos resonate best with your audience, allowing you to continuously improve your campaigns over time.

Crafting compelling creative assets—whether through images or videos—requires a strategic, thoughtful approach that balances aesthetics with functionality. Optimizing these assets for Amazon Prime viewers means using high-quality visuals, demonstrating the product's benefits, and aligning your messaging with the expectations of your audience. By investing in professional production, tailoring your content for the specific ad formats, and testing variations, you can create powerful creative assets that not only capture attention but also drive conversions and build long-term customer relationships.

LEVERAGING CUSTOM LANDING PAGES WITHIN YOUR AMAZON STORE

When it comes to driving success in e-commerce, particularly within the Amazon ecosystem, ensuring that potential customers have a seamless and engaging experience once they click on your advertisements is crucial. This experience often begins with the landing page, which serves as a critical point of conversion. For sellers looking to elevate their Amazon marketing strategy, leveraging custom landing pages within their Amazon Store is one of the most powerful ways to drive sales, foster brand loyalty, and create a memorable experience for customers. Custom landing pages allow you to take full control of how your products are presented, enabling you to craft a narrative, highlight promotions, and provide a clear path to purchase.

A custom landing page within your Amazon Store is essentially a dedicated page that you create within your Amazon storefront. Unlike product detail pages, which are primarily focused on showcasing individual items, a custom landing page offers greater flexibility and customization options. This page allows you to highlight a variety of products, build a brand story, and guide customers toward specific actions. By providing a branded, visually cohesive experience, you can make a strong first impression on shoppers and increase their likelihood of engaging with your products.

One of the most significant advantages of custom landing pages is the ability to create a more tailored and controlled shopping environment. While the standard Amazon product detail page is focused on the specific product, a custom landing page gives you the opportunity to tell a broader story about your brand or a particular product collection. For example, if you are launching a new product line, you can create a custom landing page that introduces your customers to the new products, explains their benefits, and provides information about why these products are valuable to them. A strong, clear message on the landing page can connect with potential customers in a way that encourages them to take the next step in their buying journey.

Another essential benefit of custom landing pages is the ability to showcase multiple products or product categories in a way that feels curated and intentional. Rather than simply listing products, a custom landing page allows you to group products by theme, usage, or seasonality, providing a personalized experience. This grouping helps customers to easily discover related items that they may not have otherwise encountered. For instance, if your brand specializes in skincare products, you can create a landing page that categorizes products by skin type, such as "Oily Skin Solutions" or "Anti-Aging Essentials." This type of navigation helps customers find exactly what they are looking for, without the distraction of unrelated products.

Custom landing pages can also be used to enhance the discoverability of special offers or promotions. If you are running a limited-time sale or offering exclusive deals, the landing page gives you a space to prominently display these offers. You can feature banners, countdown timers, and other visual elements that highlight the urgency and importance of these promotions, driving immediate action from customers. This strategic placement of promotional content not only helps to boost sales during a campaign but also draws attention to deals that might otherwise get lost within the broader Amazon marketplace.

Furthermore, custom landing pages allow for more detailed and engaging product descriptions. While product detail pages offer a brief description along with the usual specifications, a custom landing page allows you to go deeper into the story behind your products. This could include the brand's origin, the values behind the products, or even customer testimonials and success stories. By offering a richer narrative, you can build trust with potential buyers and differentiate your products from those of your competitors. Storytelling can be a powerful tool, especially when combined with visuals, to create a deeper emotional connection between your brand and its audience.

One of the most effective ways to enhance a custom landing page is by incorporating high-quality images and videos. Visual elements help bring your products to life, providing customers with a clearer understanding of what they are purchasing. For instance, videos that showcase your product in action or demonstrate its unique features can offer far more engagement than static images alone. Similarly, product photography that highlights the design, texture, and functionality of your products can reinforce the narrative and help customers make informed purchasing decisions. Additionally, a clean, visually appealing layout will encourage customers to stay longer on your page, exploring more of your offerings, which increases the chances of conversions.

The customization options available on Amazon also allow you to implement advanced elements such as sliders, carousels, and even personalized recommendations based on customers' browsing behaviors. These dynamic features can help capture the attention of users by offering an interactive experience. Instead of simply presenting a static collection of products, you can offer customers a more engaging and personalized shopping experience. This level of interactivity also adds a layer of professionalism to your page, helping to further elevate your brand's image.

Additionally, Amazon's built-in analytics tools allow you to track the performance of your custom landing pages. You can monitor important metrics such as click-through rates (CTR), conversion rates, and bounce rates, which provide valuable insights into how well your landing page is performing. By closely monitoring these metrics, you can identify areas of your landing page that may need refinement, whether it's improving product descriptions, adjusting the layout, or changing calls-to-action. Over time, you can test different variations of the page to optimize for the best results, making sure you're continuously improving your approach to better meet customer expectations.

To maximize the effectiveness of custom landing pages, it is essential to ensure that they are fully integrated with your overall advertising strategy. For example, if you're running a sponsored ad campaign that directs traffic to your Amazon Store, you can use a custom landing page to provide a seamless experience that aligns with the ad's messaging. When the ad leads directly to a custom landing page designed to support the campaign, you create a cohesive narrative that guides the customer from their initial interest to a final purchase. This helps reduce friction in the buying process, making it easier for customers to follow through with their decisions.

Creating and maintaining custom landing pages also involves understanding Amazon's best practices and guidelines for Storefront content. Amazon provides sellers with various design templates and layout options to help create attractive and functional pages. However, to make the most of these resources, it is essential to ensure that the landing page design is both user-friendly and responsive across devices. With many customers shopping on mobile devices, it's important to optimize your landing pages for mobile viewing to ensure that all images, text, and calls-to-action are easy to read and navigate on smaller screens.

Moreover, your landing page should reflect your brand's unique voice and aesthetic. While Amazon provides the tools for creating custom pages, how you use those tools to express your brand identity matters. A consistent and appealing design, paired with messaging that aligns with your brand values, will create a memorable experience for customers and improve the likelihood of repeat purchases. The visual consistency between your landing page and your overall Amazon Store should be maintained to reinforce brand recognition and loyalty.

Leveraging custom landing pages within your Amazon Store provides you with an invaluable opportunity to craft a tailored and engaging shopping experience for potential customers. By showcasing your products in a curated, cohesive manner, telling your brand story, and offering promotional content in a visually compelling way, you can significantly enhance your chances of conversion. Custom landing pages not only help increase sales, but they also play a pivotal role in building long-term relationships with your customers by offering them a seamless, professional, and memorable shopping experience. With the right combination of creativity, strategy, and data-driven optimization, custom landing pages are a vital tool for achieving success in the highly competitive Amazon marketplace.

KEYWORD STRATEGIES FOR SPONSORED BRANDS: BRANDED AND NON-BRANDED TERMS

When it comes to advertising on Amazon, one of the most important factors that contribute to the success of your Sponsored Brands campaigns is the effective use of keywords. Keywords are the bridge between what potential customers are searching for and the products you're trying to sell. The way you choose and manage these keywords can significantly impact the performance of your campaigns, ultimately determining how well your ads resonate with the right audience. Within the context of Sponsored Brands, there are two main categories of keywords to focus on: branded and non-branded terms. Both types of keywords serve different purposes and, when strategically combined, can create a well-rounded and highly effective advertising campaign that drives relevant traffic and maximizes your sales.

Branded keywords refer to search terms that include the name of your brand, product, or specific product lines. These keywords are highly relevant when targeting customers who are already familiar with your brand and are actively searching for your products or brand-specific offerings. Branded terms allow you to capture high-intent traffic from customers who are either already aware of your brand or have previously interacted with your business in some capacity. By targeting branded keywords, you position your products directly in front of customers who are looking for exactly what you offer. This high relevance often leads to higher click-through rates (CTR) and a greater likelihood of conversions, as customers already have a pre-existing interest in your brand.

Non-branded keywords, on the other hand, are search terms that do not include your brand name or any direct reference to your specific products. These keywords tend to be broader and more generic, targeting a wider audience who may be unfamiliar with your brand. While non-branded keywords can bring in more traffic, they often come with a lower intent compared to branded terms, as users may be in the discovery or research phase of their buying journey. These customers might be looking for solutions to a problem or exploring a category, but they haven't yet made a decision to purchase from a particular brand. Despite this, non-branded keywords offer great potential for capturing new customers, building brand awareness, and driving discovery among a larger, untapped audience.

The strategic combination of both branded and non-branded keywords is essential for creating a balanced approach to your Sponsored

Brands campaigns. By including both types of keywords, you can target customers at various stages of their shopping journey, from the initial stages of exploration to the final stages of purchase. Branded keywords allow you to capitalize on high-intent customers who are already familiar with your brand and products, while non-branded keywords enable you to cast a wider net and attract potential customers who may be looking for your type of product but haven't yet heard of your brand.

To get the most out of your branded and non-branded keyword strategies, it's important to first conduct comprehensive keyword research. This research will help you identify the most relevant and valuable keywords for both categories, ensuring that you're targeting the right search terms that align with customer behavior and intent. For branded terms, you can start by considering your brand name, product names, and any specific keywords related to your business. These terms will likely be the first to come to mind, but don't forget to explore variations or common misspellings of your brand name. You may also want to consider related product categories or terms that customers use when searching for your products.

For non-branded keywords, it's crucial to think about the broader context of your products. What problems do your products solve? What are the key benefits that resonate with potential customers? These questions will help guide you toward identifying non-branded search terms that are highly relevant to your target audience. Tools like Amazon's Keyword Tool, Google Keyword Planner, and third-party keyword research tools can be invaluable for uncovering new non-branded keywords and discovering trends in search behavior.

Once you have a list of potential branded and non-branded keywords, the next step is to organize them based on their relevance, search volume, and competition. High-volume, high-competition keywords can be costly and may not always yield the best return on investment (ROI). In contrast, lower-volume, less competitive keywords may offer more cost-effective opportunities to drive traffic and conversions. It's important to assess the performance potential of your keywords and allocate your budget accordingly.

Another critical aspect of keyword management is continually refining and optimizing your keyword list. Keyword performance can fluctuate over time, so it's important to regularly monitor and adjust your campaigns. For example, if a branded keyword is generating high clicks but low conversions, it might indicate that your ad copy or product detail pages need to be optimized to better match customer expectations. On the other hand, if a non-branded keyword is driving significant traffic but not converting, you may want to explore different variations or refine your targeting parameters.

In addition to organic search behavior, understanding your competitors' keyword strategies is another important step in optimizing your own campaigns. By conducting a competitive analysis, you can identify the branded and non-branded keywords that your competitors are targeting. This insight can inform your own keyword strategy and help you uncover untapped opportunities. However, be mindful of overloading your campaigns with too many broad, non-branded keywords, as this can lead to wasted spend on irrelevant clicks. Focus on quality over quantity by selecting keywords that align closely with your products and target customers.

As part of your optimization process, you can experiment with bid strategies for both branded and non-branded keywords. For branded terms, it's often more efficient to bid more aggressively, as you're targeting customers with higher purchase intent. Since branded keywords generally have less competition, bidding higher on these terms can help ensure that your products are prominently displayed in search results. For non-branded keywords, it's generally a good idea to start with a more conservative bid and adjust as you gather data on the performance of those keywords.

Ad copy plays a crucial role in driving the success of your Sponsored Brands campaigns, especially when working with a combination of branded and non-branded keywords. Your ad copy should align with the intent behind the search query, addressing the needs or desires of the customer. For branded keywords, your copy should reinforce the brand identity and highlight the unique selling points of your products. For non-branded keywords, focus on the broader benefits and features of your products that resonate with the target audience's pain points or goals. Tailoring your messaging to the specific keyword will help you capture the attention of potential customers and increase the likelihood of conversions.

Lastly, tracking key performance metrics is essential for measuring the success of your keyword strategies. Metrics such as click-through rate (CTR), conversion rate, and advertising cost of sale (ACoS) provide valuable insight into how your branded and non-branded keywords are performing. If you notice that a particular keyword is underperforming, it may be time to re-evaluate your bidding strategy, ad copy, or targeting approach. Conversely, if a keyword is driving significant traffic and generating high conversions, consider allocating more of your budget toward that keyword to maximize its impact.

Developing a strategic keyword strategy for Sponsored Brands campaigns is critical for driving relevant traffic, improving brand visibility, and increasing conversions on Amazon. By targeting both branded and non-branded keywords, you can cover a broad spectrum of customer intent and reach your target audience at various stages of their shopping journey. Through comprehensive research, optimization, and ongoing monitoring, you can ensure that your keyword strategy remains aligned with customer behavior and delivers measurable results for your business. The right combination of branded and non-branded terms, along with optimized ad copy and bidding strategies, will position your products to be discovered by the right customers at the right time, ultimately driving the success of your advertising efforts on Amazon.

UTILIZING AUDIENCE TARGETING OPTIONS FOR BRAND CAMPAIGNS

When it comes to advertising on Amazon, one of the most powerful tools available to advertisers is the ability to target specific audiences. Audience targeting has revolutionized the way brands engage with potential customers by allowing advertisers to focus their ads on the right people at the right time. This precision can result in higher engagement, improved conversion rates, and ultimately, a better return on ad spend. For brands looking to succeed on Amazon, mastering audience targeting options is a key component of an effective advertising strategy.

Audience targeting on Amazon is driven by an understanding of customer behavior, interests, and past purchasing patterns. This allows advertisers to reach not just anyone browsing the platform, but those who are most likely to engage with their products. By utilizing the various audience targeting options available on Amazon, brands can craft personalized and relevant ad experiences that resonate with potential buyers, moving them further down the purchase funnel.

One of the primary audience targeting options available on Amazon is demographic targeting. This involves reaching users based on demographic information such as age, gender, income level, and household size. While this data may seem basic, it can be incredibly powerful when used correctly. For instance, if a brand sells beauty products, targeting women within a specific age group who have shown an interest in skincare could significantly increase the likelihood of conversion. Demographic targeting helps brands hone in on potential customers who fit the profile of their ideal buyer, improving the relevance of the ads they see.

Another important targeting option is interest-based targeting, which allows brands to target customers based on their interests and browsing behaviors on Amazon. This can be an especially useful method for reaching consumers who have expressed interest in products or categories that are related to what the brand is selling. For example, if you sell fitness equipment, you might target people who have previously shown interest in health, fitness, and wellness products. This kind of targeting ensures that ads are shown to individuals who are more likely to be interested in the product being promoted, improving both engagement and conversions.

In addition to demographic and interest-based targeting, Amazon also offers a robust set of targeting options based on shopping behavior. These include targeting based on past purchase history, product category interest, and browsing activity. Customers who have purchased products similar to what you're selling are highly valuable targets. For instance, if someone has previously purchased yoga mats or dumbbells, targeting them with ads for new fitness equipment could be an excellent way to increase sales. This type of behavioral targeting ensures that brands can engage with consumers who are already in the buying mindset, increasing the likelihood of conversion.

Amazon's audience targeting also allows brands to focus on customers who have already engaged with their products or brand. This includes retargeting shoppers who have previously viewed a product but did not make a purchase. By reaching out to these consumers again, brands can remind them of the product they were interested in and provide an incentive to complete the purchase. Retargeting is particularly effective because these customers have already shown interest in the product, so they are more likely to convert when presented with a relevant ad.

Beyond behavioral and demographic targeting, Amazon provides options for targeting based on specific product categories and competitors. For example, you can target shoppers who are browsing within the same product category as yours, which allows you to introduce your brand to consumers who are actively searching for products similar to yours. You can also target competitors' products by bidding on keywords related to their offerings. This allows you to position your products in front of potential customers who are already in the decision-making process and may be considering alternatives to the product they were initially interested in.

One of the most innovative audience targeting features Amazon offers is the ability to leverage Amazon's vast data to target based on lifestyle or life stage. This targeting allows brands to reach consumers at various milestones in their lives, whether they are newlyweds, parents, or empty nesters. For example, a brand selling baby products can target parents who have recently had a baby, while a brand selling home décor might target consumers who have recently moved into a new home. Life-stage targeting is a powerful way to connect with consumers at key moments in their lives when they are most likely to need or desire certain products.

By combining several of these targeting options, brands can refine their audience reach to an even greater degree. The ability to layer demographic, behavioral, interest-based, and competitor targeting gives brands the power to fine-tune their ad campaigns for maximum precision. This approach ensures that ads are shown to the most relevant audience possible, which not only increases engagement but also boosts the chances of conversion. Moreover, by narrowing down the pool of potential customers, brands can often reduce wasted ad spend, as they are no longer targeting irrelevant or uninterested users.

In addition to targeting individual shoppers, Amazon also allows brands to target entire customer segments through Amazon's custom audience options. Custom audiences allow you to create a more personalized experience for your potential customers by uploading your own customer lists or using Amazon's data to identify lookalike audiences. For example, if you have a list of customers who have previously made a purchase or signed up for your email newsletter, you can upload that list and target those individuals with relevant ads. Similarly, lookalike audiences let you reach people who share similar characteristics or behaviors to your existing customers, making it easier to expand your customer base while maintaining relevance.

Effective use of audience targeting is also crucial for measuring and optimizing ad performance. By analyzing the data collected from targeted campaigns, brands can gain valuable insights into which audience segments are performing best. For example, you might discover that your ads targeting women between the ages of 30-45 are generating the highest conversion rates, or that ads shown to users who have previously purchased similar products tend to perform better. These insights enable brands to make data-driven decisions about where to allocate their ad spend, ensuring that the marketing budget is being used most efficiently. By continually testing and refining audience targeting, brands can optimize their campaigns over time, improving overall performance and maximizing return on investment.

Another factor to consider when utilizing audience targeting is the importance of ad creatives that resonate with the selected audience. For example, if you're targeting a specific age group or lifestyle stage, it's essential to tailor the ad copy, visuals, and messaging to appeal to that particular demographic. Personalized ads that speak directly to the interests and needs of the target audience are far more likely to engage potential customers and drive them to take action. Understanding the nuances of your audience and crafting creatives that speak to their unique desires and motivations is key to building a successful brand campaign.

Lastly, audience targeting plays a significant role in increasing brand awareness. By leveraging these advanced targeting options, brands can effectively position themselves in front of the right customers, ensuring that their products are seen by a highly relevant audience. As more consumers interact with your ads, learn about your brand, and engage with your products, the likelihood of brand recognition and long-term loyalty grows.

Audience targeting is one of the most effective ways to elevate your brand campaigns on Amazon. By understanding and utilizing the various targeting options—demographic, behavioral, interest-based, life-stage, and competitor targeting—you can connect with the most relevant potential customers, ensuring that your ads are shown to those most likely to engage with your brand. With the right combination of targeting strategies, creative assets, and data-driven optimizations, brands can drive higher engagement, increase conversions, and build long-lasting customer relationships.

CHAPTER 8
OPTIMIZING AND ANALYZING SPONSORED BRANDS PERFORMANCE

TRACKING BRAND-SPECIFIC METRICS: NEW-TO-BRAND ORDERS, BRAND LIFT

Tracking brand-specific metrics is essential for measuring the true impact of advertising campaigns, especially for those running sponsored ads or building a brand presence on a large platform. As competition continues to increase on online marketplaces, it's crucial for advertisers to understand not only how their ads are performing but also how they are contributing to the growth and recognition of their brand. Two critical metrics that provide invaluable insights into brand performance are New-to-Brand Orders and Brand Lift. These metrics help brands assess customer acquisition, retention, and overall brand awareness, giving advertisers a clearer picture of the effectiveness of their efforts.

New-to-Brand Orders is a metric that focuses on tracking how many orders come from customers who are interacting with a brand for the first time. This metric is particularly important because it helps brands gauge the effectiveness of their advertising efforts in attracting new customers. In an age where customer loyalty is harder to maintain, acquiring new customers is often seen as the lifeblood of a growing business. By measuring New-to-Brand Orders, advertisers can assess how well their campaigns are driving brand awareness and attracting customers who have not previously purchased their products. This metric provides a snapshot of how successful the brand's advertising strategy is in reaching potential customers who are unfamiliar with the brand but are now making their first purchase.

New-to-Brand Orders can be analyzed at both the individual campaign level and across larger timeframes to measure long-term trends. For instance, if a campaign's goal is to drive awareness and attract new customers, tracking this metric allows advertisers to see if their ads are successful in introducing the brand to new audiences. If a particular campaign or ad set is driving a high number of New-to-Brand Orders, it indicates that the creative and targeting strategies are resonating with potential customers who are not yet familiar with the brand. It may also reveal that the product offerings and messaging are compelling enough to convert new visitors into paying customers.

Additionally, tracking New-to-Brand Orders over time offers insights into the overall health of a brand's customer acquisition efforts. A rising trend in New-to-Brand Orders could signal that the brand is expanding its customer base effectively, while a flat or declining trend could indicate a need for changes in strategy, such as adjusting ad creatives, refining targeting parameters, or exploring new channels. By closely monitoring this metric, brands can ensure that they are not becoming stagnant and can adjust their advertising approach to maintain a steady flow of new customers.

In tandem with New-to-Brand Orders, Brand Lift is another important metric that provides an indication of the effectiveness of advertising campaigns in raising brand awareness and shifting customer perceptions. Brand Lift measures the increase in consumer awareness or consideration as a direct result of exposure to an ad. This metric focuses on how well ads are influencing potential customers' attitudes toward a brand or product, even if they haven't made a purchase yet. Brand Lift helps to quantify how successful an advertising campaign is at creating awareness, generating interest, and establishing a positive perception of a brand.

Brand Lift is typically measured through surveys or customer feedback mechanisms, where consumers who have seen the ads are asked about their awareness and perception of the brand. The idea behind this metric is that even if a customer doesn't immediately make a purchase, exposure to the brand through advertising could impact their likelihood of purchasing in the future. For example, if a customer sees a sponsored ad for a product that they have never heard of before, they may not make a purchase right away, but their familiarity with the brand increases. Later, when they are ready to buy, they may be more inclined to choose that brand over competitors due to the initial exposure.

Tracking Brand Lift is vital for understanding how effective a brand's campaigns are at fostering long-term brand loyalty. This metric is particularly useful for measuring the value of campaigns focused on building brand recognition and credibility rather than just driving immediate sales. For brands looking to establish themselves in a competitive market, Brand Lift can reveal whether their advertising strategies are improving their standing in the minds of consumers, potentially leading to increased sales over time.

To effectively use Brand Lift as a metric, it's essential to conduct the measurement at key intervals during and after an advertising campaign. Brands should track how awareness increases during the campaign and if the trend continues after the campaign ends. This allows advertisers to assess whether the ad exposure has a lasting effect on customer behavior or if the impact is short-lived. Additionally, it's important to segment the audience being surveyed by factors such as demographics, purchase history, and engagement with the ad to identify which groups experienced the most significant lift in awareness or consideration. This segmentation helps to refine targeting strategies for future campaigns.

Both New-to-Brand Orders and Brand Lift provide essential insights, but when used together, they give advertisers a more comprehensive view of the impact of their campaigns. While New-to-Brand Orders give a tangible measure of customer acquisition, Brand Lift helps to capture the more subtle influence of advertising on consumer attitudes and perceptions. By analyzing these two metrics side by side, advertisers can evaluate the effectiveness of their advertising strategies in attracting new customers and building brand awareness. If a campaign shows a high Brand Lift but low New-to-Brand Orders, it may indicate that the ads are successful in creating awareness but need adjustments in terms of conversion tactics to drive more purchases. Conversely, if New-to-Brand Orders are high but Brand Lift is low, it could mean that while the campaign is driving sales, it's not necessarily strengthening the brand in the long term.

Moreover, both metrics help in refining advertising strategies for future campaigns. By evaluating which ads or types of creatives are driving the most New-to-Brand Orders and the highest Brand Lift, advertisers can identify which strategies work best for attracting new customers and growing brand recognition. For instance, certain ad formats or messaging that resonate well with new customers can be replicated in future campaigns. Similarly, if certain products or offers are particularly effective in generating New-to-Brand Orders, advertisers can optimize their campaigns to highlight those items more prominently.

It's also important to recognize that the effectiveness of these metrics depends on the quality of the data being collected. To accurately track New-to-Brand Orders and Brand Lift, advertisers must ensure that they are using robust tracking systems and measurement tools that can provide accurate, real-time data. Inaccurate or incomplete data can lead to misinformed decisions and could hinder the effectiveness of future campaigns. Therefore, it's essential to invest in the right analytics tools and technologies that allow for precise tracking and reporting of these metrics.

Tracking New-to-Brand Orders and Brand Lift are indispensable for any brand looking to measure the true impact of their advertising campaigns on Amazon. While New-to-Brand Orders provide valuable insights into customer acquisition and sales performance, Brand Lift offers a deeper understanding of how well a brand is increasing awareness and shaping consumer perceptions. Together, these metrics give brands the tools they need to fine-tune their advertising strategies, attract new customers, build lasting relationships, and ultimately drive long-term success in the marketplace. By constantly monitoring and analyzing these metrics, brands can ensure that their advertising efforts are not only bringing in new customers but also enhancing their reputation and presence in a crowded digital space.

ANALYZING SEARCH TERM REPORTS FOR BRAND INSIGHTS

One of the most valuable tools available to advertisers on Amazon is the Search Term Report, a resource that allows brands to understand exactly what customers are searching for when they encounter their ads. This report reveals the search terms that led customers to click on an ad and eventually make a purchase. By analyzing the data within these reports, advertisers can gain crucial insights into consumer behavior, optimize their advertising campaigns, and adjust their strategy to ensure that they are reaching the right audience at the right time. For any brand looking to improve its performance on Amazon, understanding and leveraging search term data is essential for refining marketing efforts and maximizing the effectiveness of advertising investments.

At its core, the Search Term Report provides information on which keywords, phrases, and queries resulted in a click on an ad. This data can help uncover new keyword opportunities, optimize existing targeting strategies, and identify trends that might not have been initially apparent. By drilling down into the specific search terms that customers use when discovering products, brands can assess whether their ads are appearing for relevant searches or if adjustments are needed. Analyzing this report enables advertisers to see which search terms lead to the highest conversion rates, which can guide the refinement of targeting and the allocation of advertising budget toward the most profitable keywords.

The first key insight that can be gained from search term data is the identification of highly relevant or underutilized keywords. Often, advertisers may only target a broad set of keywords, leaving potential opportunities untapped. Search term reports allow brands to dig deeper into the queries that are directly leading to customer engagement. For instance, a brand might discover that certain niche terms are driving significant traffic to their listings, yet those terms were not part of their initial targeting strategy. This can provide valuable clues about untapped segments of the market that are more likely to convert. By adding these high-performing terms to their keyword targeting or adjusting ad copy to include them, brands can increase their reach and effectiveness.

Equally important is the identification of irrelevant or low-performing search terms. These are terms that may lead to clicks but do not necessarily result in conversions. For example, if an advertiser's ad is appearing for generic searches that are too broad or not closely related to the product, it might attract clicks from users who are not actually interested in purchasing. By filtering out these irrelevant search terms, advertisers can ensure that their ads are being shown to a more qualified audience. This is especially critical for maximizing return on ad spend (ROAS) and minimizing wasted budget on low-converting keywords. Identifying and eliminating irrelevant terms is key to refining the overall targeting strategy, ensuring that ads are more effectively aligned with customer intent.

Beyond identifying high-performing and irrelevant keywords, analyzing search term data can help brands uncover customer intent and purchasing behavior. The exact wording of a search query can provide valuable insights into how potential customers are approaching their purchase journey. For example, a customer searching for "affordable running shoes for beginners" is likely at an earlier stage of the buying process, looking for value-driven options. Meanwhile, someone searching for "best running shoes for marathon" is likely further along in their journey and may have a stronger intent to make a purchase. By understanding the subtle differences in search intent, brands can tailor their advertising messages and product listings to better address the needs and concerns of each audience segment.

Moreover, search term data can reveal seasonal or trending behaviors, allowing advertisers to stay ahead of market shifts. For example, if a particular search term suddenly spikes in volume, it could indicate a growing trend or seasonal demand that the brand may want to capitalize on. Advertisers can use this information to adjust their bids, targeting, and creative strategy to align with shifting customer interest. This is particularly useful for brands that sell products tied to seasons or specific events, such as holiday decorations, fitness gear, or back-to-school items. By analyzing search term trends over time, brands can anticipate changes in consumer behavior and adjust their strategy proactively.

When analyzing search term data, it's also important to consider the overall performance of different keyword categories. This can include branded versus non-branded search terms, which can offer insights into how well the brand is resonating with customers. Branded search terms refer to queries that include the brand name or specific product names, such as "Nike running shoes." Non-branded terms are more generic and do not include the brand name, such as "best running shoes." Brands that perform well with branded search terms are likely building strong brand recognition and customer loyalty, while strong performance with non-branded terms suggests that their products are being discovered through more general searches. Striking a balance between branded and non-branded keywords is essential for driving both brand awareness and direct sales.

By regularly reviewing search term reports, brands can optimize their bidding strategies as well. The data provides insight into which search terms are driving the most sales or clicks, which can inform bid adjustments. For example, if a particular search term is delivering high sales at a low cost per click (CPC), the brand may choose to increase the bid for that term to capture more traffic. Conversely, if certain search terms are underperforming, the brand may decrease the bid or pause them altogether. Adjusting bids based on search term performance ensures that the advertising budget is being spent efficiently and in a way that maximizes returns.

Search term analysis also provides an opportunity for A/B testing. Advertisers can experiment with different variations of keywords or ad copy to determine what resonates most with their target audience. By tracking how certain search terms perform when paired with specific messaging or creative assets, brands can fine-tune their campaigns and identify winning combinations. This continuous cycle of testing and optimization helps ensure that advertising efforts remain relevant and effective over time, even as market dynamics change.

Another key benefit of search term reports is the ability to track competitive performance. By monitoring the search terms that are driving traffic to competitor products, brands can gain insights into the types of keywords and phrases that their competition is targeting. This information can inform their own keyword strategy and help identify gaps or opportunities in the market. If a competitor is consistently capturing traffic for a particular search term, it may be worth considering how to better position the brand to compete for that term, whether through more compelling ad copy, optimized listings, or improved product offerings.

Search term reports can also help advertisers refine their product listings. If a certain term is consistently driving traffic, it may be an indication that the product title, bullet points, or descriptions could be better optimized to align with what customers are searching for. Making sure that the right keywords are incorporated into product listings can improve organic search ranking and enhance the overall visibility of the product on Amazon.

Analyzing search term reports is an essential part of any advertising strategy on Amazon. The insights derived from these reports provide a clear view of customer behavior, keyword performance, and overall campaign effectiveness. By identifying high-performing and irrelevant terms, understanding customer intent, capitalizing on trends, optimizing bids, and refining product listings, brands can make data-driven decisions that lead to higher conversions and more efficient use of advertising spend. Regularly monitoring and adjusting based on search term data ensures that campaigns remain competitive, relevant, and successful, ultimately driving growth and profitability.

REFINING HEADLINES AND CREATIVE BASED ON PERFORMANCE DATA

The success of any advertising campaign depends largely on how well its creative elements resonate with the audience. One of the most pivotal creative aspects of advertising on Amazon is the headline and its ability to capture the attention of potential customers. As advertising platforms evolve, so do the expectations of consumers. Therefore, the process of refining headlines and creative elements based on performance data is crucial to maintaining and enhancing the effectiveness of any ad campaign. For any brand or seller aiming to maximize their reach and conversion rates, continuous optimization of headlines and creative content using performance insights is essential.

When it comes to refining headlines and creative content, the starting point is understanding the underlying performance data. Performance metrics provide insights into how well an ad is performing across various dimensions, including click-through rates (CTR), conversion rates, cost-per-click (CPC), and return on ad spend (ROAS). These data points allow advertisers to gauge the effectiveness of their current creative, identify potential areas for improvement, and make informed decisions about how to adjust their content.

One of the first steps in refining creative is to look at the click-through rate (CTR), which reflects how many users clicked on the ad after seeing it. A low CTR often indicates that the headline is not compelling enough to draw in potential customers. If the CTR is underperforming, it is a strong signal that the headline might not be communicating the value of the product or offering effectively. For example, a headline that is too vague or generic may fail to grab attention, while a headline that is too specific might alienate a broader audience. In such cases, the headline can be tested and optimized for clarity, specificity, and relevance. Introducing a sense of urgency, highlighting a key benefit, or using action-oriented language can improve engagement and drive more clicks.

In addition to improving CTR, analyzing conversion rates is another critical step in refining headlines and creative elements. A headline may lead to a high CTR, but if it doesn't translate into conversions, then the ad is likely missing a critical element in the customer journey. This could be due to the mismatch between the expectations set by the headline and the content of the landing page or product listing. For instance, if the headline promises a 20% discount, but the customer does not find any mention of a discount on the landing page, the conversion rate may suffer. In such instances, the headline and the product listing should be aligned to ensure that the ad's messaging accurately reflects what the customer will encounter after clicking through.

Performance data also reveals the relative effectiveness of different creative formats. It may be that your headline is working well with one style of creative but not another. For example, an image-heavy ad might require a more concise headline, while video ads could benefit from longer, more detailed messaging. By testing various creative formats, marketers can uncover what resonates best with their audience. A refined headline can make a difference in the performance of different creative formats by providing a consistent message across all touchpoints, thus ensuring a cohesive and effective user experience.

Moreover, optimizing headlines based on performance data also means understanding the competitive landscape. It is essential to continually monitor how competing brands and products are positioning their ads. If competitors are seeing success with specific words, phrases, or emotional triggers, brands can incorporate similar techniques into their headlines, but with a unique twist that reflects their product's unique selling propositions (USPs). This could involve emphasizing features that competitors overlook or offering a stronger value proposition that sets the brand apart. However, it's important to ensure that the headlines remain truthful and aligned with the brand's values and promises. The goal is to stand out from the competition by being more relevant, clearer, or more engaging to potential customers.

A powerful tool in headline optimization is A/B testing. A/B testing allows advertisers to create multiple variations of a headline to determine which one performs the best. For example, an A/B test might involve comparing a headline that emphasizes a discount versus one that highlights the quality of the product. By running such tests on a regular basis, advertisers can refine their messaging to identify what best resonates with their audience. Over time, this process helps build a library of high-performing headlines that can be used across different campaigns.

Another important aspect to consider when refining creative is the use of customer feedback and sentiment analysis. Performance data on clicks and conversions is valuable, but feedback from customers can provide insights into how well the headline aligns with their needs and interests. For example, reviews and comments left by customers can reveal what they liked or disliked about the product, which can directly inform future headline choices. Analyzing this feedback alongside performance data allows advertisers to create more compelling and targeted messaging that appeals to the emotions and needs of their audience.

The choice of language in the headline is also paramount. Using strong, action-driven words like "exclusive," "limited-time," or "must-have" can evoke a sense of urgency or desire, encouraging users to click through and make a purchase. Words that trigger emotional responses, such as "luxury," "affordable," or "innovative," can also significantly influence how users perceive the product and its value. It's important to experiment with different language styles based on performance data to uncover which types of language have the most impact on your target audience.

When refining creative elements, it's also important to consider the context in which the ad is being displayed. A headline that works well on desktop might not perform as effectively on mobile devices, where users' attention spans tend to be shorter. Mobile ads may benefit from more concise, punchy headlines that quickly convey the product's value, while desktop ads can afford a bit more detail. Performance data across platforms can guide these adjustments, ensuring that the headline resonates with users, regardless of the device they are using.

The role of images and videos in advertising is crucial in tandem with headlines. While the headline communicates the product's benefits or key message, visuals serve to reinforce that message and capture attention. If the visuals are mismatched with the headline, or if they fail to make an impact, the overall performance of the ad can suffer. For example, if a headline promises a new innovative product but the image shows an outdated design, the ad may confuse or alienate potential customers. Testing different image styles or video formats alongside headline changes can help identify the most effective combinations. Videos that showcase a product in action, or images that highlight its key features, can complement an engaging headline and provide a clearer, more compelling reason for users to click through.

As advertisers continue to refine their campaigns based on performance data, it's crucial to maintain an agile approach. The digital landscape is constantly evolving, and consumer preferences can shift quickly. What works well today may not perform as effectively in the future. As a result, advertisers should continuously monitor their campaigns, test new creative ideas, and make adjustments to keep up with these changes. This iterative process of refinement ensures that campaigns stay relevant, engaging, and effective over time.

Refining headlines and creative elements based on performance data is an ongoing and essential process for any brand looking to succeed in advertising. By analyzing key performance metrics such as click-through rates, conversion rates, and customer sentiment, advertisers can make data-driven decisions to optimize their messaging and visual content. Whether through A/B testing, analyzing competitor strategies, or leveraging customer feedback, the goal is to ensure that the headlines and creative assets are aligned with customer needs and expectations. By continuously optimizing creative elements, advertisers can increase engagement, drive conversions, and ultimately achieve better results from their campaigns.

INTEGRATING SPONSORED BRANDS WITH OTHER ADVERTISING EFFORTS

In the ever-evolving world of digital advertising, it's essential to recognize that no single ad format operates in isolation. The integration of Sponsored Brands with other advertising efforts on Amazon can amplify the reach and effectiveness of your campaigns, driving better results and ensuring that your marketing efforts work cohesively toward a common goal. This integration allows brands to harness the power of multiple ad types, leveraging their unique strengths to engage customers at different points in the buying journey.

Sponsored Brands are designed to drive brand visibility by showcasing multiple products or a specific product offering, typically at the top of search results. When integrated effectively with other advertising efforts, such as Sponsored Products, Sponsored Display, and even external marketing channels like social media or email campaigns, the potential to enhance brand awareness, increase conversions, and improve customer loyalty significantly increases.

One of the primary benefits of integrating Sponsored Brands with other advertising efforts is the ability to create a consistent and unified brand message across multiple touchpoints. When you synchronize your Sponsored Brands campaigns with Sponsored Products, for example, you ensure that customers are exposed to a cohesive narrative. Sponsored Products ads typically show individual products in search results, often tied to specific keywords, while Sponsored Brands showcase a collection of products, helping to reinforce your brand identity and provide a broader view of your offerings. By running both types of campaigns in parallel, you create a seamless customer experience, allowing shoppers to easily move from discovering individual products to exploring your entire product line.

To integrate these ad types effectively, it's crucial to ensure that the products featured in your Sponsored Brands ads are strategically selected to complement your Sponsored Products campaigns. For example, you might promote a product with high conversion rates in a Sponsored Product ad, while using a Sponsored Brand ad to showcase a curated selection of related products or a brand store. This helps drive traffic to your product listings and landing pages while reinforcing your brand's messaging.

Additionally, Sponsored Display ads are another powerful tool to integrate with your Sponsored Brands campaigns. Sponsored Display ads are particularly effective for retargeting customers who have already shown interest in your products or similar products on Amazon. By combining Sponsored Brands with Sponsored Display, you can re-engage customers who have clicked on your Sponsored Brand ads but haven't yet converted. Sponsored Display ads can remind them of your products and encourage them to complete their purchase. This integration works particularly well when paired with the use of audience targeting and product targeting, ensuring that you're reaching the right people at the right time.

When you integrate Sponsored Brands with Sponsored Display, it's vital to align your targeting strategies. Sponsored Brands typically rely on keyword-based targeting, while Sponsored Display ads can leverage both product and audience targeting. By aligning these strategies, you can create a more personalized experience for customers, reaching them with the right message at each stage of their buying journey. For example, if a shopper views your Sponsored Brand ad for a specific product, a Sponsored Display ad can follow them, showcasing related products or offering a discount on the item they viewed, nudging them towards a purchase.

Incorporating external marketing channels into your advertising efforts on Amazon can also provide a significant boost when integrated with Sponsored Brands. Social media platforms, such as Facebook, Instagram, and YouTube, can be effective tools for raising awareness about your products and brand. By creating content that directs traffic to your Amazon listings or brand store, you can generate interest in your offerings and build a strong customer base outside of Amazon's ecosystem.

To maximize the effectiveness of this integration, ensure that your messaging is consistent across all channels. For example, if you're running a Sponsored Brands campaign on Amazon to promote a specific product bundle, your social media ads and email campaigns should highlight the same bundle with similar messaging. This consistency helps to reinforce your brand identity, making your products more memorable to potential customers.

Beyond social media, email marketing can also play a critical role in driving traffic to your Amazon listings and brand store. Once you've captured customer interest through Sponsored Brands, you can use email campaigns to keep customers engaged with personalized offers, reminders, and product recommendations. By segmenting your email list and targeting customers who have interacted with your Sponsored Brands ads, you can send relevant content that nudges them closer to making a purchase.

While integrating Sponsored Brands with other advertising efforts is crucial for reaching customers across multiple touchpoints, it's equally important to consider the timing and sequencing of your campaigns. For example, if you're running a time-sensitive promotion, such as a flash sale, you might want to run a Sponsored Brands campaign to create initial brand awareness, followed by Sponsored Products ads that focus on individual items included in the sale. You could also use Sponsored Display ads to retarget customers who interacted with your Sponsored

Brands or Sponsored Products ads but didn't complete a purchase. This multi-phase approach creates a well-rounded strategy that builds awareness, drives interest, and encourages conversions.

To ensure your integration efforts are successful, you must continuously analyze performance data and adjust your campaigns accordingly. Amazon's robust advertising reports offer valuable insights into how your ads are performing across various metrics, such as impressions, clicks, and conversions. By examining these metrics for each type of ad, you can determine which strategies are working and where there's room for improvement. For example, if your Sponsored Brands campaign is generating a lot of clicks but low conversion rates, you may want to examine your product listings to ensure they are optimized for conversions. Alternatively, if your Sponsored Products ads are generating a high ROI but you're not seeing significant brand awareness, you may need to invest more in Sponsored Brands to increase visibility.

Another key consideration when integrating Sponsored Brands with other efforts is budget allocation. Each advertising format has its unique strengths, so it's important to allocate your budget in a way that supports your overall strategy. Sponsored Brands typically require a larger budget to achieve the necessary visibility, as they are often placed at the top of search results. Sponsored Products, on the other hand, tend to be more cost-effective since they are often tied to specific keywords and product listings. By balancing your budget allocation between these formats, you can maximize both visibility and conversions, ensuring that your advertising efforts are working together efficiently.

Testing and optimization should be a constant focus when integrating Sponsored Brands with other advertising efforts. A/B testing your creative assets, targeting strategies, and budget allocation can provide valuable insights into which combinations yield the best results. Running continuous tests across your Sponsored Brands, Sponsored Products, and Sponsored Display ads allows you to refine your approach over time, ensuring that your advertising efforts remain aligned with your goals and responsive to changes in consumer behavior.

Integrating Sponsored Brands with other advertising efforts on Amazon allows brands to create a more cohesive and effective advertising strategy that reaches customers at various stages of their purchasing journey. By aligning Sponsored Brands with Sponsored Products, Sponsored Display ads, and external marketing channels, brands can enhance visibility, increase engagement, and drive more conversions. However, successful integration requires careful planning, consistent messaging, data analysis, and ongoing optimization. By adopting a comprehensive approach to advertising on Amazon, brands can significantly improve their chances of success in a competitive marketplace.

SCALING YOUR BRAND PRESENCE ON AMAZON PRIME

Scaling your brand presence on Amazon Prime is a crucial step toward achieving long-term success on the platform. As the world's largest e-commerce marketplace, Amazon offers an unparalleled opportunity to grow your brand, reach a vast customer base, and increase sales. However, with such immense competition, it is essential to adopt a strategic approach to not only introduce your brand to potential customers but also to ensure that it continues to grow and evolve over time.

The first step in scaling your brand on Amazon Prime is to establish a solid foundation by creating a professional and cohesive brand identity. This includes building a well-organized Amazon Store that reflects your brand's values, showcases your best products, and provides a user-friendly experience for shoppers. Your Amazon Store should act as a digital storefront, offering an immersive brand experience through rich visuals, compelling messaging, and easy navigation. Optimizing your product listings with high-quality images, detailed descriptions, and accurate keywords is also a fundamental aspect of scaling your brand on Amazon. Product listings that are optimized not only attract the right audience but also improve your chances of appearing in relevant searches, which is vital for gaining visibility and driving sales.

Once your foundation is solid, the next step in scaling your brand presence is to leverage Amazon's advertising capabilities. Amazon offers a range of advertising options, such as Sponsored Products, Sponsored Brands, and Sponsored Display, each of which can play a vital role in increasing your brand's reach. Sponsored Products ads are a great way to target customers who are already looking for products similar to yours, while Sponsored Brands allows you to showcase your entire product range and drive brand recognition. Sponsored Display ads, on the other hand, can be particularly effective in retargeting customers who have shown interest in your products, bringing them back to complete a purchase.

To scale your brand effectively, you must make use of these advertising formats in combination. Sponsored Products ads are excellent for driving immediate sales, but to truly build brand recognition, it's essential to integrate them with Sponsored Brands campaigns. By showcasing a curated collection of products, Sponsored Brands ads increase brand visibility at the top of search results and on product detail pages, helping customers discover your full product range. Sponsored Display ads complement this strategy by retargeting customers who have previously interacted with your brand, nurturing those relationships and encouraging repeat purchases.

Scaling your brand presence also involves continuously analyzing and optimizing your advertising campaigns. To do this effectively, you must track key performance metrics such as ACoS (Advertising Cost of

Sale), CTR (Click-Through Rate), conversion rates, and impressions. By regularly reviewing these metrics, you can identify which campaigns are working well and which areas need improvement. For example, if a Sponsored Brands campaign has a high click-through rate but a low conversion rate, it might indicate that your product listings need optimization to better convert traffic into sales. Conversely, if your Sponsored Products ads are generating low impressions, you may need to adjust your bid strategy or expand your keyword targeting to increase visibility.

One of the most powerful tools for scaling your brand presence on Amazon Prime is Amazon's Brand Analytics, which offers valuable insights into customer behavior and competitor performance. By analyzing this data, you can identify trends, spot opportunities, and refine your targeting strategies. For instance, you can gain insights into which keywords are driving the most traffic and sales, allowing you to adjust your advertising campaigns accordingly. Additionally, you can monitor how your brand is performing compared to competitors, providing a benchmark for where you stand in the marketplace and revealing areas where you can outpace the competition.

Another key aspect of scaling your brand on Amazon Prime is building a loyal customer base. While acquiring new customers is essential, retaining existing customers is equally important for long-term growth. One of the most effective ways to foster customer loyalty is by offering exceptional customer service. Promptly addressing customer queries, providing fast and reliable shipping, and handling returns smoothly are all critical factors in enhancing customer satisfaction. Additionally, incorporating product reviews and ratings into your product listings builds trust and helps new customers make informed purchasing decisions. Engaging with customers through personalized follow-up emails or promotional offers can also strengthen relationships and encourage repeat business.

To further enhance your brand presence, it's important to expand beyond Amazon's core search and advertising features. Amazon Prime offers several opportunities to engage with Prime members, who are some of the most loyal and high-value customers. As part of your scaling strategy, you can explore Prime Day promotions, Lightning Deals, and other Amazon events that give your products increased visibility during high-traffic periods. Participating in these events not only boosts brand awareness but can also significantly increase sales, especially when paired with strategic advertising campaigns.

Beyond Amazon's advertising and promotional tools, a strong content strategy can also contribute to scaling your brand. High-quality, informative, and engaging content can help establish your brand as an authority in your niche, attracting customers and driving traffic to your listings. You can utilize Amazon's A+ Content feature to provide rich media, such as comparison charts, lifestyle images, and enhanced product descriptions, which make your listings more appealing and informative. Leveraging video content can also significantly boost engagement. Videos showcasing your products in action, explaining their benefits, or offering tutorials can provide customers with a deeper understanding of your brand and offerings, ultimately leading to higher conversion rates.

Building your brand on Amazon Prime is also about expanding your presence across the platform, including in the Amazon marketplace's international regions. By selling in international Amazon marketplaces, you can reach a global audience and increase sales. However, this comes with its own set of challenges, including the need to adapt your content and marketing strategies to different languages, cultures, and shopping behaviors. Fortunately, Amazon's Global Selling program makes it easier to reach international customers by offering tools for language translation, global shipping, and local customer support.

To scale your brand presence successfully on Amazon Prime, it is important to understand the balance between paid advertising and organic growth. While Amazon's advertising tools are indispensable for driving traffic and sales, organic rankings are just as important for long-term success. Organic growth on Amazon is achieved through product reviews, sales volume, and optimized listings. By consistently offering high-quality products, excellent customer service, and a seamless shopping experience, your brand can increase its organic visibility on Amazon. Over time, this will result in more customers discovering your products without the need for paid advertising, ultimately reducing your overall advertising spend and increasing profitability.

Lastly, as your brand grows on Amazon, it's important to maintain scalability by streamlining your operations. Efficient inventory management, responsive customer support, and automated advertising adjustments can help keep your business running smoothly as it scales. Amazon provides a variety of tools and features to automate certain aspects of your business, such as Amazon's Automated Campaigns, which can adjust your bids and keywords automatically based on performance. This allows you to focus on strategy and growth while ensuring that your campaigns are optimized for success.

Scaling your brand presence on Amazon Prime requires a combination of solid foundational work, strategic advertising, continuous optimization, and a customer-centric approach. By leveraging Amazon's powerful tools, such as Sponsored Brands, Brand Analytics, and A+ Content, and by expanding your reach through Prime-specific promotions and global selling, you can maximize your brand's visibility and sales potential. By adopting a comprehensive, data-driven approach to scaling your brand, you can ensure long-term success on the platform, establishing your brand as a leader in your niche and building a loyal customer base.

PART 4

Reaching Shoppers Beyond Search with Amazon Sponsored Display Ads

CHAPTER 9
EXPLORING THE POTENTIAL OF SPONSORED DISPLAY

UNDERSTANDING DIFFERENT SPONSORED DISPLAY TARGETING OPTIONS

Understanding the different targeting options available within Sponsored Display advertising is essential for optimizing your campaigns on Amazon. Sponsored Display is a powerful tool that allows you to reach potential customers at multiple touchpoints across the Amazon ecosystem. By utilizing the targeting capabilities effectively, you can increase your visibility, drive traffic to your product listings, and ultimately, boost sales. Two primary targeting options that advertisers should be familiar with are audience targeting and product targeting. Both offer unique benefits and can be leveraged in combination to maximize the effectiveness of your campaigns.

Audience targeting is one of the most versatile and powerful targeting options within Sponsored Display ads. This option enables advertisers to target specific customer groups based on their behaviors and interests, ensuring that their ads reach the most relevant audience. Amazon provides several audience segments for targeting, including retargeting customers who have previously viewed your products, as well as those who have shown interest in similar products or categories.

One of the most beneficial aspects of audience targeting is the ability to reach customers who have already interacted with your brand or products. Retargeting, for example, allows you to display ads to users who have visited your product detail pages or added items to their carts without making a purchase. This strategy can significantly increase the likelihood of converting these potential customers, as they are already familiar with your products. By keeping your brand in front of them through Sponsored Display ads, you can remind them of their interest and encourage them to complete their purchase.

Another important audience segment is the one focused on similar products. Through this type of targeting, you can reach shoppers who have shown interest in products similar to yours, even if they haven't yet interacted with your brand. This is particularly useful for expanding your reach beyond your current customer base, attracting users who are looking for solutions that align with what you offer. By targeting these customers, you can increase the chances of capturing new buyers and expanding your brand's reach in a competitive marketplace.

Amazon also provides audience targeting based on shopping behaviors. These segments are built around customers' purchasing patterns and interests, such as those who are likely to make a purchase in a particular category or those who frequently engage with specific types of products. This allows you to tailor your ads to reach users with high purchase intent, making your ad spend more efficient by targeting customers who are most likely to convert. The ability to reach highly relevant customers is crucial in a marketplace as large as Amazon, where competition for attention is fierce.

In addition to audience targeting, product targeting is another vital option for Sponsored Display campaigns. Product targeting allows you to target specific products, categories, or brands directly. This targeting option is especially powerful because it allows you to place your ads on the product detail pages of competing or complementary products. By targeting a competitor's product page, you can place your ad directly in front of customers who are actively browsing and considering similar products. This provides an excellent opportunity to capture the attention of shoppers who are already in the decision-making process and are likely to consider alternative options.

Product targeting also allows you to refine your strategy by focusing on specific categories or individual products that align with your offerings. For example, if you sell accessories for smartphones, you can target your ads to appear on the detail pages of popular smartphone brands or in the "Frequently Bought Together" section of related products. This gives you the chance to attract customers who are in the process of making a purchase decision related to your product category, increasing the likelihood of capturing their attention and influencing their decision.

By selecting individual ASINs (Amazon Standard Identification Numbers), you can further refine your product targeting strategy. This allows you to target specific products, even within a broader category, and display your ad alongside them. This is particularly beneficial if your product offers a unique value proposition or if it competes directly with specific brands or products. For instance, if you have a premium phone case brand, you can target ads to appear on pages for well-known but less premium phone case brands. This can help you attract budget-conscious customers who may be looking for a higher-quality alternative.

Another useful feature of product targeting within Sponsored Display is the ability to target by specific categories or brands. By selecting categories, you can ensure that your ads are shown to users who are browsing within the same or related product categories as your offerings. This type of targeting is beneficial if you want to ensure that your ads are being displayed to the right audience but don't necessarily want to target specific products. It's a great way to gain visibility within a broader product category while still reaching shoppers who are interested in products similar to yours.

The combination of audience and product targeting provides advertisers with a unique opportunity to implement a highly tailored advertising strategy. Audience targeting allows you to reach customers who have already interacted with your products, while product targeting enables you to position your ads directly on competitor pages or relevant categories. By using both targeting options in tandem, you can create a multi-layered approach that captures both new customers and those who are already familiar with your brand. This approach ensures that your ads reach the most relevant shoppers, maximizing the likelihood of conversion.

When utilizing both targeting options, it's essential to keep in mind the importance of continuous monitoring and optimization. Even though these targeting options are powerful, they need to be regularly reviewed to ensure their effectiveness. By analyzing key performance metrics, such as click-through rate (CTR), conversion rate, and return on ad spend (ROAS), you can identify which targeting options are driving the best results and adjust your strategy accordingly. For example, if you find that product targeting is generating higher conversion rates than audience targeting, you may want to shift more of your budget toward product-based targeting to take advantage of its effectiveness. Conversely, if audience targeting is producing better results, you can further refine your audience segments to capture even more relevant customers.

To refine targeting strategies even further, you can also take advantage of Amazon's reporting tools to gather insights into customer behavior and campaign performance. The detailed reports provided by Amazon will give you a clear understanding of how your ads are performing across different audience segments and product targets. You can use this data to identify trends, make adjustments to your campaigns, and optimize your ads to maximize return on investment (ROI).

Another key aspect of optimizing Sponsored Display ads is testing. Amazon allows advertisers to run A/B tests on different targeting options, creatives, and bidding strategies. By experimenting with various targeting methods, you can gain valuable insights into what resonates best with your audience. For example, you may find that a specific combination of audience targeting and product targeting yields better results than when either is used alone. A/B testing allows you to continually refine your approach and find the best-performing strategies for your brand.

To fully leverage the power of Sponsored Display advertising, it's essential to take a holistic approach that integrates both audience targeting and product targeting. By doing so, you can create campaigns that target the right customers at the right time with the right message. Whether you're retargeting customers who have interacted with your products or targeting shoppers browsing similar products, Sponsored Display provides a wide range of options that can help you grow your brand, increase sales, and expand your reach on Amazon. By constantly analyzing performance data and optimizing your campaigns, you can ensure that your advertising efforts are always working toward your brand's goals, driving long-term success on the platform.

REACHING SHOPPERS ON AND OFF AMAZON

In today's competitive landscape, businesses must go beyond merely relying on Amazon's marketplace to capture the attention of shoppers. As e-commerce continues to evolve, it has become increasingly important for brands to create strategies that not only engage customers within the Amazon ecosystem but also extend their reach to potential shoppers outside of it. Successfully reaching shoppers both on and off Amazon presents a significant opportunity to increase brand awareness, drive traffic to your listings, and ultimately boost sales.

To understand how to reach shoppers effectively both within and outside of Amazon, it's essential to grasp the full scope of advertising tools available on the platform. Amazon provides various ad types that allow advertisers to target consumers at different stages of their buying journey. However, the power of these tools is amplified when combined with off-Amazon strategies that help you engage a broader audience, increase your brand's visibility, and strengthen customer loyalty.

On Amazon, the primary focus of many advertisers is to capture the attention of customers who are actively searching for products or browsing categories relevant to their interests. Amazon offers several ad formats, including Sponsored Products, Sponsored Brands, and Sponsored Display, that can be highly effective for targeting users based on their browsing behaviors and purchasing intent. By strategically placing ads on Amazon's search results pages, product detail pages, and even within the broader Amazon network, you can capture customers while they are most engaged in the shopping process.

One powerful tool for reaching shoppers on Amazon is Sponsored Products. This ad type allows you to promote individual product listings and appear within search results and product detail pages. Sponsored Products ads are triggered by specific search terms that are relevant to your product, which means that you are essentially targeting customers who have already expressed interest in similar products. This form of targeting enables advertisers to reach customers who are in a ready-to-buy state, increasing the likelihood of conversion.

Similarly, Sponsored Brands ads offer another effective way to engage Amazon shoppers. These ads allow you to showcase your brand

and multiple products at once, creating a more comprehensive experience for potential customers. Sponsored Brands ads appear in prominent locations on Amazon's search results pages, often at the top of the page, ensuring visibility to high-intent shoppers. By creating compelling and eye-catching ads, you can drive traffic directly to your Amazon storefront or specific product detail pages. Sponsored Display ads also allow you to target shoppers with specific interests and behaviors, whether they are browsing similar products or have previously interacted with your brand.

However, focusing solely on in-Amazon advertising misses out on a significant opportunity. While Amazon's marketplace is incredibly powerful, it is only one channel within a broader digital landscape. To truly scale your brand and increase your reach, it's essential to extend your advertising efforts to off-Amazon platforms. Reaching shoppers off Amazon involves targeting audiences on external websites, social media platforms, and other digital channels where consumers are actively engaging with content. By doing so, you can connect with potential buyers before they even consider shopping on Amazon, build brand awareness, and guide them to your Amazon listings.

One of the most effective off-Amazon strategies involves using Amazon's own advertising products to reach shoppers across the web. Amazon offers a range of tools, such as Amazon DSP (Demand-Side Platform), which allows advertisers to run display ads on third-party websites, mobile apps, and other digital media. With Amazon DSP, you can access exclusive audience insights and leverage Amazon's vast data to deliver highly targeted ads to potential customers based on their behaviors, interests, and demographic information. This can significantly increase your brand's visibility, reaching customers who might not be actively searching for your products on Amazon but are likely to be interested in them.

Through Amazon DSP, you can also implement retargeting campaigns, which display ads to users who have previously interacted with your brand, either through visiting your Amazon listings, viewing specific products, or even adding items to their shopping carts. Retargeting is particularly effective because it allows you to re-engage potential customers who are already familiar with your products, increasing the chances of conversion. These retargeting ads can appear on various websites and apps across the web, reminding users of their interest in your products and encouraging them to complete a purchase on Amazon.

In addition to Amazon's DSP, social media platforms like Facebook, Instagram, and Pinterest are excellent channels for reaching shoppers off Amazon. These platforms offer highly advanced targeting capabilities, allowing advertisers to segment audiences based on specific interests, behaviors, location, and even purchasing intent. Running ads on social media provides a unique opportunity to build brand awareness and engagement, reaching consumers who may not be actively shopping for products but are open to discovering new brands. By leveraging the visual nature of social media, you can create compelling ads that showcase your products, highlight customer reviews, and feature promotions to entice users to visit your Amazon listings.

Facebook and Instagram, for example, allow advertisers to run both image and video ads, giving you the flexibility to craft engaging content that resonates with your target audience. Video ads, in particular, are highly effective in showcasing products and demonstrating their value. Whether it's a product demonstration, a customer testimonial, or a behind-the-scenes look at how your products are made, video content on social media allows you to connect with consumers on a deeper level, building trust and interest in your brand.

Moreover, Google Display Network (GDN) offers another off-Amazon channel that can significantly expand your brand's reach. Through GDN, you can display banner ads, text ads, and even interactive ads on millions of websites across the web. GDN uses Google's vast data on users' browsing habits to target customers based on their interests, demographics, and previous interactions with your brand. By running display ads through GDN, you can increase visibility and drive traffic to your Amazon listings, reaching potential customers who might not have otherwise discovered your products.

The power of combining on-Amazon and off-Amazon advertising cannot be overstated. Using a multi-channel approach helps ensure that your brand stays top of mind for consumers at every stage of the buying process. By targeting shoppers both within Amazon's ecosystem and across the broader web, you increase the likelihood of capturing attention from a wider audience, building brand recognition, and ultimately, increasing conversions. Additionally, integrating both on-Amazon and off-Amazon strategies provides valuable opportunities to create a seamless shopping experience for consumers, guiding them from initial discovery through to purchase.

It is also crucial to track and measure the performance of your advertising efforts both on and off Amazon. Monitoring key performance metrics such as return on ad spend (ROAS), click-through rate (CTR), and conversion rate will help you understand the effectiveness of each campaign. By analyzing the data, you can identify trends, optimize your targeting strategies, and make data-driven decisions to continually improve your advertising efforts. A/B testing is also an invaluable tool for comparing different ad creatives, targeting methods, and bidding strategies to determine the most effective approach.

Ultimately, the goal of reaching shoppers both on and off Amazon is to create a comprehensive, integrated advertising strategy that drives brand growth, increases visibility, and enhances customer acquisition efforts. By strategically using Amazon's internal advertising tools alongside external platforms, you can ensure that your brand is consistently exposed to potential customers, maximizing your opportunities for success in the competitive world of e-commerce.

UTILIZING DIFFERENT AD FORMATS: IMAGE AND VIDEO ADS

Advertising on Amazon has evolved beyond simple product listings and text-based ads, with dynamic visual formats now playing a pivotal role in capturing customer attention and enhancing engagement. The rise of image and video ads on the platform has transformed how brands reach their target audience, offering opportunities to build deeper connections and tell a more compelling story. Whether you're looking to showcase your products in an eye-catching way or create an emotional connection with potential buyers, utilizing image and video ads can be highly effective in driving customer actions and increasing conversions.

The first step in understanding how to leverage image and video ads on Amazon is to recognize the power of visual content. In an online shopping environment, where consumers are bombarded with a multitude of product choices, visuals are often the deciding factor in attracting attention. A well-designed image or video ad not only highlights your product but also communicates its benefits, quality, and value in a manner that resonates with potential buyers. It serves as a hook, pulling customers in by offering a glimpse of what they can expect if they choose your brand.

Image ads are one of the most widely used ad formats on Amazon. These ads are primarily static, but they have the advantage of being simple yet visually striking. Images can showcase your product in its best light, either through high-quality product shots, lifestyle images that show the product in use, or even a combination of both. The key to an effective image ad is clarity and relevance. Your image needs to be crisp, high-resolution, and focused on showing the product's key features or its most appealing aspects. For example, if you're advertising a kitchen gadget, showing the product in use—perhaps being used to prepare food in a home kitchen—can help the customer visualize how it will enhance their everyday life.

Amazon's Sponsored Brands format allows you to utilize image ads that appear at the top of search results, providing prime visibility to potential customers who are actively browsing for similar products. These image ads are highly effective for showcasing a selection of products, such as a product line or related items. Sponsored Brands also lets you pair your product images with a custom headline, which can help create a strong brand identity and offer a more personalized touch. Using these ads, you can not only drive traffic directly to your product detail pages but also build awareness for your brand as a whole.

While image ads are powerful, video ads provide an even more dynamic and immersive experience that can capture the audience's attention in ways that static images simply cannot. Video ads are particularly effective in showcasing the benefits and features of a product, as they allow you to tell a story, explain complex concepts, and demonstrate the product in action. Videos also provide a better opportunity to build an emotional connection with your audience. For example, a video ad for a fitness product can show someone using the product in a real-life workout scenario, highlighting its effectiveness while connecting with viewers on a personal level.

Video ads can be a game-changer in terms of customer engagement. They tend to have higher engagement rates than static ads because they allow you to incorporate sound, movement, and a narrative element that captures attention. The visual nature of videos makes it easier to communicate a compelling message about your product, especially when it comes to showcasing its value, how it works, and why it's a better choice compared to competing products. In fact, studies have shown that video content is one of the most effective forms of advertising, as it can increase customer recall, boost engagement, and improve conversion rates.

On Amazon, Sponsored Brands video ads appear in the search results and product detail pages, offering a highly visible opportunity to reach customers who are actively researching products. These video ads are shown alongside the search results, allowing you to promote your products in a manner that feels more natural and less intrusive. When creating a Sponsored Brands video ad, you need to keep in mind that Amazon limits these ads to a duration of 6-15 seconds, so it's important to communicate your message quickly and efficiently. The video should grab the viewer's attention immediately, highlight key features or benefits, and include a clear call to action.

One of the primary advantages of video ads is their ability to showcase a product's real-world use, which is something that image ads can't do as effectively. For instance, if you're advertising a product like a skincare cream, a short video can demonstrate how it's applied, its texture, and how it absorbs into the skin. Seeing the product in action helps the potential customer understand how it fits into their lifestyle, increasing the chances of them clicking on the ad and ultimately making a purchase.

When incorporating video ads into your Amazon advertising strategy, it's important to consider not only the creative quality but also the targeting of the ads. Just as with image ads, targeting plays a crucial role in the success of your video campaigns. You can target specific audiences based on their browsing and purchasing behaviors, ensuring that your video ad reaches those most likely to convert. For example, you could target consumers who have previously shown interest in similar products or those who have viewed similar video content related to your product category.

Another factor to consider when using video ads is the emotional impact they can have on your audience. Video ads are particularly effective at conveying a sense of storytelling. For example, a video ad for a charity-focused brand might show how purchasing a product helps support a cause, tugging at viewers' heartstrings and prompting them to make a purchase. The ability to tell a story through video is an incredibly powerful tool for building a connection with customers, as it allows you to communicate your brand's values, mission, and personality in a way that resonates on a deeper level.

To get the most out of both image and video ads, you must prioritize quality and consistency across your campaigns. Each ad must align with your brand's identity, ensuring a seamless experience for the customer from the moment they see your ad to when they make a purchase. Your images and videos should be visually appealing, professionally crafted, and on-brand to enhance recognition and foster trust. Additionally, it's important to optimize these assets for mobile viewing, as a significant portion of Amazon shoppers are browsing via mobile devices. Whether it's an image or a video, the ad must display properly on mobile screens and load quickly to ensure a smooth viewing experience.

One of the most effective ways to test and optimize your image and video ads is through A/B testing. This involves testing different versions of your ads to determine which performs better. For example, you might test various headlines, images, or video formats to see which one resonates most with your target audience. By continuously analyzing and refining your ad assets, you can improve their performance over time, increasing the likelihood of achieving your advertising goals.

Both image and video ads are powerful tools for engaging potential customers and driving traffic to your Amazon listings. Each ad format offers unique advantages, with image ads being highly effective for showcasing product features and video ads offering a more immersive experience that can build emotional connections and boost customer engagement. By using a combination of these ad formats and optimizing your creative assets, you can create a compelling and effective advertising strategy that attracts, engages, and converts shoppers on Amazon. Whether you're looking to increase brand awareness or drive direct sales, incorporating high-quality image and video ads into your Amazon campaigns can lead to significant results and help you stand out in a crowded marketplace.

LEVERAGING RETARGETING STRATEGIES TO ENGAGE PRIME MEMBERS

Retargeting strategies have become an essential tool in the digital advertising landscape, especially when trying to re-engage potential customers who have already interacted with your brand in some way. On Amazon, retargeting offers a unique opportunity to reach Prime members—those who are particularly valuable due to their high engagement and propensity to make frequent purchases. Leveraging these retargeting strategies effectively can increase your brand's visibility, drive conversions, and ensure that your products stay top-of-mind for shoppers who are likely to convert. Understanding how to target Prime members through retargeting can significantly enhance your overall advertising success on the platform.

Prime members, with their high purchasing frequency and loyalty, represent an ideal audience for retargeting campaigns. These customers are already committed to Amazon's ecosystem, which means they are familiar with the platform and trust its services. By utilizing retargeting strategies, you can specifically target these engaged consumers and increase the likelihood that they will make a purchase. Retargeting on Amazon allows you to reach shoppers who have previously viewed your product, added it to their cart, or visited your product pages but did not complete the purchase. These consumers have already shown interest in your product, so they are more likely to convert if you deliver the right message at the right time.

One of the primary ways to implement a retargeting strategy on Amazon is through Sponsored Display ads. These ads are specifically designed to help advertisers reach potential customers who have interacted with their brand but have not yet made a purchase. Sponsored Display ads can be displayed both on and off Amazon, making them incredibly versatile in targeting Prime members across different touchpoints. By using Sponsored Display, you can engage shoppers who have viewed specific product pages or added products to their cart but didn't follow through with the purchase.

One key element of a successful retargeting campaign is the use of dynamic retargeting, which involves displaying personalized ads based on the shopper's behavior. For example, if a shopper viewed your product but did not purchase it, you can retarget them with an ad that shows the exact product they viewed, along with additional product recommendations or incentives, such as a discount or a limited-time offer. By creating dynamic and personalized ads, you increase the likelihood of a conversion, as you're catering to the individual's specific interests and previous actions.

The ability to target specific customer actions, such as abandoning a shopping cart, makes retargeting especially powerful. Amazon's platform allows you to set up retargeting campaigns that focus on shoppers who have left items in their cart, a behavior that often signifies strong intent to purchase. By re-engaging these customers with targeted ads, you remind them of the products they were interested in, providing a gentle nudge to complete their purchase. This kind of retargeting can be highly effective in driving sales, as it directly addresses a point in the customer journey where a transaction was almost made but was abandoned for some reason.

Beyond cart abandonment, you can also retarget Prime members who have interacted with your brand in other ways, such as viewing a product detail page or watching a product video. These shoppers are already familiar with your products and are likely further along in the buying process. By showing them relevant ads that remind them of your offerings, you keep your products visible and increase the chances that they'll return to make a purchase. When retargeting these customers, it's crucial to create ads that are relevant to their previous behavior. For instance, if they watched a video about your product or read customer reviews, your ad should highlight features that were mentioned in the video or emphasize the benefits discussed in the reviews. This level of relevance increases the likelihood of capturing their attention and driving a conversion.

Another powerful strategy for retargeting Prime members is to use a sequential approach to ad delivery. Rather than showing the same ad repeatedly to a customer, a sequential retargeting strategy involves showing a series of ads that gradually lead the customer toward a purchase. This method works by nurturing the customer through the buying process, providing them with different touchpoints that build on their previous interactions. For example, a first ad could introduce the product, a second ad could highlight its key features, and a third ad could offer a special discount or promotion. This progressive approach to retargeting keeps the customer engaged without overwhelming them with the same messaging.

Additionally, creating urgency in your retargeting ads can be highly effective in driving conversions. Since Prime members are accustomed to fast shipping and a seamless shopping experience, adding time-sensitive offers to your retargeting ads can prompt action. For example, you could run a limited-time discount or emphasize fast, free shipping to appeal to the fast-paced nature of Amazon shoppers. Urgency is a key driver of conversions, and by incorporating it into your retargeting strategy, you can compel shoppers to act quickly before the offer expires.

Data plays a critical role in the success of any retargeting campaign. By analyzing the behavior of shoppers who interact with your products, you can segment your audience based on specific actions, such as viewing a product, adding it to the cart, or making a purchase. This segmentation allows you to create more targeted and relevant ads, ensuring that you're reaching the right customers with the right message. Furthermore, you can track the performance of your retargeting campaigns and make adjustments based on metrics like click-through rate (CTR), conversion rate, and return on ad spend (ROAS). Continuous optimization is key to maximizing the effectiveness of your retargeting strategy.

It's also important to consider the frequency and timing of your retargeting ads. If you show the same ad too many times, you risk overwhelming your potential customers and causing ad fatigue, which can lead to diminishing returns. On the other hand, if you don't show your ads enough, you may miss the opportunity to engage potential customers who are ready to make a purchase. Finding the right balance in ad frequency is essential to keep your brand in front of the right people without oversaturating them with repetitive messaging.

While Sponsored Display ads are an excellent tool for retargeting on Amazon, it's also important to integrate your retargeting efforts with other advertising strategies to ensure a cohesive approach. For example, you can use Sponsored Brands ads in conjunction with Sponsored Display to create a more comprehensive retargeting strategy. Sponsored Brands ads can help raise brand awareness by featuring your brand logo and product images at the top of search results, while Sponsored Display ads can focus on converting users who have already shown interest in your products. By using both ad formats in tandem, you can guide shoppers through the entire customer journey, from brand discovery to conversion.

Lastly, it's worth considering the broader customer journey when designing your retargeting campaigns. While Prime members may be highly engaged, it's essential to recognize that they may not convert immediately. Retargeting provides an opportunity to remain visible to potential customers throughout their decision-making process, helping to nurture leads and guide them toward making a purchase when they're ready. By using retargeting strategically and tailoring your ads to the behaviors and preferences of Prime members, you can significantly improve your chances of success and maximize the impact of your campaigns.

Leveraging retargeting strategies to engage Prime members on Amazon is a powerful way to drive conversions and grow your brand. By utilizing Sponsored Display ads, dynamic and personalized ad creatives, and data-driven segmentation, you can re-engage shoppers who have already shown interest in your products and increase the likelihood of a sale. Additionally, using sequential ad strategies, creating urgency, and integrating retargeting with other advertising efforts can further enhance the effectiveness of your campaigns. Retargeting is a critical tool for reaching customers who are on the verge of making a purchase, and with the right approach, it can yield significant returns and help you build lasting relationships with Prime members.

UNDERSTANDING THE BENEFITS OF CONTEXTUAL TARGETING

Contextual targeting is a powerful advertising strategy that leverages the context of content viewed by potential customers to deliver relevant ads. This method tailors the messaging based on the content surrounding the advertisement, ensuring that the right products are shown to the right people at the right moment. Understanding the benefits of contextual targeting can significantly enhance the effectiveness of your advertising campaigns, especially on platforms like Amazon Prime, where the competition for consumer attention is fierce, and the stakes for driving sales are high. By strategically aligning your ads with content that resonates with your target audience, you can create a more engaging, personalized experience that leads to higher conversion rates and stronger brand affinity.

The primary advantage of contextual targeting is its ability to deliver relevance. Consumers are more likely to engage with ads that align with their current interests or the content they are consuming. For example, if a shopper is browsing a cooking show or reading an article about healthy eating, showing them an ad for kitchen appliances, organic food, or meal prep services makes sense. This relevance not only increases the likelihood that the shopper will click on the ad, but it also enhances the overall user experience. Contextual targeting ensures that advertisements are integrated seamlessly into the browsing or viewing experience, making them feel less intrusive and more helpful. By aligning the ad content with the user's current activity, you reduce the chances of annoying the viewer with irrelevant messaging and, instead, provide them with something that is useful and timely.

Moreover, contextual targeting helps you avoid wasting your advertising spend on audiences who are unlikely to engage with your product. Traditional targeting methods often rely on broad demographic data, which may not always align with the interests or behaviors of the consumer. For instance, demographic targeting might suggest showing ads for sports equipment to a group of people aged 18-34, but this group could have a mix of interests that doesn't reflect the specific preferences of your ideal customer. Contextual targeting, on the other hand, focuses on the actual content the user is engaging with at the moment, ensuring that your ad reaches those who are already in a mindset to purchase products similar to what you're offering. This approach minimizes the risk of irrelevant ad impressions, leading to a more efficient use of your budget.

In addition to ensuring that your ads are shown to relevant users, contextual targeting also increases the chances of conversion by aligning your product with the intent of the user. Intent is a critical factor in any purchasing decision. Consumers are often in different stages of the buying journey when they browse content—some may just be browsing, while others are actively looking for a solution to a problem. Contextual targeting helps identify these moments of intent by delivering ads based on the content the user is consuming, which can be indicative of their interests and current needs. For instance, if a user is reading a review about wireless headphones, they might be in the decision-making phase and ready to purchase. Serving an ad for your wireless headphones in this context increases the likelihood that they will click on the ad, visit your product page, and ultimately make a purchase.

Another key benefit of contextual targeting is its ability to drive brand awareness in a more organic and non-intrusive way. Because the ad is contextually relevant to the content the user is viewing, it feels like a natural part of their experience rather than an interruption. This creates a more positive perception of your brand, as consumers appreciate advertising that adds value to their experience rather than detracting from it. For example, a well-timed ad for a camera while someone is watching a photography tutorial video might feel like a helpful recommendation rather than a bothersome interruption. This positive association can lead to higher brand recall and improved customer sentiment over time.

Contextual targeting also allows advertisers to take advantage of specific trends and seasonal moments. For instance, during the holiday season, many consumers are actively searching for gifts and are more open to receiving ads that fit their current needs. If you sell winter coats, showing ads for your products during cold weather-related content can be an effective strategy. Similarly, if there's a major sporting event, contextual targeting allows you to show ads for related products, such as fan merchandise, snacks, or beverages, at the right moment when viewers are most engaged with the event. By aligning your ad placements with seasonal trends and real-time events, you can create a sense of urgency and relevance, which can increase engagement and sales.

One of the critical aspects of contextual targeting is its ability to work seamlessly across various types of content, whether it be video, articles, or even social media. On platforms like Amazon Prime, shoppers are not only watching video content but may also be browsing product detail pages, reading reviews, or engaging with other types of media. By placing ads in these contexts, you can reach consumers when they are most receptive to your messaging. For instance, when a customer is watching a product demo video, showing an ad that highlights the unique features of your product can reinforce the message they're already absorbing and encourage them to take the next step in their purchase journey. Similarly, if someone is reading an article about skincare, an ad for your skincare line will likely resonate more than a general, untargeted ad for a completely different product category.

Another advantage of contextual targeting is that it respects user privacy by relying on the content the user is interacting with rather than personal data. In an era where privacy concerns are paramount, consumers are increasingly cautious about how their data is used by advertisers. Contextual targeting mitigates these concerns by ensuring that ads are shown based on the environment the consumer is engaging with rather than tracking their personal information. This makes it a more privacy-conscious approach to advertising, which can enhance your brand's reputation and foster trust with your audience.

As a brand, contextual targeting also provides valuable insights into consumer behavior and preferences. By analyzing which types of content your ads perform best with, you can gather data about your audience's interests and behaviors. This can help you refine your targeting strategy for future campaigns. For example, if you notice that your ads for kitchen products perform exceptionally well during cooking shows or recipe content, you can adjust your advertising strategy to target similar types of content in the future. Over time, this data-driven approach allows you to optimize your campaigns, making them more effective and cost-efficient.

Contextual targeting on Amazon Prime and other platforms also helps advertisers stand out by making ads feel more native and integrated into the overall user experience. Instead of bombarding users with generic ads that disrupt their browsing, contextual ads blend naturally into the content, making them less likely to be ignored. This native feel can improve ad engagement rates and lead to better overall campaign performance. Additionally, with Amazon's sophisticated algorithms, advertisers can refine their contextual targeting strategy based on real-time data, optimizing ad placements for maximum visibility and impact.

Ultimately, the key to success with contextual targeting lies in its ability to deliver timely, relevant, and personalized ads to consumers in a non-intrusive way. By aligning your product with the content consumers are already engaging with, you increase the chances of capturing their attention, driving higher engagement, and boosting conversions. Whether you're aiming to increase brand awareness, drive sales, or foster deeper customer relationships, contextual targeting provides a powerful tool to achieve these goals. When done right, it enhances the overall consumer experience, respects privacy, and ensures that your ads are working as effectively as possible to help your brand thrive.

CHAPTER 10

IMPLEMENTING EFFECTIVE SPONSORED DISPLAY CAMPAIGNS

CHOOSING THE RIGHT TARGETING STRATEGY FOR YOUR GOALS

When it comes to advertising on platforms like Amazon Prime, one of the most crucial decisions you will make is selecting the right targeting strategy to achieve your specific business goals. This is not a one-size-fits-all decision; different strategies can be leveraged depending on whether you want to drive brand awareness, boost conversions, or retarget potential customers who have interacted with your product. The key to success lies in understanding the nature of your goals and aligning them with the most effective targeting tactics that will yield the best results.

The first step in choosing the right targeting strategy is defining your primary objective. Do you want to introduce your brand to a new audience, encourage users who are already aware of your product to make a purchase, or re-engage previous customers who haven't made a purchase in a while? Each of these objectives requires a unique approach to targeting. Once your goal is clear, you can begin to evaluate the various targeting strategies available on Amazon Prime and other advertising platforms.

If your goal is to increase brand awareness, one of the most effective strategies is broad targeting. Broad targeting allows your ads to reach a wide range of potential customers, including those who may not be familiar with your brand or products. This strategy casts a wide net to ensure maximum exposure. With broad targeting, Amazon's algorithms automatically display your ads to users who have demonstrated a potential interest in similar categories, behaviors, or search terms. The advantage of this approach is that it exposes your brand to new audiences, helping you increase visibility and start building a presence on the platform. It's ideal when you're in the early stages of building your brand or introducing a new product, as it helps you reach users who are more likely to be interested in your offerings but haven't yet discovered them. However, one drawback to broad targeting is that it can result in higher costs if the audience you're targeting is too general or irrelevant. Therefore, it's essential to continuously monitor and refine your targeting based on performance data to ensure that you're reaching the right audience and optimizing your ad spend.

On the other hand, if your objective is to drive conversions and increase sales, a more refined targeting strategy may be necessary. In this

case, targeting users based on specific behaviors or interests is highly effective. Amazon offers several options for behavior-based targeting, such as keyword targeting and product targeting. Keyword targeting involves selecting specific search terms that potential customers may use to find products like yours. When users enter those terms into Amazon's search bar, your ad appears in the search results, directly connecting your brand with people actively looking for products in your category. This strategy is particularly beneficial if you have a clear understanding of the types of keywords that align with your product's features and benefits. For example, if you sell high-performance running shoes, targeting keywords such as "best running shoes" or "trail running shoes" can help you appear in front of users who are already in the buying mindset and looking for similar products.

Product targeting, on the other hand, allows you to target specific products or product categories that are closely related to what you're selling. This strategy enables you to reach shoppers who are already considering a similar product but might be open to a better alternative or an upgrade. For example, if a shopper is browsing a competitor's product, your ad could appear, showcasing the unique features or advantages of your own product. Product targeting is particularly useful when you want to position your brand as a viable alternative to other products, providing potential customers with an opportunity to discover something new that may better meet their needs. This strategy can lead to higher conversion rates because it focuses on customers who are already in the purchase phase of the buyer journey.

If you are targeting existing customers or potential repeat buyers, remarketing or retargeting is a strategy that works effectively for this goal. Retargeting allows you to reach users who have previously interacted with your brand but haven't yet completed a purchase. These users may have added products to their cart or visited your product detail pages but left the site without purchasing. Retargeting ensures that your brand stays top of mind and encourages users to come back and complete the purchase. Amazon offers retargeting options through its Sponsored Display ads, which allow you to reach users both on and off Amazon. For instance, if a user previously viewed your product but didn't purchase, retargeting ads can display that product to the user across other websites they visit, reminding them of their interest in your brand. This form of remarketing is effective for nurturing leads and bringing potential customers back to finalize their decision.

For businesses focused on building long-term relationships with customers, targeting strategies that emphasize customer loyalty and engagement may be a good fit. This approach involves focusing on users who have previously made a purchase and are more likely to return for future purchases. By targeting customers who have already interacted with your brand or made a purchase in the past, you can deepen customer loyalty and increase lifetime value. Amazon offers the ability to target audiences based on past purchases, so you can encourage repeat purchases from satisfied customers or introduce them to new products they may be interested in. These strategies are perfect for businesses that sell consumables, accessories, or products that require regular replenishment.

In addition to these targeting strategies, another consideration when choosing your approach is the use of demographic targeting. While many targeting strategies are centered around user behavior, demographic targeting allows you to reach specific age groups, genders, or even household income levels. This can be especially valuable for products that appeal to specific demographic groups. For example, luxury goods may perform better when targeted at individuals with higher income levels, while children's toys may resonate more with parents within certain age ranges. Demographic targeting ensures that your ads are more finely tuned to the specific characteristics of your ideal customer, increasing the likelihood of conversion by aligning the ad content with their personal attributes and preferences.

The success of your targeting strategy is also highly dependent on the data available and how you leverage it. Amazon's advertising platform provides extensive data and analytics that can help you understand which targeting methods are working best for your specific goals. Regularly analyzing the performance of your campaigns allows you to make informed decisions about which strategy to focus on. For example, if you notice that keyword targeting is driving high conversion rates, you might choose to allocate more of your budget to that strategy. Conversely, if you find that your broad targeting campaign isn't performing as expected, you can refine your approach by narrowing your target audience or incorporating additional behavioral signals.

Choosing the right targeting strategy is a dynamic and ongoing process. As your brand grows and your goals evolve, you may need to adjust your targeting strategy to stay aligned with changing market conditions and consumer behavior. It's crucial to continually assess the performance of your campaigns and make data-driven decisions to ensure that your targeting is working as efficiently as possible. With the right strategy in place, you can maximize the effectiveness of your Amazon advertising campaigns and achieve the business objectives you've set for your brand. By carefully selecting and refining your targeting approach, you will be able to connect with the right audience at the right time and drive the results you desire.

DESIGNING VISUALLY APPEALING DISPLAY ADS

In the digital advertising world, the importance of designing visually appealing display ads cannot be overstated, especially when you are trying to capture the attention of a diverse and ever-changing online audience. On platforms like Amazon Prime, where competition is fierce and the landscape constantly evolving, the visual appeal of your display ads plays a pivotal role in determining their success. Display ads are your opportunity to make a lasting impression on potential customers, guiding them to engage with your brand, products, and services. But how can you create display ads that truly stand out in a crowded marketplace? The answer lies in understanding key design principles, making thoughtful decisions about visual elements, and leveraging data to optimize for engagement and conversion.

The foundation of a visually appealing display ad is the careful use of color, typography, and imagery. Color choices, in particular, have the power to influence emotions and perceptions. For example, the use of bold and bright colors such as red or yellow can evoke excitement and urgency, while softer tones like blue and green can inspire feelings of trust and calm. Choosing the right color scheme for your display ads is not just about aesthetics, but also about aligning with the emotional response you want to elicit from your audience. For instance, if you are promoting a luxury product, a more understated, elegant color palette like black, gold, or silver may be appropriate. On the other hand, for a product aimed at a younger audience, vibrant and playful colors may resonate better. It's essential to ensure that the colors you use not only represent your brand identity but also create a cohesive and compelling visual narrative.

In addition to color, typography is another key element in display ad design. The font you choose can significantly impact how your ad is perceived. Fonts should be legible, clear, and consistent with your brand's voice. A modern, sans-serif font might work well for a tech product, while a more formal serif font might be appropriate for a financial or educational product. Beyond font choice, the size and spacing of your text are just as important. Text that is too small can be difficult to read, especially on mobile devices, while text that is too large can overwhelm the design. Proper hierarchy is essential—make sure that your most important message, like a promotional offer or call-to-action, stands out with a larger, bolder font. By controlling the visual flow of your ad with thoughtful typography, you can guide the viewer's eye toward the most important information and increase the likelihood that they will take the desired action.

Imagery also plays a vital role in designing effective display ads. When selecting images, it's crucial to choose visuals that are high quality, relevant to your product or service, and resonate with your target audience. A picture is worth a thousand words, so the images you use in your display ads should clearly communicate your product's benefits and appeal to the consumer's needs or desires. For example, if you're advertising a clothing item, using high-resolution images of models wearing the clothes in natural, relatable settings can help potential customers envision themselves using the product. Lifestyle imagery—where the product is shown in use—tends to be more engaging than static product shots because it connects the viewer with the product on a deeper emotional level. High-quality images help convey professionalism and trustworthiness, two attributes that are essential when trying to convert viewers into customers.

However, simply using appealing colors, fonts, and images is not enough. The overall layout and design of your display ad must be organized in a way that ensures a smooth visual flow and guides the viewer's attention to the most important elements. Start by prioritizing the key components of your ad: the product image, headline, call-to-action, and any promotional offers or benefits. These elements should be arranged in a way that makes sense logically, with the most important pieces taking center stage. The call-to-action (CTA), in particular, must be clear and compelling. Phrases like "Shop Now," "Learn More," or "Get Yours Today" should be bold and placed in a location that naturally draws the viewer's eye. When designing your ad, consider the device your audience is likely using. A display ad on a desktop monitor may have more space to work with, allowing for a more detailed layout, while mobile display ads require a streamlined design with easy-to-read text and larger, more prominent buttons for quick interaction.

A strong visual hierarchy is critical to ensuring that viewers can absorb the information in the correct order. Begin by placing your most important message at the top or center of the ad, as these areas naturally draw the viewer's attention. Use contrast—between text and background, or between different elements in the ad—to make sure that the most crucial information stands out. A high-contrast color palette can work wonders to highlight key messages or actions. However, too much contrast or too many elements competing for attention can lead to visual clutter. Therefore, balance is essential. An ad that is too busy can overwhelm the viewer, while an ad that lacks enough contrast may fail to grab attention. Keep the design clean, simple, and focused on a single objective to maximize its effectiveness.

In terms of performance, the visual elements of your display ads should be tested and optimized regularly. Testing different designs, colors, headlines, and CTAs can provide valuable insights into which visual components resonate best with your audience. A/B testing is a powerful tool in this regard, allowing you to compare the effectiveness of multiple variations of your ads to see which design performs better. For example, you might test two versions of an ad—one with a bold red CTA button and another with a green CTA button—to see which color drives more clicks. It's also important to monitor how different visual elements perform across various devices. What works well on desktop might not translate as effectively to mobile, and vice versa. By continuously evaluating your ad designs and iterating based on performance data, you can optimize your display ads for maximum engagement and conversion rates.

Another important aspect to consider is the integration of your display ads within the broader advertising ecosystem. Display ads are often just one part of a larger marketing strategy, and they should work seamlessly with other forms of advertising such as search ads, video ads, and social media campaigns. Consistency across all of your ads—whether they are on Amazon Prime, your website, or social media—is essential for building brand recognition and trust. The visual elements of your display ads should align with your overall branding, creating a unified and cohesive experience for your customers. From the colors and fonts to the imagery and messaging, consistency helps reinforce your brand's identity and ensures that your customers easily recognize your products across different platforms.

As consumer preferences evolve and advertising trends change, staying current with design best practices is crucial. The digital advertising landscape is constantly shifting, and staying up to date with the latest trends, tools, and technologies can give you an edge over competitors. Incorporating interactive elements, such as animations or dynamic images, can capture attention in new ways and keep your display ads fresh and engaging. However, it's important to balance innovation with usability; while interactive features can be exciting, they should never detract from the ad's clarity or user experience.

Designing visually appealing display ads requires a combination of creativity, strategic thinking, and data-driven decision making. The ultimate goal is to create ads that not only catch the eye but also drive conversions by compelling users to engage with your brand. By carefully selecting color schemes, fonts, imagery, and layout, while ensuring a seamless user experience across devices, you can craft display ads that not only stand out but also deliver tangible results for your business. With continuous optimization and attention to performance data, your display ads will become an integral part of your broader advertising strategy, helping you build a strong and lasting presence on Amazon Prime.

SETTING APPROPRIATE BIDS AND BUDGETS FOR DISPLAY CAMPAIGNS

Setting appropriate bids and budgets for display campaigns is a critical part of any advertising strategy, particularly when aiming to maximize visibility and drive conversions on Amazon Prime. The decisions you make regarding bids and budgets directly influence the performance and effectiveness of your campaigns. Without proper adjustments, even the most creative and compelling display ads may fail to generate the desired results. This section will delve into the key considerations and strategies involved in setting bids and budgets that are aligned with your goals, ensuring that your display campaigns are not only cost-effective but also impactful.

The process of setting bids and budgets starts with understanding the broader dynamics of the auction system on Amazon. Display campaigns operate within a competitive environment where multiple advertisers vie for the same audience. Amazon's advertising system uses a bidding model, where you are essentially bidding for the opportunity to have your ad displayed to specific shoppers based on targeting criteria such as interests, behaviors, or demographics. When setting bids, you are determining how much you are willing to pay for a specific action or outcome, such as a click or an impression.

Bidding is a key factor in determining how often and where your display ads will appear. Higher bids typically increase the chances that your ads will be shown more frequently or in higher-visibility placements, while lower bids may result in fewer impressions or less prominent placements. However, setting bids too high can lead to overspending, while setting them too low may result in missed opportunities. Striking the right balance between these two extremes requires a deep understanding of your campaign objectives, competitive landscape, and the lifetime value of a customer.

The first step in determining appropriate bids is understanding your campaign's objective. Are you focused on brand awareness, driving traffic to your product page, or encouraging conversions? Each of these goals may require a different approach to bidding. For example, if your goal is to raise brand awareness, you may prioritize reaching as many people as possible. In this case, setting a lower bid that stretches your budget and maximizes your exposure could be an effective strategy. On the other hand, if your goal is to drive conversions or sales, you may want to prioritize bidding higher to ensure your ads appear in more prominent positions where they are likely to attract the most relevant traffic. By aligning your bid strategy with your specific objectives, you can optimize your ad performance without overspending.

Another important factor to consider when setting bids is your competition. Amazon Prime is a highly competitive platform, with numerous advertisers targeting the same audiences. Therefore, understanding the competitive landscape is crucial. Research the average bids for your product category and audience segment, and adjust your bids accordingly. If your competitors are bidding aggressively for a similar target audience, you may need to increase your bids to ensure your ads are shown in competitive placements. However, you should avoid blindly increasing your bids without considering the impact on your overall return on investment (ROI). Bidding too high can result in higher costs without necessarily driving a corresponding increase in sales or brand engagement.

Once you have determined an appropriate bid amount, it is time to set your budget. Your budget is the amount you are willing to spend on your display campaign over a specific period. Setting the right budget requires careful consideration of both your financial resources and your campaign objectives. If you have a limited budget, you may need to focus your efforts on a narrower audience or a more targeted set of keywords. Alternatively, if you have more flexibility in your budget, you may choose to cast a wider net and target a larger audience. In any case, it is essential to ensure that your budget is large enough to allow for meaningful data collection and performance analysis.

One common approach to budgeting is setting a daily or lifetime budget. A daily budget is the maximum amount you are willing to spend per day, while a lifetime budget is the total amount you are willing to spend for the entire duration of the campaign. Both options have their advantages. A daily budget provides more control over your spending and allows you to adjust your bids on a daily basis based on performance data. However, a lifetime budget offers more flexibility, especially for longer campaigns, as it allows your budget to be distributed more evenly across the entire campaign period. It's important to monitor the performance of your campaigns regularly, regardless of the budget type you choose, to ensure that your ad spend is aligned with your goals.

While setting a budget is important, so is ensuring that your budget is allocated effectively across different campaign segments. In some cases, you may want to allocate more of your budget to specific product categories, geographic regions, or audience segments that are showing higher engagement or conversion rates. In other cases, you may want to test different targeting options to determine which ones deliver the best results. By segmenting your budget and allocating resources where they will have the most impact, you can optimize your display campaigns for better performance and more cost-effective results.

Monitoring and adjusting your bids and budgets over time is crucial to the success of your display campaigns. Advertising on Amazon

Prime is not a set-it-and-forget-it process. As you collect more data on campaign performance, you will gain insights into which bids and budget allocations are delivering the best ROI. For example, if you notice that certain ad placements or audience segments are performing well, you can increase your bid for those areas to capture more impressions and clicks. Conversely, if certain segments or placements are underperforming, you may want to lower your bid or reallocate your budget to more effective areas. Regular monitoring and optimization will help you make data-driven decisions and avoid wasting resources on underperforming ads.

It's also essential to take into account the seasonality of your products and the broader marketplace. Different times of year, such as peak shopping seasons like Black Friday or the holiday shopping rush, may require adjustments to your bids and budget. During periods of heightened competition, you may need to increase your bids to remain competitive in the auction process. Alternatively, during slower periods, you may be able to reduce your bids and still maintain visibility. By anticipating shifts in demand and adjusting your bids and budget accordingly, you can capitalize on both high and low periods of traffic to maximize your campaign's success.

When it comes to display ads, there is no one-size-fits-all approach to setting bids and budgets. Each campaign is unique, and the right bid and budget strategies will depend on your specific goals, competition, and resources. However, by aligning your bids and budgets with your campaign objectives, monitoring performance data, and being flexible with adjustments, you can ensure that your display campaigns on Amazon Prime are not only cost-effective but also optimized for success. Effective bidding and budgeting are crucial to ensuring that your ads are seen by the right audience at the right time, leading to increased engagement, conversions, and ultimately, long-term business growth.

UTILIZING AMAZON AUDIENCES

In the increasingly competitive world of digital advertising, one of the most effective ways to ensure your ads reach the right people is by leveraging Amazon's robust targeting capabilities. The platform offers various audience-based targeting options, which allow advertisers to engage specific segments of shoppers based on their behaviors, interests, and demographics. These targeting strategies, such as views retargeting, purchase retargeting, interest-based audiences, and demographics targeting, provide an invaluable opportunity to create more personalized and effective ad campaigns. Understanding how to use these audience segments efficiently can greatly enhance your advertising performance on Amazon.

One of the most potent tools available is **views retargeting**. This strategy focuses on users who have interacted with your ads but have not yet made a purchase. These shoppers have shown interest in your products by viewing your ads, whether through video, display, or product detail pages, but for some reason, they have not followed through with a purchase. Views retargeting allows you to serve ads to these individuals again, reminding them of your product and encouraging them to revisit their decision. It's a way of nurturing potential customers who are already familiar with your brand, keeping your products top-of-mind as they continue their shopping journey.

The key advantage of views retargeting lies in its ability to capture the attention of an audience that has already expressed some level of intent. These users are further along in the buyer's journey, meaning they are more likely to convert than new, completely unaware shoppers. By re-engaging them with targeted messaging or special offers, you increase the chances of turning interest into action. For example, you can offer discounts or promote features that emphasize the value of your product in a way that addresses any hesitations the viewer may have had during their initial interaction with the ad. With views retargeting, you're able to strategically bring your brand back into their consideration set, which can lead to higher conversion rates and lower cost per acquisition.

On the other hand, **purchase retargeting** focuses on consumers who have already made a purchase from your store or viewed a particular product but haven't yet made a repeat purchase. This strategy is designed to increase customer lifetime value by bringing back customers who have already bought from you. For instance, if someone purchased a camera from your store, you could retarget them with ads for related products, such as camera accessories, lenses, or tripods. By leveraging purchase retargeting, you can encourage additional purchases, expanding the relationship with the customer beyond a one-time transaction.

Purchase retargeting also helps to build brand loyalty by continuously delivering personalized ads that remind customers of the value of your offerings. With Amazon's large pool of data, advertisers can craft specific ads based on the user's past purchase behavior, making it easy to show them products they are likely to need next. By anticipating customer needs and presenting the right offer at the right time, purchase retargeting enables businesses to maintain a connection with past buyers, reducing the likelihood of customer churn and increasing repeat sales.

Another key audience segment for advertisers is **interest-based audiences**. Interest-based targeting allows you to reach customers based on their shopping behaviors and interests, even if they haven't previously interacted with your brand. This type of targeting leverages Amazon's vast data on consumer behavior to identify potential buyers who have shown an interest in categories similar to your products, such as electronics, home improvement, fashion, or fitness. By targeting these individuals, you can introduce your products to consumers who are already engaged in a shopping journey related to your industry or niche, even if they haven't specifically visited your product page or interacted with your ads before.

Interest-based targeting is highly effective because it allows advertisers to cast a broader net while still targeting people with relevant purchasing behaviors. For example, if you sell organic skincare products, you can target individuals who have shown interest in health, wellness, or beauty products. This type of audience targeting allows you to increase visibility for your products among shoppers who are more likely to resonate with your offerings. Additionally, because Amazon gathers insights based on real shopping behavior, the quality of the audience is usually high, which means that your ad spend is more likely to lead to conversions.

Demographic targeting on Amazon further refines this strategy by allowing you to target shoppers based on specific demographic characteristics, such as age, gender, income, or household size. This type of targeting is especially useful for businesses that have a clearly defined customer profile and want to ensure they are reaching individuals who fit that profile. For example, a company selling luxury watches may choose to target high-income earners, while a brand selling baby products may want to focus on households with young children.

Demographic targeting provides another layer of precision for advertisers, helping to narrow down the audience pool to those who are most likely to convert based on factors beyond shopping behaviors or interests. It's particularly useful when your product appeals to a specific age group, gender, or income bracket. The ability to create such targeted campaigns ensures that your budget is spent efficiently, allowing you to reach the most relevant consumers for your brand. Furthermore, demographic targeting can also work well in combination with other targeting strategies, such as interest-based targeting, to ensure that your ad is being shown to individuals who not only fit the demographic profile but also have relevant shopping interests.

A key benefit of utilizing these audience targeting strategies is the ability to optimize your campaigns for greater relevance. Each audience segment—whether it's based on views, purchase history, interests, or demographics—represents a different stage in the buyer's journey. By tailoring your ad content and approach based on these factors, you can create more personalized experiences for each consumer. This personalization can result in higher engagement rates, increased click-through rates, and ultimately, a better return on investment.

Amazon's audience targeting options also allow for more granular reporting and measurement. As you implement these strategies, you can track the effectiveness of each audience segment in terms of impressions, clicks, conversions, and other key performance indicators. This data allows you to continually refine your ad campaigns, adjusting your bids and creative assets to optimize performance. Additionally, the more data you collect on the effectiveness of your audience targeting, the better equipped you become at predicting which audience segments are most likely to perform well in the future.

Ultimately, successful use of Amazon's audience targeting options is about finding the right balance between broad and narrow targeting. While interest-based and demographic targeting may help you reach a wider audience, retargeting strategies—such as views and purchase retargeting—can help you focus on the most engaged users who are already familiar with your brand. The key to success is not just about using one targeting option over another, but about strategically combining different audience segments to create a cohesive and highly effective ad campaign.

Understanding and leveraging Amazon's audience targeting options—including views retargeting, purchase retargeting, interest-based audiences, and demographics—can dramatically improve the performance of your advertising campaigns. By tailoring your targeting strategy to align with specific customer behaviors, interests, and characteristics, you can create more personalized and relevant ads that drive engagement and conversions. Whether you are nurturing leads, driving repeat purchases, or expanding your reach to new potential customers, utilizing these advanced targeting strategies is essential for building a successful advertising presence on Amazon.

TARGETING SPECIFIC PRODUCT CATEGORIES AND ASINS

In the fast-paced world of digital advertising, one of the most effective strategies for boosting visibility and increasing sales on Amazon is targeting specific product categories and ASINs (Amazon Standard Identification Numbers). This form of precise targeting allows advertisers to zero in on audiences who are already interested in a particular type of product or a specific item within a broader category. By honing in on these niches, brands can ensure that their ads are reaching the most relevant shoppers, which can lead to higher conversion rates, reduced advertising spend, and increased return on investment (ROI).

Targeting specific product categories involves selecting the broader grouping of products under which your offerings are classified on Amazon. For example, if you sell fitness equipment, you can target shoppers browsing the "Sports & Outdoors" category or, more specifically, the "Exercise & Fitness" subcategory. This type of targeting enables advertisers to reach individuals who have shown an interest in products similar to theirs, increasing the chances of engagement and eventual sales.

Given the immense variety of products available on Amazon, the platform provides advertisers with a powerful tool to effectively segment and engage potential customers who are already predisposed to making purchases in a specific area.

The advantage of targeting product categories is that it enables brands to cast a wide net while still focusing on relevant consumers. Rather than targeting random users who may or may not be interested in your products, you can direct your ads toward individuals who are actively engaged in a shopping journey within a category that aligns with your offerings. For instance, someone who is looking at various types of yoga mats or workout machines is far more likely to be interested in purchasing your brand's yoga accessories or resistance bands, than someone who is browsing unrelated products like electronics or home décor.

Moreover, the competitive landscape on Amazon often means that reaching shoppers through category-based targeting can also enhance your brand's visibility, especially if you're advertising in a popular or trending category. By positioning your product within a relevant category, you place it in front of consumers who are in the mindset to buy, making it easier for them to discover and engage with your offerings.

While targeting product categories is an effective way to engage with broad groups of relevant shoppers, **targeting specific ASINs** can provide an even more granular approach to reaching potential customers. An ASIN is a unique identifier for products sold on Amazon, and each individual product listed on the platform has its own ASIN. With ASIN targeting, advertisers can choose to display their ads only on the product detail pages of specific items, ensuring that their ads appear in front of users who are actively viewing a particular product. This can be an incredibly effective way to capture the attention of shoppers who are already considering similar products to yours.

For example, if you sell a specific brand of coffee maker, targeting the ASINs of competing coffee makers could position your product as a viable alternative for customers already considering a purchase. By advertising directly on the detail pages of competing products, you are essentially placing your brand in front of customers at a critical point in their decision-making process. These shoppers have already expressed an interest in the category or product, and your ad serves as a gentle nudge that encourages them to consider your offering as well.

One of the key benefits of ASIN targeting is the ability to focus on competitors' products. By identifying products that are similar to yours or belong to the same market segment, you can target their ASINs and ensure that your ads show up on their product detail pages. This strategy is particularly useful if you believe your product offers unique features, better pricing, or superior quality compared to your competitors. By capturing the attention of consumers who are already evaluating similar items, you increase the chances of your brand standing out and persuading them to switch to your offering.

However, targeting specific ASINs is not limited to competing products. You can also target complementary products that pair well with your own. For example, if you sell a high-quality blender, you could target ASINs for smoothie ingredients, recipe books, or other kitchen appliances that are often purchased by users of blenders. By targeting these complementary products, you can introduce your offering to customers who are in the right mindset to make an additional purchase, thus expanding the reach of your brand to a broader audience within the same shopping journey.

When deciding between targeting product categories or ASINs, it is essential to understand the level of control and precision each strategy offers. Category targeting provides a broader scope and allows advertisers to reach a larger audience, while ASIN targeting offers a much more focused approach, placing ads directly in front of shoppers who are most likely to convert. For some brands, combining both approaches can provide a balanced strategy that casts a wider net while also ensuring that highly relevant shoppers are targeted with personalized ads.

For example, a brand selling organic skincare products could target the "Beauty & Personal Care" category to reach shoppers browsing skincare products in general. At the same time, the brand could also target specific ASINs for products that compete directly with their own, ensuring that their ads are placed on the product detail pages of those competing items. This dual strategy ensures that the brand's ads are shown to both a broad audience interested in skincare, as well as to consumers who are actively considering similar products, making it a highly effective way to increase visibility and drive conversions.

Moreover, Amazon's advertising platform provides powerful reporting tools that allow advertisers to track the performance of both product category targeting and ASIN targeting. By analyzing data such as impressions, clicks, and conversions, you can evaluate which targeting strategy is providing the best return on investment and make adjustments accordingly. If you find that targeting product categories is delivering higher impressions but lower conversion rates, it may be time to focus more on specific ASINs to drive more qualified traffic. Conversely, if your ASIN-targeted campaigns are seeing success, but you want to expand your reach, you can consider incorporating category-based targeting to attract new potential customers.

Beyond just driving direct conversions, targeting specific product categories and ASINs can also be valuable for increasing brand awareness and building a more robust presence on the platform. Even if customers do not immediately purchase your product after seeing your ad, the exposure can help to familiarize them with your brand and increase the likelihood of future sales. By consistently showing up in relevant categories or alongside complementary or competing products, your brand stays top-of-mind, which can translate into higher customer lifetime value and increased loyalty over time.

Targeting specific product categories and ASINs is a powerful way to maximize your advertising reach on Amazon, ensuring that your ads are shown to the most relevant and engaged audiences. Whether you're targeting a broad category of products or honing in on specific items or competitors, these strategies provide valuable opportunities to increase visibility, drive conversions, and strengthen your brand presence. By understanding how to leverage both category-based and ASIN-targeted strategies, advertisers can effectively manage their campaigns and optimize performance, ultimately ensuring that their brand gets the attention it deserves on Amazon's vast marketplace.

CHAPTER 11
MEASURING AND OPTIMIZING SPONSORED DISPLAY CAMPAIGNS

ANALYZING VIEW-THROUGH CONVERSIONS AND OTHER KEY METRICS

Understanding how advertising influences shopper behavior goes beyond immediate clicks and direct purchases. In the realm of Amazon Prime advertising, analyzing view-through conversions and other essential performance metrics offers a more complete picture of campaign impact. View-through conversions provide advertisers with the ability to measure how many conversions occur after a shopper has seen an ad but not clicked on it. This type of metric is crucial in evaluating the true influence of an advertisement, particularly in campaigns where exposure and brand recall matter just as much as direct engagement.

View-through conversions (VTCs) track the number of customers who are exposed to a display ad, do not immediately interact with it, but end up making a purchase within a specified attribution window. This window, often set at 14 days by default on Amazon, captures the delayed behavioral response that many customers exhibit in their buying journey. Not every shopper clicks on an ad at first glance. In fact, many engage with brands through multiple touchpoints before converting. They may see an ad on their smart TV while browsing Amazon Prime Video, take note of the brand or product subconsciously, and return days later to make a purchase through organic search, voice command via Alexa, or even in-store.

This delayed conversion path is common in today's fragmented media environment, where consumers are constantly absorbing content across devices and channels. View-through conversions help quantify this behavior. They give advertisers the ability to understand how top-of-funnel activities influence bottom-of-funnel outcomes. Without VTCs, these conversions would be invisible, attributed to organic channels or dismissed entirely. When measured and analyzed correctly, view-through data validates the branding impact of campaigns and can help justify continued or increased investment in display advertising.

To accurately evaluate view-through conversions, it's important to interpret them in context. A high number of VTCs might indicate strong brand recall and product resonance, especially if your ads are designed with a storytelling or awareness focus. However, these metrics should not be evaluated in isolation. The effectiveness of view-through conversions is best assessed when viewed alongside other key indicators, such as total sales, new-to-brand metrics, and click-through rate. Doing so ensures a holistic view of campaign performance and helps to distinguish whether your ads are contributing to overall lift or merely benefiting from coincidental conversions.

One of the challenges in analyzing VTCs is understanding attribution. Amazon uses last-touch attribution for many of its reporting structures, meaning the last ad a customer interacted with before converting is given credit for the sale. However, in the case of view-through conversions, credit is assigned even if the user never clicked on the ad. This means advertisers must be careful in interpreting these figures and should ensure that their broader strategy considers the role of assisted conversions and brand influence. A robust campaign will often include multiple layers of exposure before the shopper is convinced to buy. View-through tracking makes these layers visible and measurable.

In addition to VTCs, other key metrics are critical in evaluating the health and success of a campaign. Impressions, for instance, indicate how often your ad is shown. While impressions alone don't confirm engagement, they provide insight into your reach and exposure. High impressions combined with low conversions might prompt a creative review—perhaps your ad visuals or message aren't compelling enough to drive action. Conversely, steady impressions with growing VTCs could point to increasing brand familiarity and long-term interest, which are valuable especially in competitive markets.

Click-through rate (CTR) is another central metric that complements view-through data. A high CTR suggests that your ad is relevant and engaging enough to prompt direct interaction. Comparing CTR with VTC allows advertisers to assess how many users are acting immediately versus those who need more time or multiple exposures. If your CTR is low but VTC is high, your ad may still be successful in influencing purchases, just not in real time. This is particularly common in industries like electronics or fashion, where shoppers often spend time researching and comparing products before making a final decision.

Conversion rate (CVR), calculated by dividing conversions by clicks, is a valuable performance metric that highlights the efficiency of your landing page or product listing. A strong CVR combined with healthy view-through numbers suggests that your ad not only generates interest but also leads to persuasive product pages that close the sale. If CVR is weak, even with solid VTC or CTR, it could indicate that something in the purchase path—perhaps the pricing, reviews, or product details—needs refinement.

Another metric that aligns with view-through analysis is the cost-per-acquisition (CPA). This figure shows how much you're spending to acquire each customer. View-through conversions can significantly improve the perceived efficiency of a campaign by revealing additional conversions that weren't captured through direct interaction. If CPA seems high when counting only click-based conversions, integrating VTC can lower this number and provide a more realistic measure of campaign performance.

Return on ad spend (ROAS) remains the ultimate gauge for many advertisers. It reflects the revenue generated for every dollar spent. View-through data helps enhance the accuracy of ROAS calculations, especially in branding campaigns where clicks might be fewer but exposure is meaningful. When VTCs are properly integrated into ROAS analysis, brands can more confidently invest in high-funnel tactics that may not pay off immediately but build valuable momentum over time.

To make the most of these insights, it's essential to segment your performance data. Look at how VTCs vary across ad formats, audience segments, and campaign types. Some campaigns might be better suited for generating clicks, while others may excel in long-term influence through impressions and view-throughs. For instance, video ads on Amazon Prime Video might yield fewer direct clicks but can drive significant view-through conversions as shoppers recall the ad later while browsing the site. Static display ads on the homepage may have lower conversion rates but still play a key role in brand recognition and retargeting success.

Seasonality and timing also play a role in VTC behavior. During peak shopping periods like Prime Day, Black Friday, or back-to-school season, shoppers are bombarded with ads and often delay decision-making. This delay inflates the importance of VTCs, as many consumers will return to Amazon days later to finalize their purchases. Monitoring how view-through metrics fluctuate during these periods can help advertisers fine-tune their campaigns and allocate budget more effectively.

Data analysis should not end with metric collection. The key lies in translating insights into action. If your VTCs are rising while clicks remain stagnant, consider enhancing your call-to-action or experimenting with different creative formats. If your view-through audience is converting at a high rate, you might explore additional ways to expand that audience segment, perhaps by using lookalike audiences or leveraging interest-based targeting. Data without interpretation is noise. Insight, when turned into strategic direction, becomes power.

Ultimately, the goal of analyzing view-through conversions and other key performance indicators is to construct a more nuanced understanding of how advertising shapes shopper behavior. In a landscape as complex and competitive as Amazon, visibility alone isn't enough. Advertisers must look beyond the obvious and measure what truly matters—not just who clicks, but who buys, when they buy, and how the journey unfolded. When view-through conversions are seen not as peripheral, but as central to campaign success, advertisers unlock the full potential of their efforts and move one step closer to sustained growth and deeper customer engagement.

EVALUATING AUDIENCE AND PRODUCT TARGETING PERFORMANCE

Evaluating the performance of audience and product targeting on Amazon Prime is a crucial step in any advertising strategy that aims to move beyond guesswork and into data-driven precision. Understanding how different segments of shoppers respond to specific campaigns, creative formats, and product placements offers valuable insights into how to refine marketing efforts and increase return on investment. The difference between a campaign that merely exists and one that thrives often lies in how well it connects the right message with the right person at the right moment. Audience and product targeting are the twin engines that power this alignment, and evaluating their performance is how you keep them calibrated for optimal output.

Audience targeting on Amazon allows advertisers to serve ads to defined groups of users based on shopping behavior, interests, purchase history, or demographic details. These can include retargeting pools such as viewers of a product detail page who didn't purchase, or more exploratory segments like those interested in similar products or categories. Product targeting, on the other hand, focuses on aligning ad placements with specific ASINs or product categories. This enables advertisers to place their products next to competitors, complementary items, or within broader thematic spaces where their offering naturally fits.

Performance evaluation begins with a clear understanding of campaign goals. Whether the objective is brand awareness, customer acquisition, competitive conquesting, or repeat purchase encouragement, each targeting strategy should be measured against its intended outcome. Metrics such as click-through rate (CTR), conversion rate (CVR), cost per acquisition (CPA), return on ad spend (ROAS), and new-to-brand (NTB) orders all serve as indicators of how well your targeting efforts are functioning.

For audience targeting, CTR is often the first metric to analyze. A high CTR typically indicates that your ad is reaching a relevant audience who finds your messaging or offer compelling enough to explore further. However, CTR alone does not confirm success. It must be followed by strong conversion metrics to validate that interest leads to action. If CTR is high but conversions are low, it may indicate that while the audience is intrigued, the product or landing page does not meet their expectations.

In this case, further refinement of either the creative content or the audience parameters may be necessary.

Conversion rate provides deeper insight into whether the selected audience is in a buying mindset. Retargeting audiences often exhibit higher CVR because they are already familiar with the product. In contrast, interest-based audiences may have lower initial conversion rates, as they are less familiar with the brand or need more time in the consideration phase. Analyzing performance over a longer attribution window helps reveal delayed conversions and better reflects the true effectiveness of targeting these exploratory audiences.

CPA is especially important in evaluating the cost-efficiency of audience targeting. While broader audience pools might deliver more impressions and even clicks, the cost per conversion may be higher compared to more refined, retargeted segments. Evaluating this metric over time and across campaigns helps balance scale with efficiency. Similarly, ROAS offers a comprehensive view of return on investment and should be tracked across all targeted audience types. High ROAS in a narrowly targeted audience pool may justify increasing the budget for that segment, while lower ROAS might suggest reallocating spend elsewhere.

New-to-brand metrics add another dimension to audience targeting evaluation. If your goal is customer acquisition, it is important to track how many conversions come from shoppers who have never purchased from you before. A campaign with a modest ROAS but a high percentage of NTB orders might be more valuable in the long run than one that yields better short-term returns but only engages repeat buyers. Understanding where these new customers are coming from, and which audience segments are driving their acquisition, allows advertisers to scale with greater confidence.

When evaluating product targeting, the analysis shifts slightly to consider the relevance and competitiveness of the placements. In product targeting campaigns, CTR can reflect how well your ad stands out in comparison to adjacent listings. Placing an ad next to a higher-priced or lower-reviewed product might yield higher engagement, as shoppers perceive greater value in your offering. Conversely, if CTR is low, it may be that your product doesn't stand out or lacks a compelling differentiator in that specific placement context.

Product-level performance should be assessed across a range of competitor and complementary ASINs. Identifying which specific ASIN placements are yielding conversions at a reasonable CPA or high ROAS helps fine-tune the target list. You may find that certain competitor listings drive excellent results, while others underperform or drain budget without meaningful return. Amazon allows for refinement at the ASIN level, so pruning or expanding your product target list based on performance data is an essential part of campaign optimization.

In evaluating product category targeting, it's useful to segment performance by subcategories, pricing tiers, or brand groups. Categories with high shopper intent and lower competition may yield better results than more saturated segments. If your product belongs to a premium niche, targeting budget categories may not drive high conversions, even if impressions are plentiful. Conversely, targeting complementary products—such as running shoes alongside athletic socks—may introduce your brand to relevant customers without directly competing on the same product function.

Another key aspect of product targeting evaluation is geographic and demographic alignment. Different product placements may perform better in specific regions or among particular shopper segments. If Amazon provides demographic insights, use these to understand whether your product performs better among certain age groups, income brackets, or household types. Aligning product targeting with these demographic insights can sharpen campaign relevance and increase efficiency.

Performance over time is another critical lens through which to evaluate targeting. Early results from a campaign may not fully reflect its potential. It is important to allow enough data to accumulate, particularly for audience segments with longer consideration cycles. Look at week-over-week trends, comparing early engagement to later-stage conversions. In some cases, campaigns need time to mature as Amazon's algorithm optimizes delivery or as repeated exposures increase brand familiarity. If performance trends upward over time, it may suggest that your targeting is working even if the initial numbers were modest.

Cross-comparison is another powerful tool in evaluating audience and product targeting. By setting up test campaigns with slightly different audience definitions or ASIN placements, you can compare their performance side-by-side. This form of A/B testing can reveal surprising insights, such as which customer segment is most responsive to a new product launch or which competitor ASIN placements are most vulnerable to conquesting. Over time, this process of testing, learning, and refining becomes a feedback loop that sharpens your overall targeting strategy.

Ultimately, evaluating audience and product targeting performance is about connecting data with business strategy. Metrics on their own are simply numbers, but when interpreted through the lens of your brand goals and customer understanding, they become a roadmap for growth. The most successful advertisers do not just collect performance data—they act on it. They evolve their campaigns, adapt to shopper behavior, and reallocate budget based on what the numbers are telling them. This process is not static but dynamic, as shopper preferences shift, competitors evolve, and new opportunities arise within the platform.

In a landscape as competitive and fast-moving as Amazon Prime, the difference between mediocre and outstanding campaign performance often lies in the diligence of evaluation. By consistently measuring, analyzing, and adjusting audience and product targeting, brands can build campaigns that don't just perform well in bursts, but generate sustainable, compounding returns over time. This level of attention to performance isn't just about optimizing ads—it's about mastering the connection between your brand and the customer, and ensuring that connection grows stronger with every impression, every click, and every conversion.

A/B TESTING DISPLAY CREATIVE FOR OPTIMAL ENGAGEMENT

A/B testing display creative is one of the most powerful methods available to advertisers seeking to optimize engagement, reduce waste, and increase returns on Amazon Prime's advertising ecosystem. In a marketplace where consumers are exposed to a constant flow of visual stimuli, standing out requires more than guesswork. Success depends on informed decisions, data-driven iterations, and a willingness to test assumptions. A/B testing enables brands to move beyond subjective preferences and get direct answers about what works and what doesn't in the eyes of real shoppers.

At its core, A/B testing is the process of comparing two or more variations of a creative asset to determine which one performs better in a live environment. This could mean testing two different headline messages, color palettes, call-to-action buttons, product imagery, or even video lengths and formats. By isolating variables and analyzing how shoppers respond to each version, advertisers can identify the elements that resonate most with their audience and make confident decisions on which creative to scale.

The first step in effective A/B testing is establishing a clear hypothesis. This requires understanding not just what is being tested, but why. For instance, if the hypothesis is that a product-centric image will outperform a lifestyle image because it showcases more detail, then the test should be structured specifically to measure the performance difference between those two visual approaches. Without a clear hypothesis, tests can become unfocused, and results may be misinterpreted or inconclusive. Every test should aim to answer a specific question that informs future creative development.

Timing and traffic allocation are also critical in A/B testing. Display ads operate in a dynamic, high-velocity environment where user behavior can shift depending on the time of day, day of the week, or seasonal events. Therefore, both variations must be exposed to a statistically significant audience under comparable conditions to yield meaningful insights. Uneven delivery or external influences like promotional events can skew results and lead to incorrect conclusions. Ideally, the test period should allow both versions to accumulate enough impressions, clicks, and conversions to assess differences with confidence.

The success of display creative often hinges on visual hierarchy—the arrangement of elements that guide the viewer's attention. A/B testing helps uncover which layout or focal points capture interest most effectively. Some shoppers may respond better to clean, minimalistic layouts that emphasize the product, while others may engage more with busy visuals that tell a story or create a sense of urgency. By experimenting with visual priorities—whether it's the placement of the logo, size of the product image, or prominence of the call-to-action—brands can learn how to direct shopper attention in a way that increases engagement.

Headline and messaging are other vital components to test. Even a few words can significantly impact how a shopper perceives an ad. Messaging that emphasizes benefits like "fast shipping" or "limited-time discount" may prompt action in a way that a more generic message like "premium quality" does not. Emotional appeal versus rational appeal is another axis worth exploring. Some audiences might be drawn to messages that evoke excitement or exclusivity, while others respond to factual, benefit-driven language. A/B testing different headline styles reveals not just what performs better, but what kind of messaging aligns with a brand's customer base.

Color psychology also plays a role in how display ads are perceived. Colors evoke specific emotions and can influence attention and recall. A bold red background may create urgency, while a calming blue may suggest trust and reliability. Testing color variations across creative assets can reveal unexpected patterns. Perhaps a subtle background color outperforms a vibrant one because it doesn't compete with the product image. Or perhaps a branded color scheme reinforces recognition and boosts performance. Small changes in color can produce disproportionately large effects on click-through and conversion rates.

The same principle applies to video ads within display formats. Elements such as opening frames, pacing, transitions, soundtracks, and overlay text can all be tested to refine video effectiveness. A fast-paced video with upbeat music might catch attention quickly but lose viewers before the key message is delivered. Alternatively, a slower-paced video with clear narration might maintain interest and convert better, especially with older demographics or higher consideration products. Testing different video intros, hooks, and closing messages helps determine which sequences drive the highest engagement and conversions.

When testing interactive or animated creative elements, it's important to consider not just engagement metrics but also post-click behavior. An ad might attract more clicks due to motion or animation, but if users bounce immediately after clicking, it suggests the creative overpromised or misled the viewer. In these cases, A/B testing can help strike the right balance between drawing attention and setting realistic expectations. The most effective creative entices clicks and delivers on its promise post-click, creating a seamless experience from impression to purchase.

Another layer of A/B testing lies in audience segmentation. The same creative asset may perform very differently across demographic groups, interest segments, or even device types. A creative that performs exceptionally well with a younger audience might fall flat with older shoppers. A layout optimized for mobile may not translate as effectively on desktop. By running A/B tests segmented by audience attributes or device type, advertisers can tailor future campaigns for maximum relevance. This insight is particularly useful for brands looking to personalize at scale or expand into new customer segments.

Post-test analysis is where the real learning begins. It's not enough to know which version "won"—the deeper value lies in understanding why. Analyzing engagement patterns across different stages of the customer journey can uncover the nuances behind shopper behavior. Did one version attract more new-to-brand shoppers while the other performed better with return customers? Did engagement improve in certain geographic regions? Was there a correlation between ad exposure and repeat visits to the product page? These deeper questions lead to smarter creative development and more efficient ad spend in future campaigns.

Moreover, successful A/B testing is never a one-and-done effort. The digital advertising landscape—and consumer behavior with it—is constantly evolving. What works today may be less effective tomorrow as audiences grow accustomed to certain messages or visuals. Maintaining a habit of regular creative testing ensures that campaigns remain fresh, engaging, and aligned with changing shopper expectations. It also fosters a culture of curiosity and continuous improvement, which is essential in a data-driven marketing environment.

There's also a cumulative effect to creative testing. Insights gained from one campaign inform the next, allowing advertisers to build a library of learnings that drive increasingly effective strategies. Over time, this leads to a refined creative playbook—a proven set of principles, visuals, and messaging cues that consistently resonate with the brand's core audience. Instead of reinventing the wheel with every campaign, advertisers can draw from this repository and adapt with precision.

Ultimately, A/B testing display creative is a discipline of experimentation and insight. It rewards brands that approach advertising as a science, not just an art. By systematically testing and analyzing creative elements, advertisers gain a clearer understanding of what makes their audience take notice, engage, and convert. In the hyper-competitive environment of Amazon Prime advertising, where every impression counts and every click costs, this precision is not just beneficial—it's essential. A/B testing empowers advertisers to make decisions grounded in performance, driven by real customer behavior, and aligned with long-term growth goals.

REFINING RETARGETING STRATEGIES BASED ON CUSTOMER BEHAVIOR

Retargeting is one of the most valuable tools in the modern advertiser's arsenal, especially in a marketplace as dynamic and saturated as Amazon Prime. Shoppers are rarely linear in their buying behavior. They browse, compare, read reviews, abandon carts, revisit, and sometimes purchase weeks after their initial interaction. Understanding and leveraging these nuanced behavioral patterns allows brands to refine their retargeting strategies with precision and empathy, turning passive browsers into loyal customers.

The first and most fundamental shift in thinking when refining retargeting strategies is to move away from a one-size-fits-all approach. Not all visitors are the same, and not all shoppers abandon for the same reason. Some may have been doing preliminary research, others may have been distracted or deterred by price, and some may have added to cart but opted to purchase a competitor's product instead. The key to unlocking higher conversions lies in segmenting these behaviors and responding with tailored retargeting approaches that align with the shopper's current place in the funnel.

Behavioral signals are the digital footprints that customers leave behind. These include page visits, time spent on listings, clicks on alternative products, frequency of visits, search queries, and interaction with specific content like videos or A+ detail pages. Each behavior offers insight into intent. A shopper who repeatedly visits a product detail page but never adds it to cart is expressing a different kind of interest than one who added the item but never completed checkout. By distinguishing between high-intent and low-intent behaviors, advertisers can calibrate the intensity, format, and message of their retargeting efforts accordingly.

A customer who viewed a product once may only need a subtle reminder, such as a soft display ad featuring the item in a carousel with other recommendations. Someone who viewed the product several times, read reviews, and lingered may benefit from a more direct and persuasive retargeting message—perhaps a short video ad reinforcing the product's value or showcasing user testimonials. For those who abandoned their cart, urgency-based messaging, such as highlighting limited stock or time-sensitive promotions, can help nudge them back across the line. Recognizing the behavioral nuances behind these actions helps avoid generic, repetitive retargeting that risks annoying potential buyers rather than winning them over.

The timing of retargeting is equally crucial. Serving an ad too quickly after a visit might come across as pushy, while waiting too long may result in lost interest or forgotten intent. The optimal window varies depending on the product category and customer journey. For impulse buys or low-cost items, retargeting within a few hours might be effective. For high-ticket items or complex purchases, spacing out the follow-up and reinforcing key decision-making factors over a few days or weeks may yield better results. Advertisers need to analyze customer behavior patterns over time and adjust the frequency and cadence of retargeting efforts to avoid fatigue.

One of the most powerful ways to enhance retargeting is by incorporating additional layers of data, such as customer purchase history, interest categories, and demographic information. For example, if a customer has previously purchased high-end kitchen appliances, and recently browsed a new blender but didn't buy, a retargeting message that emphasizes the product's premium features and aligns with their past behavior is more likely to resonate. This form of behavioral layering— combining past actions with recent signals—creates a more accurate picture of shopper intent and facilitates more effective personalization.

The context in which ads appear also influences retargeting effectiveness. Ads that are displayed while the shopper is actively browsing related categories on Amazon have a much higher likelihood of engagement than those served off-platform without context. For this reason, advertisers should prioritize on-Amazon retargeting placements when refining strategies. However, when using off-Amazon retargeting, such as through Amazon DSP's external inventory, it's essential to maintain continuity in messaging and creative design. The shopper should immediately recognize the ad as a follow-up to their previous interest, creating a seamless psychological bridge between the past engagement and the present ad.

Refinement also involves consistent testing and iteration. Just because one retargeting strategy worked for a particular segment or product doesn't mean it will scale universally. A robust strategy involves ongoing A/B testing of ad creatives, formats, copy, and timing. Does a static image with a product benefit outperform a short video? Does a carousel showcasing related items yield more engagement than a single-product display? These are the types of questions that regular testing can help answer. Continuous analysis of metrics like click-through rate (CTR), return on ad spend (ROAS), and view-through conversions offers the feedback loop needed to optimize further.

Another dimension to refining retargeting strategies is understanding when not to retarget. Not every visitor is a qualified lead, and not every abandoned session indicates purchase intent. Some shoppers are simply window-shopping or researching for someone else. Continuously retargeting low-probability visitors wastes budget and risks diminishing brand perception. Setting exclusion parameters based on behavior—such as visitors who bounced quickly or viewed unrelated categories—helps keep campaigns focused on high-intent users.

A particularly effective form of refined retargeting is sequential messaging, where ads evolve based on the user's interaction history. If a shopper sees an initial reminder ad and clicks through but still doesn't convert, the next ad served can provide deeper information, such as product comparisons, FAQs, or user testimonials. If they engage again but hesitate, a third ad could highlight a limited-time offer or customer review. This progression mimics a personalized sales funnel and aligns the messaging with the shopper's increasing familiarity and engagement with the product.

For returning customers or those who've already made a purchase, retargeting can transition from re-acquisition to brand reinforcement or upselling. If someone bought a pair of headphones, they might later be shown matching accessories or complementary products like charging docks or carrying cases. Retargeting here becomes an extension of customer experience rather than a re-engagement tool. This post-purchase behavioral retargeting encourages repeat purchases and enhances customer lifetime value.

Transparency and privacy considerations are also important when refining retargeting efforts. While behavioral data can drive personalization, it's vital that shoppers feel their experience is being enhanced—not manipulated. Ads should feel relevant and helpful, not invasive or overly persistent. Amazon's own advertising framework places strong emphasis on user privacy, so adhering to best practices around frequency capping, clear opt-outs, and respectful messaging is essential to maintaining customer trust.

Ultimately, refining retargeting strategies based on customer behavior is about precision and empathy. It's about understanding why a shopper didn't convert, what might persuade them to return, and how to deliver that message in the most relevant, respectful, and effective way possible. It requires a blend of data analysis, creative thinking, and continuous experimentation. When done right, refined retargeting bridges the gap between browsing and buying, between hesitation and action. It not only recaptures lost sales but builds a deeper relationship with shoppers, increasing the likelihood that they return, not just to buy once, but to buy again and again.

INTEGRATING SPONSORED DISPLAY WITH YOUR OVERALL MARKETING FUNNEL

Integrating Sponsored Display into your broader marketing funnel requires a comprehensive understanding of how each stage of the buyer journey interacts with the tools available within Amazon's advertising ecosystem. Sponsored Display ads are not isolated promotional bursts—they are dynamic components that, when placed strategically within the larger framework of a brand's marketing strategy, can enhance awareness, drive consideration, and ultimately increase conversions. The effectiveness of these ads multiplies when they are not just run independently, but synchronized with other campaign types, off-Amazon marketing efforts, and brand storytelling initiatives.

At the top of the marketing funnel, the primary goal is to attract attention and generate interest. This is where Sponsored Display ads play a crucial role in casting a wide net. They offer the unique capability of reaching audiences both on and off Amazon, allowing brands to introduce themselves to potential customers during casual browsing or even while they're engaging with competitor products. Unlike Sponsored Products, which rely heavily on keyword-driven visibility and are more focused on conversion, Sponsored Display can be deployed proactively to influence early-stage shoppers before they've even begun a serious buying process. By delivering compelling visuals, concise value propositions, or promotional hooks, Sponsored Display supports brand discovery, which is essential for long-term growth.

But for Sponsored Display to truly contribute to the top of the funnel, the creative elements and targeting strategy must align with brand-level messaging. Ads should focus less on pushing a transaction and more on educating the shopper or introducing the brand's personality. This can mean highlighting a product's unique lifestyle application, showcasing awards or customer accolades, or tying the message to broader themes like sustainability or innovation. These tactics build emotional resonance, which not only primes consumers for eventual purchase but also lays the foundation for a relationship that extends beyond a single transaction.

As potential buyers move from the awareness phase into consideration, the role of Sponsored Display becomes more sophisticated. At this stage, shoppers may have already viewed product detail pages, compared multiple listings, and engaged with other media—either on Amazon or externally. Sponsored Display can act as a bridge that follows the user across this fragmented journey, keeping the brand top-of-mind while reinforcing key messages tailored to their stage in the funnel. If a shopper looked at a particular item but didn't add it to their cart, a retargeting campaign can re-engage them with timely follow-ups. The power of this format lies in its ability to reach audiences based on behavior and interest, making it a seamless continuation of a shopper's experience rather than an abrupt interruption.

What further distinguishes Sponsored Display in the consideration phase is its flexibility. It allows advertisers to retarget shoppers who have viewed specific ASINs, categories, or even competitor products. This level of granularity enables brands to serve highly relevant creative tailored to an individual's previous interactions. For example, if someone viewed a coffee maker but didn't convert, Sponsored Display could later show that shopper a banner with the product's top customer review, or a new limited-time discount, effectively nudging them further down the funnel with contextual persuasion.

As the funnel narrows toward conversion, Sponsored Display becomes a potent tool for reinforcement and final persuasion. In this phase, every impression matters, and messaging should aim to remove friction or resolve last-minute objections. Here, advertisers might leverage Sponsored Display to offer value-based messaging, such as fast shipping via Prime, bundle deals, or customer support guarantees. The creative strategy should reflect the urgency and intent typical of this stage, with calls to action that encourage immediacy—such as "Buy Now," "Last Chance," or "Low Stock."

The integration of Sponsored Display at the bottom of the funnel is not just about driving a single transaction. It's also about setting the stage for post-purchase engagement and repeat business. After conversion, the advertising strategy doesn't end. Sponsored Display enables advertisers to continue engaging with customers by showing them complementary or upgraded products, encouraging product reviews, or reinforcing brand affinity with messaging that thanks them for their trust. This transforms the ad unit into more than a sales driver—it becomes a relationship-builder.

Where Sponsored Display truly shines is in its ability to harmonize with off-Amazon marketing initiatives. For brands that are already running social media campaigns, email marketing flows, or influencer partnerships, Sponsored Display offers a parallel digital touchpoint that aligns with external messaging while maintaining the native advantages of Amazon's ecosystem. A potential customer might first see a product recommended on Instagram, then later encounter a Sponsored Display ad featuring the same product while browsing a news website. That ad might take them directly to the Amazon listing, creating a smooth, frictionless path from inspiration to transaction. This type of cross-channel consistency reinforces credibility and reduces the drop-off that typically occurs when shoppers must jump between platforms or unfamiliar purchasing flows.

Successful integration of Sponsored Display into a broader funnel also relies on internal coordination across marketing teams. Brand teams, performance marketers, and content creators must align their strategies, ensuring that messaging is consistent across every channel. Sponsored Display campaigns should not be treated as afterthoughts or supplementary—they must be built into the campaign calendar, synchronized with major product launches, promotional periods, and seasonal themes. This ensures that when a shopper sees a Sponsored Display ad, it resonates with other touchpoints they've experienced elsewhere, creating a sense of coherence and reinforcing the message with every impression.

Measurement and attribution are key to refining this integration over time. Sponsored Display provides insights into metrics like view-through conversions, click-through rates, and audience engagement. These data points allow advertisers to determine how well each ad contributes to different stages of the funnel. If an ad performs well in driving clicks but has a low conversion rate, it may be best suited for the awareness or consideration stages. Conversely, if an ad consistently drives purchases, it may be more effective when deployed toward the bottom of the funnel. Understanding these patterns helps advertisers deploy Sponsored Display more strategically, ensuring it complements the funnel rather than cluttering it.

It's also important to adapt Sponsored Display strategies based on product lifecycle stages. For new product launches, ads may focus more on exposure and education. For established products, the emphasis might shift to competitor conquesting or upselling. In seasonal campaigns, ads could highlight limited-time deals or tie-ins with holidays and events. This adaptability makes Sponsored Display an incredibly versatile tool, capable of serving different roles within the same funnel at different times.

The key to mastering Sponsored Display as part of a broader funnel is to view every impression not in isolation but as a step in a dialogue. Each ad, whether shown on a product detail page, a third-party site, or within a mobile app, contributes to the cumulative story that a brand tells its audience. The more cohesive, intentional, and responsive this story is, the more likely it is to drive action—not just once, but repeatedly.

Ultimately, integrating Sponsored Display into the overall marketing funnel transforms it from a transactional tactic into a strategic growth engine. It allows brands to guide shoppers through every phase of their journey with relevance and precision, creating experiences that feel less like advertising and more like thoughtful, personalized guidance. This alignment between platform capabilities and strategic vision is what enables brands to fully harness the power of Sponsored Display, driving not just sales, but scalable, long-term success.

PART 5

Advanced Strategies and Amazon DSP

CHAPTER 12
INTRODUCTION TO AMAZON DSP (DEMAND-SIDE PLATFORM)

UNDERSTANDING PROGRAMMATIC ADVERTISING ON AMAZON

Programmatic advertising on Amazon represents a powerful evolution in the way brands can connect with customers at scale, using data, automation, and advanced targeting to optimize performance across the buyer journey. It marks a shift away from manual campaign management toward intelligent systems that place the right ad, in front of the right shopper, at the right moment—often in real time. Understanding this model is essential for any brand aiming to thrive in the increasingly competitive environment of digital retail, especially within Amazon's vast ecosystem.

At its core, programmatic advertising refers to the automated buying and selling of digital ad inventory. Unlike traditional methods where marketers directly negotiated placements with publishers, programmatic relies on algorithms and data signals to bid on impressions dynamically, often through real-time auctions. Within Amazon, this process is orchestrated primarily through Amazon DSP (Demand Side Platform), a tool designed to give advertisers access to a massive range of inventory both on Amazon's owned-and-operated properties and across the broader web. The real magic of Amazon's programmatic offering lies in its integration of transactional data, shopper behavior, and audience insights that few other platforms can match.

What makes Amazon's version of programmatic advertising so unique is the depth of its first-party data. Unlike third-party data aggregators that piece together behavioral signals from across the internet, Amazon directly observes real purchase behavior, product interactions, and browsing habits within its ecosystem. This provides a much richer and more reliable foundation for targeting. For example, a user who has repeatedly browsed high-end audio equipment and read reviews on related accessories might be classified into a high-intent audience segment for premium electronics. Amazon DSP can then use this information to bid on opportunities to show that user highly relevant ads, whether they are currently browsing Amazon.com or reading an article on a partner website.

The targeting options available through Amazon's programmatic platform are as robust as they are strategic. Brands can reach audiences based on lifestyle preferences, in-market behavior, demographic attributes, or even contextual signals—such as the type of content a user is engaging with at the moment an ad is served. These targeting capabilities are not just granular—they're dynamic, evolving in real time as Amazon learns more about each shopper. This means campaigns can be continually refined, ensuring that impressions are not wasted and budget is deployed as efficiently as possible.

One of the biggest advantages of using Amazon DSP is the ability to reach customers beyond the confines of Amazon's retail site. Programmatic advertising here extends into streaming content via Amazon Freevee, Fire TV, IMDb, Twitch, and other partner apps and websites. This expands the visibility of your brand to potential customers in moments of engagement that occur outside of traditional search or product detail pages. For instance, a shopper might see a product video while watching a favorite show on Fire TV or encounter a banner ad while reading a news article. These off-Amazon impressions are seamlessly tied back to Amazon's commerce engine, creating a full-circle marketing loop that starts with awareness and can end in conversion.

Creative flexibility is another hallmark of Amazon's programmatic offering. Advertisers can deploy a wide range of ad formats, including display banners, video ads, and interactive formats that encourage user interaction. Each format can be customized and tested for optimal performance across different devices and environments, from mobile phones and desktops to smart TVs and tablets. The platform also allows for dynamic creatives—ads that automatically adapt based on the audience or context. For example, a user who recently viewed a particular product might be served an ad that features that exact item with a personalized message or promotion. These creatives can be especially effective in retargeting scenarios, where familiarity and relevance drive engagement.

Measurement and attribution in programmatic campaigns are also enhanced through Amazon's unique capabilities. Advertisers have access to insights that connect ad impressions and engagement to actual purchase behavior, both online and in physical stores (if applicable). This is made possible through Amazon Attribution and proprietary pixel and tag technologies that track the entire shopper journey. Brands can monitor not just whether an ad was seen or clicked, but whether it led to a conversion—and what kind of conversion it was. This level of transparency helps advertisers make smarter decisions about how to allocate spend, which audiences to prioritize, and which creatives are delivering the strongest ROI.

A particularly powerful use case within programmatic advertising on Amazon is sequential messaging. Because Amazon can track the progression of a shopper's journey, it can serve different ads at different stages to guide the user down the funnel. A shopper might first see a general awareness video that introduces a new product line. If they engage with that content, they may later be retargeted with a carousel of specific items from the collection. As interest grows, the ads might include price promotions, customer reviews, or urgency-based messaging to drive conversion. This controlled narrative allows brands to use programmatic advertising not just as a promotional tool, but as a storytelling medium.

While the benefits of programmatic advertising are compelling, success in this domain requires a strategic mindset and technical proficiency. Campaigns must be properly structured to reflect distinct objectives, whether that's growing brand awareness, driving traffic, boosting conversions, or building customer loyalty. Budget allocation must be carefully managed, with an eye toward both top-funnel exposure and bottom-funnel efficiency. And creative assets must be continually refreshed and optimized to prevent fatigue and keep performance metrics trending upward.

There is also a learning curve when it comes to interpreting the data that comes out of programmatic campaigns. Metrics like impression share, frequency, detail page view rate, purchase rate, and new-to-brand metrics provide deep insights but require context to interpret effectively. It's not just about how many people saw an ad—it's about whether those impressions are reaching the right people, and whether those engagements are translating into long-term value for the brand. Successful programmatic advertisers take a test-and-learn approach, constantly refining their strategy based on performance data and evolving trends in shopper behavior.

One of the most underutilized aspects of programmatic advertising on Amazon is its synergy with other marketing channels. When used in tandem with Sponsored Products, Sponsored Brands, and off-Amazon campaigns like email or social media, Amazon DSP becomes a powerful connective tissue that links all your touchpoints together. A shopper who first encounters your brand in a Facebook post might later see a DSP ad that leads them to your Amazon storefront, where they engage further and eventually make a purchase. This integration reinforces messaging consistency and builds brand equity across the digital landscape.

It's important to understand that programmatic advertising on Amazon is not just for large enterprises. While Amazon DSP was originally more accessible to vendors with sizable budgets, self-service options and third-party platforms have made it increasingly approachable for smaller brands looking to scale. With careful planning, even modest campaigns can produce significant results when grounded in solid audience insights, compelling creative, and a clear understanding of the funnel.

In a digital landscape increasingly driven by automation and data, programmatic advertising on Amazon stands out as a frontier of opportunity. It's a realm where technology and strategy converge, allowing brands not only to reach their target audience, but to do so with relevance, precision, and scale. Those who master its nuances and stay attuned to its evolving capabilities will find themselves in a position to not just compete—but to lead.

BENEFITS OF USING DSP FOR ADVANCED TARGETING AND REACH

Amazon's Demand-Side Platform, commonly known as Amazon DSP, represents one of the most powerful tools in digital advertising today, especially for brands seeking to harness advanced targeting and maximize their reach across the customer journey. With programmatic precision and unparalleled access to Amazon's wealth of first-party data, DSP opens the door to highly personalized, scalable advertising that extends far beyond what traditional campaigns can deliver. The benefits of leveraging this platform go well beyond audience reach; it redefines how advertisers understand and interact with shoppers in a way that's both intelligent and outcome-driven.

At the center of Amazon DSP's advantage is the access to proprietary data sourced directly from millions of active shoppers. Unlike third-party platforms that rely on indirect data collection methods, Amazon gathers its insights from actual behaviors—what people are searching, browsing, clicking, purchasing, and reviewing. These signals are incredibly potent because they come from customers who have demonstrated real intent, often in the final stages of their decision-making process. The ability to tap into this behavior allows advertisers to identify shoppers with high conversion potential, resulting in more efficient use of ad spend and more effective audience targeting.

Amazon DSP offers granular targeting capabilities that allow brands to go far beyond broad demographic groups or general interests. Through the platform, advertisers can segment audiences based on in-market behavior, lifestyle categories, shopping frequency, brand affinity, and even recent product interactions. For example, a luxury skincare brand can target individuals who frequently shop in premium beauty categories, have recently viewed high-end moisturizers, and belong to a specific age demographic. This depth of audience definition ensures that every impression is meaningful, which not only increases the chances of engagement but also reduces wasted budget on irrelevant views.

Another critical advantage of using DSP is the ability to reach both Amazon customers and shoppers outside of the Amazon ecosystem. While Amazon's retail site and apps are central to its advertising environment, DSP also enables campaigns to appear across thousands of third-party websites and mobile apps, as well as Amazon-owned properties like IMDb,

Fire TV, and Twitch. This means that even when a shopper isn't actively browsing for a product on Amazon, your brand can still stay top-of-mind through strategically placed display and video ads. This off-site reach allows for comprehensive brand storytelling, awareness building, and retargeting, all while maintaining a connection to the commerce engine that drives conversions.

Retargeting is particularly powerful through Amazon DSP because it is directly informed by shopper intent. Advertisers can re-engage users who have viewed specific product detail pages, added items to their cart, or made similar purchases in the past. These retargeting efforts can be tailored with personalized creatives that mirror the customer's interests or highlight unique selling points that may help tip the scales toward purchase. For instance, a customer who viewed a Bluetooth speaker but didn't buy it can later be shown a dynamic ad featuring that same product, along with a discount offer or a limited-time deal. This real-time adaptation keeps the brand relevant and increases the likelihood of conversion.

One of the more understated but game-changing elements of DSP is its ability to drive new-to-brand acquisition. Through advanced audience modeling and lookalike segmentation, Amazon DSP can identify and target potential customers who share behavioral similarities with your current buyer base but have not yet interacted with your products. This allows brands to scale their reach beyond familiar audiences and build incremental growth by tapping into new segments that would otherwise be hard to find. Importantly, these audiences aren't based on superficial traits; they're crafted from complex behavioral patterns that reflect real commerce activity, making the targeting far more predictive and valuable.

When it comes to campaign execution, Amazon DSP gives advertisers control and flexibility. Whether working through a managed service or using the self-service platform, brands can fine-tune bids, optimize pacing, choose inventory types, and set frequency caps to maintain ad freshness. The dynamic nature of programmatic bidding ensures that the most relevant impressions are prioritized, and the campaign budget is allocated where it's most likely to yield results. Moreover, because DSP operates on a real-time bidding model, advertisers can continually assess performance and make adjustments on the fly based on live data.

Another substantial benefit of DSP lies in its robust measurement and attribution capabilities. Through Amazon's analytics suite, advertisers can track key metrics such as detail page view rates, purchase rates, return on ad spend (ROAS), new-to-brand orders, and even offline sales impact. This transparency provides a clear window into the actual value of each impression and allows brands to tie their advertising efforts directly to business outcomes. For marketers who need to prove ROI or justify increased investment, these insights are invaluable. The depth of measurement also enables more intelligent experimentation, with A/B testing of creative variations, audiences, and placements, leading to a continuously improving cycle of performance.

The format flexibility of DSP also contributes to its effectiveness. Advertisers can use a mix of static display ads, interactive formats, and video creatives to match the consumer's environment and attention span. Video, in particular, is an increasingly vital part of programmatic strategy, given its ability to convey brand narrative, build emotional connection, and deliver high recall. Through Amazon DSP, video ads can appear on high-traffic streaming platforms like Fire TV or Freevee, ensuring your brand is seen during moments of engagement, not distraction. When used strategically, video enhances top-of-funnel awareness while display ads guide customers through consideration and conversion stages.

The cohesive experience across touchpoints also contributes to a more unified brand presence. Amazon DSP enables sequential messaging, where users receive different ads based on their stage in the customer journey. This orchestration ensures that the messaging evolves logically— from introductory branding to persuasive product highlights and final call-to-action. It's not just about frequency—it's about relevance and timing. The ability to move users through a funnel with strategically crafted creative variations allows brands to control the narrative and encourage action at precisely the right moment.

Moreover, DSP helps align advertising efforts with larger business strategies. Whether the goal is to boost a product launch, clear out inventory, or drive subscriptions to a new Prime Video channel, DSP campaigns can be structured to support those objectives with precise audience alignment and targeted messaging. For brands that sell both on and off Amazon, DSP bridges the gap, helping to drive traffic where it's needed most—whether to an Amazon product detail page, a storefront, or an external landing page.

It's also worth noting that Amazon DSP isn't limited to products alone. Brands that offer services, entertainment content, apps, or digital subscriptions can also benefit. For example, an entertainment company promoting a new Prime Video series can target viewers who have watched similar shows, expressed interest in the genre, or frequently engage with streaming platforms. Likewise, mobile app developers can target likely downloaders based on their interaction history with similar apps or content, ensuring the ad spend is going toward a qualified audience.

As retail media continues to evolve, platforms like Amazon DSP are redefining the way advertisers think about targeting and reach. It's no longer sufficient to place an ad in front of a broad audience and hope for the best. In a world driven by performance, personalization, and precision, DSP allows advertisers to cut through the noise and deliver experiences that resonate. It empowers brands to operate with strategic clarity—knowing not only who they're reaching, but why they're reaching them, and what outcome they expect to achieve. This level of intelligence and control is not just a competitive advantage—it's a necessity for any brand looking to thrive in a digital-first economy.

EXPLORING DIFFERENT DSP AD FORMATS: DISPLAY, VIDEO, AUDIO

In the evolving world of digital advertising, understanding the unique capabilities and strengths of various ad formats is essential to unlocking the full potential of Amazon's Demand-Side Platform. Amazon DSP is not just a tool for reaching audiences—it is a dynamic ecosystem that provides multiple pathways for brands to communicate, influence, and convert. Among the most impactful features of this platform are its diverse ad formats, each serving specific objectives and optimized for different types of customer interactions. Display, video, and audio ads each bring distinct advantages, and mastering how to leverage them in context is key to building a multi-dimensional, high-performing campaign.

Display ads form the backbone of many DSP strategies. Their power lies in their flexibility, scalability, and ability to drive performance across every stage of the customer journey. Amazon DSP display ads can be highly targeted, fueled by Amazon's rich pool of first-party data, which enables advertisers to place their brand message in front of audiences that have already shown relevant shopping behaviors. These could be users who recently viewed similar items, searched for comparable products, or demonstrated category-level interest. Display ads reach these users both on Amazon-owned properties and across the broader web through third-party inventory, enabling continuity in visibility even when customers are browsing elsewhere.

What makes display ads particularly effective within DSP is their visual presence. Display creatives, when designed thoughtfully, are capable of catching the eye quickly in a cluttered digital landscape. Whether it's promoting a limited-time offer, announcing a new product launch, or simply keeping the brand top of mind, display ads serve as a reminder and reinforcement tool. With customizable sizing, rich targeting options, and clickable interactivity, they provide a direct line between brand messaging and shopper action. Their role in remarketing is also essential—display ads can be deployed to re-engage users who didn't convert on the first interaction, helping to nurture potential customers back into the purchase funnel.

Video ads, meanwhile, deliver impact through motion, storytelling, and emotion. In an era where passive scrolling is the norm, video stands out because it demands attention. Amazon DSP video formats offer brands the chance to immerse users in a narrative, explain product benefits, or convey a brand's ethos in a way that static images cannot. These video ads are shown across a variety of channels, including Amazon sites, Amazon devices such as Fire TV, and other premium streaming environments like Freevee and Twitch. This reach into high-quality, content-rich environments makes video a powerful driver of top-of-funnel objectives such as brand awareness and consideration.

Beyond awareness, video ads also play a valuable role in conversion. With Amazon DSP, brands can deploy shoppable video ads that include calls to action and product links, seamlessly combining engagement with commerce. Because Amazon's data insights inform audience selection, the viewers of these video ads are not just random browsers—they're users who are already predisposed to be interested in the content being shown. Whether it's a 15-second teaser of a product demo or a longer narrative that speaks to lifestyle alignment, video ads build emotional connections and deliver a compelling message that can drive action.

Audio ads represent the next frontier in reaching audiences within moments of intimacy and focus. Unlike visual formats that compete for attention on screens, audio ads are delivered during moments when people are listening—while cooking, commuting, working out, or relaxing. Amazon DSP's audio inventory includes placements on Amazon Music (ad-supported tier), Alexa-enabled devices, and other audio streaming platforms. This format provides a unique opportunity to connect with consumers in a screenless environment, often when they are less distracted and more receptive to auditory messaging.

The strength of audio ads lies in their ability to tap into mood and environment. Because they reach users in immersive contexts, they can leave a lasting impression through voice, tone, and sound design. For brands that rely on personality, storytelling, or sonic branding, audio offers a direct channel to communicate in a way that feels personal and authentic. Moreover, audio ads can be paired with companion display creatives that appear on the screen of the device being used, offering a dual-layer of communication that drives brand recall and encourages click-throughs.

One of the standout benefits of using all three ad formats within Amazon DSP is the potential for integrated, multi-touch campaigns. A customer's journey is rarely linear, and reaching them through only one format risks losing momentum or failing to engage at key touchpoints. By combining display, video, and audio formats strategically, brands can craft a cohesive messaging experience that evolves over time. For instance, a campaign might begin with a video ad that introduces the brand story, followed by a display ad that reinforces the product benefits, and then a retargeting audio ad that nudges the customer toward conversion. This layered approach creates consistency and familiarity, which are essential ingredients for building trust and driving results.

Amazon's DSP platform enhances this strategy by offering advanced audience segmentation, frequency capping, and cross-format performance tracking. This means that advertisers can not only control how often users are exposed to their ads but also gain insights into how each format contributes to overall campaign objectives. For example, analytics may reveal that users who first viewed a video ad and were later retargeted with a display ad had a higher conversion rate than those exposed to display alone. These insights can inform future budgeting and creative decisions, ensuring that every dollar spent delivers maximum return.

In addition to performance optimization, the use of diverse formats also supports brand storytelling across customer personas. Different segments of your audience may respond better to different forms of communication. Younger, visually driven users might engage more deeply with video ads, while multitaskers may favor audio. High-intent shoppers close to making a purchase decision might prefer clear, direct display ads with pricing and product imagery. By deploying a variety of ad types, brands can meet people where they are and tailor the message in a format that resonates most effectively with that specific behavior or need.

The creative potential within these formats also allows for experimentation and innovation. A/B testing across ad types—whether it's testing different video lengths, display layouts, or voice tones in audio— can reveal what works best for your brand in real-time. Amazon DSP supports this iterative process with data-rich reporting and flexible campaign controls. This makes it easy for marketers to refine their approach continuously, removing guesswork and replacing it with actionable insight.

Using display, video, and audio formats together within Amazon DSP is not just about variety—it's about synergy. When well-executed, each format plays a role in advancing a customer toward conversion while simultaneously enhancing brand perception. It's a holistic strategy that mirrors how people consume content in their daily lives—visually, audibly, and interactively. Brands that understand how to synchronize these channels gain a distinct advantage, presenting a consistent and compelling presence across the fragmented digital landscape.

Ultimately, the ability to explore and deploy these formats through one centralized, data-informed platform makes Amazon DSP a cornerstone of modern advertising strategy. By aligning creative execution with consumer behavior and leveraging Amazon's unparalleled targeting capabilities, marketers can transform passive exposure into active engagement. The depth and versatility of display, the emotional resonance of video, and the immersive intimacy of audio form a trifecta of tools capable of shaping perception, guiding decisions, and driving measurable business outcomes. This is not simply about reaching more people—it's about reaching the right people, at the right time, in the right way.

ACCESSING AMAZON'S EXTENSIVE DATA AND INVENTORY

Amazon's advertising ecosystem is built on the foundation of a vast and intricate data structure, providing brands with unparalleled opportunities to target, optimize, and measure the success of their campaigns. One of the key advantages of using Amazon as an advertising platform is the sheer volume and richness of data available, coupled with the expansive inventory across its various channels. This combination enables advertisers to craft hyper-targeted strategies and achieve higher levels of precision and efficiency. To fully capitalize on these advantages, it is crucial to understand how to access Amazon's extensive data and inventory and use them to fuel campaign performance.

Amazon's advertising platform offers a treasure trove of data that spans multiple categories, including shopping behavior, demographics, and user intent. This data comes directly from Amazon's vast network of customer touchpoints—spanning the retail website, Prime Video, Alexa, and Amazon's suite of devices. Each interaction, whether it's a product search, a click on an ad, or a video view, generates valuable information about a user's preferences and behaviors. Amazon collects and processes this data in real time, creating a constantly evolving picture of each customer's interests and purchasing intent. This wealth of information allows advertisers to create highly specific customer segments based on detailed behaviors and affinities.

One of the primary ways to access this data is through Amazon's robust audience targeting capabilities. Advertisers can segment their audience based on a variety of factors, such as past purchase history, browsing behavior, search queries, and even demographic information like age, gender, and location. This level of granular targeting ensures that ads are shown to users who are not just likely to be interested in a product, but who are actively in the market for something similar. For example, if a user has recently searched for hiking boots or viewed several outdoor gear listings, Amazon's advertising system can serve them targeted ads for related products, increasing the likelihood of conversion. By utilizing these audience insights, advertisers can optimize ad spend by focusing on high-intent shoppers and avoiding wasted impressions on irrelevant audiences.

Amazon's extensive inventory is another critical component of its advertising capabilities. The platform offers a wide variety of inventory sources, both within Amazon's own ecosystem and through third-party networks. Within Amazon's ecosystem, advertisers can access premium placements on high-traffic pages, such as the search results page, product detail pages, and homepage banners. These spots are prime real estate, offering maximum visibility to a highly engaged audience. Additionally, Amazon's DSP (Demand-Side Platform) enables advertisers to purchase display and video ad space on other websites and apps within Amazon's extended network, which spans across the internet and even to partner sites like Twitch and Freevee.

The breadth of Amazon's inventory also extends to other Amazon-owned properties. For example, Prime Video offers a unique advertising opportunity by allowing brands to run video ads before, during, or after content on the platform. Similarly, brands can leverage Amazon's Alexa devices and the voice assistant's growing influence in consumer decision-making. Ads within Amazon Music and on Kindle devices further extend a brand's reach beyond the traditional shopping experience. These diverse touchpoints allow advertisers to reach potential customers in a variety of contexts—whether they are actively shopping, streaming content, or engaging with voice-activated devices.

In addition to customer behavior and inventory, another valuable data set available on Amazon is performance analytics. Amazon provides detailed reporting on ad campaign performance, including impressions, clicks, conversions, and sales. By accessing these insights, advertisers can measure the effectiveness of their campaigns and make data-driven decisions on where to allocate resources. Metrics such as cost-per-click (CPC), return on ad spend (ROAS), and conversion rate provide actionable insights into campaign performance, helping advertisers identify which ads, keywords, and audiences are delivering the best results. Amazon's data analytics tools also allow for real-time optimizations, enabling advertisers to adjust bids, refine targeting strategies, and tweak creatives as needed to improve performance.

A critical advantage of accessing Amazon's data is its ability to inform bid and budget decisions. The platform's sophisticated algorithms take into account a variety of factors when determining how much an advertiser should bid for a given impression, including the level of competition for a particular keyword or audience, as well as historical performance data. By analyzing this data, advertisers can make informed decisions about how much to bid to secure prime inventory placements without overspending. Additionally, Amazon's automated bidding options allow advertisers to let the system make real-time adjustments based on performance signals, ensuring that budgets are spent efficiently and that ads are shown to the right audience at the right time.

Beyond direct campaign management, accessing Amazon's extensive data and inventory also allows for advanced audience segmentation and retargeting. Retargeting is an essential strategy in driving conversions by re-engaging users who have already interacted with a brand but have not yet completed a purchase. Amazon's data allows advertisers to track user behavior across multiple touchpoints, enabling highly personalized retargeting efforts. For instance, a user who views a product on Amazon but doesn't purchase it can be retargeted with display ads that remind them of the item they viewed, offering them an incentive or a special deal to complete the purchase. Similarly, shoppers who have added products to their cart but abandoned it can be targeted with ads designed to bring them back to finish the transaction.

The ability to use Amazon's data for cross-channel advertising is another significant benefit. Advertisers can not only target users within the Amazon ecosystem but also extend their campaigns to off-Amazon properties. The DSP allows brands to buy display and video ad placements across a range of third-party websites and apps, helping to build a wider audience beyond Amazon's own domain. This ability to create an integrated, omnichannel advertising strategy increases the chances of reaching users multiple times across different touchpoints, keeping the brand top of mind and reinforcing the message in different formats.

Additionally, Amazon's data empowers advertisers to execute more precise audience segmentation for product launches or promotions. Whether launching a new product line or running a seasonal campaign, brands can use Amazon's data to identify the right audience segments that are most likely to respond positively. For example, if a brand is releasing a new product for pet owners, they can use Amazon's data to identify users who have previously purchased pet-related items or engaged with pet-related content. This ensures that the promotional efforts reach individuals who are already interested in the category, increasing the likelihood of success.

Amazon also provides the ability to integrate external data sources with its platform, allowing brands to enhance their targeting efforts with additional customer insights. For example, businesses can incorporate data from their CRM systems to create lookalike audiences, target specific customer segments, or adjust campaigns based on offline sales data. This integration of first-party and third-party data expands the scope of targeting options, enabling brands to craft highly personalized campaigns that resonate more deeply with potential customers.

Accessing Amazon's vast inventory and data allows for unparalleled control over campaign strategy and execution. By leveraging audience insights, inventory placements, and performance metrics, advertisers can build campaigns that are finely tuned to reach the right people at the right time. This enables businesses to maximize their return on investment, enhance customer engagement, and achieve measurable business outcomes. The combination of Amazon's extensive data, advanced targeting options, and vast inventory resources creates a powerful platform for advertisers to drive sales, build brand awareness, and foster long-term customer loyalty. The key is to leverage these resources strategically and continuously refine campaigns based on real-time insights and performance data. In doing so, brands can stay ahead of the competition and navigate the dynamic landscape of Amazon advertising with confidence.

DETERMINING IF DSP IS RIGHT FOR YOUR BUSINESS

Determining whether Amazon's Demand-Side Platform (DSP) is the right fit for your business requires a comprehensive understanding of what DSP offers, how it aligns with your business objectives, and whether your current stage of growth can support and benefit from the platform's capabilities. Amazon DSP is a powerful advertising tool designed for advanced targeting and broader reach, but it is not a one-size-fits-all solution. Instead, it requires strategic alignment with your overall marketing goals, resources, and operational infrastructure.

The fundamental distinction between DSP and other Amazon advertising solutions lies in its programmatic capabilities. Unlike Sponsored Products or Sponsored Brands, which primarily focus on targeting shoppers within Amazon's retail ecosystem, DSP enables advertisers to reach audiences both on and off Amazon through a wide variety of display, video, and audio formats. This breadth of reach can be transformative for businesses seeking to elevate brand awareness, retarget potential customers across the web, and influence purchase decisions well before a shopper lands on a product detail page.

The first consideration in evaluating whether DSP is appropriate is your advertising goal. If your objective is to grow top-of-funnel awareness, nurture leads, or engage customers across different digital environments, DSP can be extremely effective. It allows you to target audiences who are not necessarily in the final stages of the purchase journey but who have demonstrated behaviors or interests that indicate potential buying intent. This includes people who have viewed similar products, searched for relevant terms, or previously interacted with your brand in some way. Because of its advanced targeting capabilities, DSP works well for both direct response campaigns and longer-term brand-building efforts.

Another critical factor is your budget. Amazon DSP typically requires a higher initial investment compared to other advertising formats. The platform is often associated with minimum spend thresholds, especially when working directly with Amazon's managed services. For this reason, DSP is generally more suitable for mid-sized to large brands or businesses with a flexible marketing budget that allows for experimentation, optimization, and long-term strategy development. If your current advertising budget is tightly constrained and primarily focused on achieving immediate conversions with limited reach, other Amazon solutions might offer a better return in the short term.

That said, there are self-service DSP options that allow for more flexibility in terms of budget and control. With a self-service model, advertisers can manage campaigns in-house or through a third-party agency without the same minimum spend requirements that typically come with managed service options. This can open the door for smaller brands that have the internal expertise or are willing to partner with external experts to manage campaigns effectively. However, to truly leverage the full potential of DSP, access to skilled personnel or agencies who understand the nuances of programmatic buying, data analysis, and creative optimization is essential.

Another important dimension to consider is the stage of your business and the maturity of your advertising operations. DSP is ideally suited for businesses that already have a firm grasp on performance advertising and are looking to expand their capabilities. If your business has already seen success with Sponsored Products and Sponsored Brands, DSP can be a natural next step to increase market share, refine retargeting strategies, and reach new customer segments. It can also be a valuable asset for brands launching new product lines, entering new geographic markets, or trying to re-engage lapsed customers.

Equally important is the level of data you want to use to shape your campaigns. One of DSP's most compelling features is access to Amazon's proprietary audience data. This includes shopping signals, search behaviors, and browsing habits across millions of Amazon users. With DSP, advertisers can create custom audiences, lookalike audiences, or target predefined segments such as lifestyle, in-market, or demographic groups. These capabilities are especially beneficial for brands that want to move beyond keyword-based targeting and toward more behavioral, interest-based marketing. If your brand thrives on precision marketing and data-driven decisions, DSP provides the sophistication needed to execute such strategies.

Retargeting is another area where DSP shines. For brands that experience high traffic but low conversion rates, DSP offers a mechanism to re-engage visitors long after they've left your product or storefront page. Unlike Sponsored Display retargeting, which is limited to Amazon-owned properties, DSP extends your reach to external websites, mobile apps, and other platforms across the internet. This creates a cohesive advertising journey, following potential customers wherever they go online and maintaining brand visibility throughout the decision-making process. If your goal is to increase the frequency and depth of touchpoints with your audience, DSP offers unmatched capabilities to support that strategy.

However, the effectiveness of DSP is highly contingent upon your ability to interpret and act on performance data. The platform provides a wealth of insights, from view-through conversions to detailed audience overlap reports. But with this depth comes complexity. If your team lacks experience in analyzing programmatic data or optimizing display and video campaigns, you may not realize the full potential of your investment. Therefore, businesses considering DSP must assess not only their budget and goals but also their internal capabilities. Access to skilled analysts, creative strategists, and campaign managers is a critical success factor.

The creative assets you can produce also play a significant role. DSP supports a variety of ad formats, including dynamic display ads, custom creatives, and streaming video. If your brand has the resources to create high-quality visuals, compelling storytelling, and engaging messaging, DSP can amplify those efforts across multiple channels. On the other hand, if your creative resources are limited or if your ads are not optimized for attention and engagement, even the best targeting will fall flat. High-performing DSP campaigns depend on synergy between audience selection, ad format, message design, and landing page experience.

Moreover, consider your long-term marketing strategy. DSP is not typically a set-it-and-forget-it channel. It thrives on continuous optimization, frequent A/B testing, and iterative learning. Brands that view advertising as a short-term lever for sales may struggle with DSP's longer conversion timelines and broader focus. Those that see advertising as a sustained investment in brand equity, customer acquisition, and market dominance are better positioned to benefit from DSP's features. The platform offers tools to build long-term customer relationships, from prospecting and engagement to loyalty and reactivation, but it demands patience, experimentation, and strategic clarity.

Geographic expansion is another use case where DSP delivers distinct advantages. If your business is moving into international markets or targeting multilingual audiences, DSP allows you to deploy localized campaigns with native-language creatives and region-specific targeting. Amazon's reach across North America, Europe, Asia, and beyond provides a launchpad for global brand visibility. This is especially valuable for consumer goods, tech products, or entertainment services looking to scale their presence across borders with tailored messaging.

In evaluating whether DSP is right for your business, also consider how it integrates with your broader media mix. Brands that run omnichannel campaigns—combining social, search, email, and offline advertising—will find that DSP can serve as a central component of an integrated strategy. It can reinforce messaging across multiple channels, deliver consistent branding, and synchronize your customer journey. When used alongside tools like Amazon Marketing Cloud or other third-party analytics platforms, DSP can enhance your attribution modeling and provide deeper visibility into customer interactions.

Ultimately, the decision to adopt DSP should be driven by your business objectives, readiness, and capacity to manage complexity. It is not the right tool for every brand at every stage, but for those prepared to embrace its advanced capabilities, DSP offers a powerful pathway to scale advertising efforts, reach new audiences, and build lasting brand value. Careful evaluation, strategic planning, and a willingness to invest in both time and resources are essential to unlocking the platform's full potential.

CHAPTER 13

LEVERAGING AMAZON DSP FOR PRIME-FOCUSED CAMPAIGNS

UTILIZING ADVANCED AUDIENCE SEGMENTS FOR PRIME MEMBERS

When it comes to advertising on Amazon Prime, one of the most powerful tools available to marketers is the ability to target highly specific audience segments. These segments allow businesses to engage with Prime members in a way that is both personalized and relevant, ultimately driving more meaningful interactions and better conversion rates. Amazon Prime members represent a premium audience—individuals who are not only dedicated to the platform but also have access to a wide range of benefits, including fast shipping, streaming services, exclusive deals, and more. By tapping into advanced audience segments, advertisers can tailor their campaigns to meet the unique needs and preferences of these members, leading to more efficient and effective advertising outcomes.

To truly leverage Amazon's advanced audience targeting capabilities, it's crucial to first understand the different types of audience segments available. The platform offers a range of options that allow advertisers to narrow down their target groups based on specific behaviors, interests, and demographic characteristics. These segments include but are not limited to, past shopping behaviors, browsing history, demographic information such as age and gender, geographic location, and even lifestyle preferences. Each segment can provide valuable insights into how Prime members interact with products and services, enabling advertisers to craft highly relevant campaigns that speak directly to the needs and desires of these members.

One of the key advantages of using advanced audience segments for Prime members is the ability to target shoppers who have already shown interest in your product or category. For instance, Amazon's retargeting capabilities allow advertisers to reach users who have visited their product pages, placed items in their shopping cart, or engaged with their brand in some way but did not complete the purchase. This type of audience is highly valuable because these shoppers are already familiar with the brand, making them more likely to convert. By serving them personalized ads that remind them of the product they showed interest in or offering an incentive to complete their purchase, businesses can increase the likelihood of driving a sale.

Beyond retargeting, advanced audience segments allow businesses to reach new, high-potential customers by targeting individuals who exhibit similar behaviors to their best existing customers. Amazon's lookalike audience capabilities take the data from an advertiser's current customer base and find Prime members who share similar shopping habits, preferences, and demographic characteristics. This type of audience is incredibly valuable for businesses looking to expand their reach without wasting resources on irrelevant or uninterested shoppers. By utilizing lookalike segments, advertisers can target individuals who are more likely to engage with their brand and convert, resulting in a higher return on investment (ROI).

In addition to shopping behaviors and demographics, geographic location is another powerful tool when it comes to targeting Prime members. Advertisers can segment their audience based on where Prime members live, allowing businesses to tailor their campaigns to specific regions, cities, or even neighborhoods. This can be especially useful for brands that are running region-specific promotions or offering localized products and services. By honing in on customers in a particular area, businesses can craft messaging that speaks directly to local preferences and needs, ultimately increasing the relevance of their ads and driving stronger engagement.

Another powerful advanced targeting tool is the ability to segment Prime members by their interests and lifestyle preferences. Amazon offers an array of interest-based segments that allow advertisers to target users based on the categories they browse or products they purchase. For example, if a Prime member frequently browses and purchases fitness-related products, advertisers can target that individual with ads for health supplements, workout gear, or gym memberships. Similarly, advertisers can use lifestyle-based segments to target individuals with specific hobbies, such as cooking, gaming, or home improvement. This level of precision allows businesses to deliver highly personalized ads that are aligned with the interests and passions of their target audience, leading to increased engagement and higher conversion rates.

The power of Amazon's advanced audience segments also lies in their ability to provide a deeper understanding of customer behavior. By analyzing the performance of different segments, advertisers can identify which groups are most likely to engage with their ads, as well as which types of messaging and creatives resonate best with each segment. This data-driven approach allows businesses to continuously refine their targeting strategies, ensuring that they are consistently reaching the most relevant and high-value customers.

It's important to note that while advanced audience segmentation provides powerful targeting capabilities, it also requires careful planning and optimization to ensure maximum effectiveness. Simply selecting an audience segment is not enough to guarantee success. Advertisers must also consider the creative aspects of their campaigns, ensuring that the messaging, visuals, and calls to action align with the needs and preferences of the targeted group. For example, ads targeting fitness enthusiasts should feature images and messaging related to health and wellness, while ads targeting home improvement enthusiasts should showcase DIY projects and tools. By tailoring the creative to the specific segment, businesses can increase the chances of capturing the attention of Prime members and driving action.

Moreover, tracking and analyzing the performance of these advanced segments is crucial for ongoing optimization. Amazon's advertising platform offers a wealth of performance metrics, such as click-through rates, conversion rates, and return on ad spend, that provide valuable insights into how well different segments are performing. By regularly reviewing these metrics, advertisers can identify trends and make data-driven adjustments to their campaigns to improve performance over time. For example, if a particular audience segment is underperforming, advertisers can tweak their targeting criteria, adjust their bidding strategy, or experiment with different creatives to improve results.

Another benefit of using advanced audience segments for Prime members is the ability to scale campaigns based on performance. Once advertisers identify high-performing segments, they can allocate more of their advertising budget to those groups to maximize their reach and impact. Conversely, underperforming segments can be adjusted or eliminated to prevent wasted spend. This flexibility allows businesses to continuously optimize their advertising strategy and focus resources on the most profitable audience segments.

Advanced audience segmentation also enables advertisers to create highly effective remarketing campaigns. By tracking user behavior and segmenting Prime members based on their interactions with previous ads, websites, or product pages, businesses can re-engage users who may not have converted on their initial visit. Remarketing ads can remind these users of the products they viewed, offer additional incentives, or provide personalized recommendations based on their previous interactions. This type of targeted advertising helps keep the brand top of mind and encourages users to complete their purchases.

Ultimately, utilizing advanced audience segments for Prime members enables businesses to connect with a highly engaged, valuable group of shoppers in a way that is both efficient and cost-effective. By targeting the right audiences with the right message, businesses can significantly improve their advertising performance, increase conversions, and drive more sales. The ability to reach Prime members at various stages of the customer journey—whether through retargeting, lookalike audiences, interest-based segments, or location-based targeting—ensures that businesses can engage with potential customers in a way that is both relevant and personalized. By continuously optimizing and refining their audience segments and creative strategies, advertisers can build stronger relationships with their customers, increase brand loyalty, and drive long-term growth.

CREATING CUSTOM AUDIENCES BASED ON PURCHASE HISTORY AND BEHAVIOR

In the rapidly evolving world of digital advertising, one of the most effective ways to engage customers is by creating custom audiences based on purchase history and behavior. This strategy allows businesses to craft highly personalized ad campaigns that target consumers who have already demonstrated an interest in specific products or categories. Amazon, as one of the world's largest e-commerce platforms, offers powerful tools to help advertisers leverage purchase history and customer behavior to optimize their targeting efforts. By creating custom audiences tailored to these behaviors, businesses can significantly improve the relevance and effectiveness of their ad campaigns, ultimately boosting sales and fostering stronger customer relationships.

Purchase history is one of the most valuable sources of data when it comes to audience segmentation. It provides insight into the types of products a customer has bought, how frequently they make purchases, and the price points they are most comfortable with. This level of detail allows businesses to create highly specific audience segments, ensuring that the ads they serve are relevant to the customer's past buying habits. For example, if a customer has consistently purchased fitness equipment, an advertiser can target them with ads for related products, such as supplements, workout gear, or gym memberships. Similarly, if a consumer frequently buys electronics, they can be targeted with promotions for the latest tech gadgets or accessories.

By targeting customers based on their purchase history, advertisers can not only improve the chances of conversion but also increase the lifetime value of a customer. Personalized ads that reflect a customer's past purchases show that the business understands their preferences and needs, making the ad feel more relevant and less intrusive. This can lead to increased brand loyalty, as customers are more likely to return to a brand that consistently offers them products they are interested in.

In addition to purchase history, customer behavior also plays a crucial role in shaping custom audiences. Behavior-based targeting involves analyzing how customers interact with a brand, whether through browsing history, product views, or engagement with previous ads. For instance, if a customer has recently viewed a product but has not yet made a purchase, they can be added to a custom audience for retargeting. By showing them a tailored ad that highlights the benefits of the product or offers a special discount, businesses can encourage the customer to complete their purchase. This type of behavior-based targeting helps businesses capture sales that might have otherwise been lost due to cart abandonment or lack of follow-through.

Another example of behavior-based targeting is identifying customers who have added products to their shopping cart but failed to complete the purchase. These individuals are prime candidates for retargeting campaigns, as they have already shown strong intent to buy. By creating a custom audience of shoppers who abandoned their carts, businesses can deliver personalized ads that remind them of the items they left behind, offer discounts or promotions, or highlight related products that might encourage them to finalize their purchase.

Creating custom audiences based on purchase history and behavior also allows businesses to tap into the power of lookalike audiences. By identifying customers whose behaviors and purchases closely resemble those of high-value customers, businesses can create lookalike audiences that have a higher likelihood of converting. Amazon's platform enables advertisers to upload their customer lists and create lookalike segments based on shared traits, such as shopping habits, interests, or demographics. This approach enables businesses to expand their reach to new customers who are most likely to be interested in their products, based on the behaviors of their existing customer base.

Custom audiences based on purchase history and behavior are not limited to targeting individuals who have already made a purchase. Advertisers can also use this data to target potential customers who are in the consideration phase of the buying journey. For example, a customer who has recently browsed a specific product category but has not yet made a purchase may be interested in receiving more information or seeing a comparison of products. By targeting these customers with ads that provide educational content, product demonstrations, or customer reviews, businesses can move them further down the sales funnel, ultimately driving conversions.

In addition to the obvious benefit of improved targeting, creating custom audiences based on purchase history and behavior also allows advertisers to optimize their ad spend. Rather than casting a wide net and hoping to capture the attention of random shoppers, businesses can focus their budgets on reaching individuals who are already engaged or interested in their products. This targeted approach not only reduces wasted spend but also increases the return on investment (ROI) for each ad campaign. By spending less on irrelevant impressions and more on highly qualified prospects, businesses can make their advertising dollars go further.

Moreover, the use of custom audiences can help advertisers identify trends and patterns in customer behavior that may not be immediately obvious. By analyzing the performance of different custom audiences, businesses can gain valuable insights into which products or categories are most popular among their customers, which types of ads are most effective, and how different customer segments respond to different messages. This data can inform future marketing strategies, allowing businesses to continuously refine their targeting efforts and improve the performance of their campaigns over time.

To get the most out of custom audience targeting, businesses must also ensure they are using the right creative elements in their ads. The power of custom audiences lies in their ability to deliver highly relevant and personalized content, so the ad's messaging, images, and call-to-action (CTA) should all be tailored to the specific audience. For example, an ad targeting customers who recently purchased kitchen appliances might feature an offer for kitchen accessories or complementary products. Alternatively, an ad targeting customers who have shown interest in fitness-related products could feature a limited-time discount on a new workout program or gym equipment. The more closely the ad aligns with the customer's past behavior and interests, the more likely it is to drive engagement and conversions.

Additionally, it is essential to track and measure the effectiveness of custom audience campaigns. Amazon's advertising platform provides detailed reporting tools that allow businesses to monitor the performance of their campaigns, including metrics such as click-through rates, conversion rates, and cost-per-click. By analyzing these metrics, businesses can assess which custom audiences are delivering the best results and which areas need improvement. This data can be used to fine-tune targeting strategies, adjust bids, or experiment with different creative formats to optimize performance.

As part of a comprehensive advertising strategy, creating custom audiences based on purchase history and behavior allows businesses to build a deeper connection with their customers. By delivering ads that reflect a customer's unique preferences and past interactions with the brand, businesses can improve customer satisfaction, enhance engagement, and ultimately drive more sales. With the ability to retarget previous customers, reach new prospects through lookalike audiences, and optimize ad spend for maximum ROI, custom audience targeting is an invaluable tool for businesses looking to succeed in the competitive world of Amazon advertising.

Custom audiences based on purchase history and behavior provide businesses with a powerful way to target the right customers with the right message. By leveraging Amazon's robust targeting capabilities, businesses can create highly personalized campaigns that resonate with their audience and drive conversions. Whether targeting previous buyers, retargeting abandoned cart shoppers, or expanding reach through lookalike audiences, businesses can use purchase history and behavior data to craft ads that are relevant, timely, and effective. The ability to continually optimize and refine these custom audiences ensures that advertisers can stay ahead of the competition and deliver exceptional results.

IMPLEMENTING ADVANCED RETARGETING STRATEGIES ACROSS DEVICES

In the digital age, consumers interact with brands across a multitude of devices—smartphones, tablets, desktops, and even connected televisions. For advertisers, this presents both a challenge and an opportunity. Advanced retargeting strategies, when effectively implemented across these devices, can significantly enhance the impact of an advertising campaign. By leveraging the power of cross-device retargeting, advertisers can engage their audience consistently, increase conversions, and ensure their messaging reaches consumers at the most opportune moments in their buying journey. This kind of strategy involves the seamless integration of various advertising efforts across multiple touchpoints, creating a unified and cohesive experience for potential buyers.

To begin with, understanding the behavior of consumers across devices is essential for creating effective retargeting campaigns. Consumers may start their shopping journey on one device, such as a smartphone, by browsing for products or reading reviews, and then later return to a different device, such as a laptop or desktop, to finalize their purchase. This fragmented behavior presents a challenge for advertisers, as it makes it harder to track and engage consumers effectively across different platforms. However, with advanced retargeting strategies, businesses can ensure that they follow their customers through the entire decision-making process, no matter where they are or which device they're using.

The core idea behind cross-device retargeting is to identify and track users as they move from one device to another. In the past, advertisers might have relied on cookies or device-specific identifiers to track a user's behavior on a single device. However, these methods often fell short when it came to cross-device tracking. Today, advanced tracking technologies—such as Amazon's advertising platform—allow advertisers to monitor user behavior across devices by linking their activity to a unique user identifier. This ensures that an individual's interaction with an ad on one device can trigger a retargeting campaign on another device, creating a continuous and personalized experience.

The first key benefit of implementing advanced retargeting strategies across devices is the ability to increase reach and engagement. A single consumer may interact with a brand multiple times over the course of their purchasing journey, and each of these interactions may occur on a different device. For instance, a shopper may first come across a product on their smartphone while commuting, then later decide to research it in more depth on their tablet at home. Without cross-device retargeting, the brand may miss the opportunity to continue engaging this shopper across these various touchpoints. However, by utilizing advanced tracking methods, an advertiser can ensure that their retargeting efforts follow the shopper wherever they go. This increases the likelihood of converting that shopper into a paying customer, as the business remains top-of-mind throughout the entire journey.

Moreover, advanced retargeting strategies across devices allow advertisers to create more tailored and personalized experiences for their audience. By understanding which devices a user is interacting with, businesses can customize their messaging to match the context in which the user is engaging. For example, a shopper who views a product on their desktop during a lunch break might be in a different mindset than someone browsing the same product on their mobile phone during a commute. By leveraging cross-device retargeting, advertisers can create ads that are optimized for the device the consumer is currently using, enhancing the relevance of the message and increasing the likelihood of conversion. This level of personalization helps create a seamless user experience, as consumers feel that the ads they see are tailored to their needs and preferences.

In addition to personalization, cross-device retargeting can also improve the overall efficiency of an advertising campaign. Traditionally, advertisers may have run separate campaigns targeting different devices, which could lead to fragmented messaging and redundant ads. For instance, the same user might see the same ad on their smartphone and again on their desktop, leading to ad fatigue and wasted spend. By implementing advanced retargeting strategies that connect all devices, businesses can streamline their advertising efforts, ensuring that their messages are delivered strategically at key moments across a user's journey. This minimizes redundancy and maximizes the effectiveness of the ad spend, ultimately improving the return on investment (ROI) of the campaign.

One of the most effective retargeting strategies is to create a tailored customer journey that spans across devices, with each step of the journey carefully designed to meet the user's needs and intent. For example, a customer who has viewed a product on a mobile device might then be retargeted with an ad on their desktop, featuring more in-depth product information or a discount offer. This can encourage the customer to make a purchase by moving them from the awareness phase to the consideration or decision phase. The key is to ensure that the message evolves as the customer moves across devices, addressing their changing needs and behaviors.

Another aspect of cross-device retargeting is the importance of timing. For example, if a user has abandoned a cart on their mobile phone, they should not only be retargeted with a display ad encouraging them to complete the purchase on their phone but should also be reminded on their desktop device when they later return to their computer. By strategically timing these reminders across devices, advertisers can increase the chances that the user will return to finalize their purchase. The goal is to stay engaged with the customer at every touchpoint, ensuring that they are continually reminded of the value of the product and the benefits of completing the transaction.

Cross-device retargeting also has significant implications for the types of ads that businesses use in their campaigns. Since different devices have different user experiences, the format of the ad needs to be optimized for each platform. For instance, mobile ads may benefit from more concise messaging and interactive formats, such as swipeable carousels or product demos, while desktop ads may have more room for longer-form content or detailed product descriptions. By leveraging advanced retargeting strategies, advertisers can dynamically serve ads that are best suited to the device on which they are being viewed, improving both user experience and engagement.

Despite the clear advantages of cross-device retargeting, it is important for businesses to be mindful of the challenges and complexities that can arise when implementing this strategy. One of the primary challenges is the reliance on user data and privacy concerns. With increasing regulations surrounding data privacy, businesses must ensure they are compliant with relevant laws and policies when tracking customer behavior across devices. Transparency and user consent are essential to building trust, and businesses should prioritize respecting privacy preferences while still optimizing their ad targeting strategies.

Additionally, effective cross-device retargeting requires a sophisticated technological infrastructure that can handle the complexities of tracking user behavior across multiple touchpoints. Businesses must ensure they have the right tools and platforms in place to gather and analyze data from different devices and integrate it into their advertising efforts. This requires a seamless connection between data collection, ad serving, and analytics platforms, which can be a significant undertaking for businesses that lack the necessary resources or technical expertise.

Implementing advanced retargeting strategies across devices can be a game changer for businesses looking to maximize their advertising impact. By ensuring a consistent and personalized experience for consumers, businesses can increase engagement, drive conversions, and improve their return on investment. However, it is essential for businesses to be aware of the challenges involved, particularly regarding privacy concerns and the technical complexity of cross-device tracking. With the right tools, data strategy, and commitment to delivering a seamless customer experience, businesses can unlock the full potential of cross-device retargeting and significantly enhance the performance of their advertising campaigns.

RUNNING VIDEO ADS TO ENGAGE PRIME VIEWERS ON AND OFF AMAZON

Video advertising has become one of the most powerful tools in digital marketing, especially for engaging highly targeted audiences such as Prime members. As Prime viewers are often more engaged and willing to make purchases, video ads offer an opportunity to not only capture their attention but also deliver a compelling message that drives them toward conversion. Running video ads to engage Prime viewers on and off Amazon requires a strategic approach, understanding of user behavior, and the ability to craft messages that resonate across different touchpoints and devices.

To begin, it's important to understand the unique power of video ads within the context of Amazon Prime. Prime members are typically loyal and engaged consumers, often seeking exclusive content, fast shipping, and additional benefits such as Prime Video access. This customer segment is highly valuable because they are already accustomed to the convenience and value Amazon provides. Video ads, particularly those that are well-targeted and contextually relevant, have the ability to deepen this connection by offering not just a product, but an experience that fits seamlessly within the customer's existing habits.

Running video ads to engage Prime viewers requires a robust understanding of the platform's ad tools and capabilities. Amazon offers various ad types, including display, video, and audio ads, but video ads stand out due to their visual and auditory appeal. They allow advertisers to tell a story, showcase products, and demonstrate use cases in a way that text and images cannot. Video content is particularly effective for introducing new products, explaining product features, or conveying brand values. For example, a brand launching a new kitchen gadget may use a video ad to demonstrate its functionality in real-time, showing viewers how it simplifies cooking tasks. These types of immersive ads are highly effective at engaging Prime members, who are already in a shopping mindset and likely to respond positively to content that feels personalized and relevant.

One of the first considerations when running video ads on Amazon is ensuring that the content is aligned with Amazon's unique ecosystem. Prime members engage with a variety of content on Amazon, from shopping to watching exclusive shows or movies. This diverse ecosystem offers a wealth of targeting opportunities for video ads. For instance, advertisers can create video ads specifically tailored to Prime Video viewers, capitalizing on moments when viewers are already highly engaged with content. Ads can be served before, during, or after a program, offering a seamless experience that doesn't disrupt the content consumption but instead complements it.

The next critical factor in running video ads is targeting the right audience. Amazon offers sophisticated targeting options that allow advertisers to reach Prime members based on various factors such as past purchase behavior, browsing history, and even demographic data. Additionally, advertisers can target audiences based on specific interests, such as fitness, technology, home improvement, or fashion. This level of targeting is particularly valuable for Prime viewers, as it ensures that video ads are highly relevant to the individual, increasing the likelihood of engagement and conversion.

Furthermore, running video ads on Amazon allows advertisers to extend their reach beyond just Amazon.com and Prime Video. With Amazon's extensive advertising network, including Amazon DSP (Demand-Side Platform), advertisers can target Prime members across a variety of off-Amazon sites and platforms. By using Amazon's vast inventory, businesses can serve their video ads on third-party websites, mobile apps, and even connected devices like Fire TV, creating a cross-platform ad experience that maximizes visibility and engagement. This extension of reach is crucial for increasing brand awareness and driving conversions, as it ensures that video ads are seen not only on Amazon but across a user's entire digital ecosystem.

To optimize the effectiveness of video ads, it is essential to craft content that resonates with the Prime audience both in terms of the message and the format. The tone, style, and length of the video should be carefully tailored to fit the target audience and the platform. For instance, a Prime viewer may appreciate a concise 15-second ad during a movie or TV show, but a longer 30-second or 60-second ad may be more effective on a product detail page or in the middle of an engaging shopping session. Moreover, the video content should be visually compelling, with high-quality production values and a clear call-to-action that guides the viewer toward the next step, whether it's making a purchase, signing up for a service, or simply learning more about the brand.

The integration of strong storytelling is another key element of successful video ads. Prime members are accustomed to high-quality video content through their access to Prime Video and other Amazon services. As such, they expect a level of sophistication and polish in the video ads they encounter. Storytelling can be used effectively in video ads by highlighting how a product or service can improve a viewer's life, solve a problem, or fulfill a desire. For example, a video ad for a new fitness tracker could show various people of different ages and fitness levels using the product to track their workouts and improve their health, creating an emotional connection with the viewer. This approach not only captures attention but also fosters trust by positioning the product as a practical solution that aligns with the viewer's lifestyle.

Another strategy for maximizing the effectiveness of video ads is to use retargeting. With Amazon's vast data on customer behaviors, it is possible to retarget viewers who have previously interacted with the brand or shown interest in a particular product. For example, if a Prime member watches a video ad about a new smart speaker but doesn't make a purchase, they can later be retargeted with a follow-up video ad on a different device, reminding them of the product and highlighting new features or special offers. This reinforces the product's value and nudges the consumer further down the purchase funnel. Retargeting can also be used to offer personalized discounts or limited-time promotions, increasing the likelihood of conversion.

One of the most effective ways to engage Prime viewers is through interactive video ads that encourage users to take immediate action. These types of ads can include clickable elements such as product links, exclusive offers, or interactive calls-to-action that invite users to explore more. For example, a video ad for a new pair of headphones could include a "Shop Now" button that directs users to the product page, enabling them to quickly make a purchase without leaving the video player. These interactive features enhance the user experience and provide a frictionless path to conversion, making it easier for viewers to act on their interest.

Moreover, measuring the performance of video ads is critical to understanding their impact and optimizing future campaigns. Amazon provides advertisers with a wealth of analytics and reporting tools to track key metrics such as view-through rates, click-through rates, engagement, and conversions. By analyzing these metrics, advertisers can gain insights into how their video ads are performing, which elements are resonating with viewers, and where there may be opportunities for improvement. Continuous testing and optimization are key to refining video ad strategies and ensuring they deliver the best possible results.

Running video ads to engage Prime viewers both on and off Amazon is an effective strategy that can significantly boost engagement, brand awareness, and conversions. By leveraging Amazon's robust targeting options, high-quality content, and cross-platform reach, advertisers can deliver highly relevant, personalized video ads that capture the attention of Prime members at the right time and place. With thoughtful targeting, compelling storytelling, and ongoing optimization, businesses can maximize the power of video advertising to drive success in the competitive landscape of Amazon's advertising ecosystem.

INTEGRATING DSP WITH YOUR EXISTING AMAZON ADVERTISING EFFORTS

Integrating Amazon's Demand-Side Platform (DSP) with your existing advertising efforts on the platform is a strategic approach that allows for a more cohesive, efficient, and effective advertising strategy. DSP offers robust tools that can amplify your reach, refine your targeting, and optimize your budget, all while seamlessly connecting with other aspects of your Amazon advertising campaigns. Understanding how to integrate DSP with your current advertising efforts is crucial to maximizing your potential for growth, improving the customer experience, and driving conversions.

One of the first steps to integrating DSP into your existing Amazon advertising strategy is understanding its capabilities and how it complements the other ad types available on the platform. Amazon offers a variety of advertising solutions, including Sponsored Products, Sponsored Brands, and Sponsored Display, each catering to different objectives and tactics. While these solutions are highly effective on their own, DSP allows you to extend your reach beyond Amazon's immediate ecosystem, accessing Amazon's vast data and inventory to display ads across other websites, mobile apps, and even streaming services like Amazon Prime Video. By integrating DSP with your current advertising approach, you can create a more unified campaign that not only targets users on Amazon but also reaches them across the web, on their mobile devices, and even on connected devices such as Fire TV.

To get started, it's essential to map out how DSP can complement your existing Amazon advertising efforts. Sponsored Products and Sponsored Brands are great tools for promoting specific products directly on Amazon's site, driving traffic to your product listings, and generating sales. However, DSP extends the reach of these campaigns by allowing you to target users outside Amazon's ecosystem, ensuring that your brand and products are seen in a wider context. For example, if you are running a Sponsored Brand campaign that showcases your product line on Amazon's search results or product detail pages, integrating DSP allows you to retarget users who have interacted with your brand but haven't yet converted. This retargeting can happen across Amazon's network and off-

Amazon properties, reinforcing your brand's presence and nudging potential customers closer to making a purchase.

One of the key benefits of DSP is its advanced targeting capabilities. You can use DSP to create highly customized audience segments based on data-driven insights, allowing you to reach customers based on their shopping behavior, interests, demographics, and even life events. By combining this data with your existing Amazon advertising campaigns, you can create more sophisticated, highly personalized ad experiences that resonate with users on a deeper level. For example, if you are running a Sponsored Product ad for a specific skincare item, DSP can help you target customers who have previously browsed skincare products, visited beauty-related pages, or made similar purchases. This audience targeting allows for more precise, effective advertising, improving your chances of conversion.

Another powerful feature of DSP is the ability to run display, video, and audio ads across multiple devices and platforms. This flexibility allows you to build a more integrated cross-channel campaign that includes video ads on Amazon Prime Video, display ads across third-party websites, and audio ads on streaming services like Amazon Music. By integrating DSP into your existing campaigns, you can create a comprehensive advertising experience that follows potential customers as they move across devices and platforms, ensuring that your brand remains top-of-mind as they interact with various forms of content. Running video ads, for instance, is a great way to engage customers who have already interacted with your products on Amazon, while display ads can help you target those browsing similar products on third-party websites, driving awareness and retargeting them to convert.

To integrate DSP effectively with your current efforts, you'll also need to leverage Amazon's unified reporting tools. Amazon offers comprehensive reporting and analytics that allow you to track and measure the performance of both your DSP and traditional ad campaigns in one place. By analyzing the performance of your DSP campaigns alongside your other ads, you can identify trends, measure return on investment (ROI), and pinpoint areas for optimization. This integration of data provides a more holistic view of your campaigns, helping you refine your strategies, adjust bidding strategies, and allocate budgets more effectively. The ability to monitor performance across various ad types and platforms helps you maximize the impact of each ad dollar spent, ensuring that every aspect of your advertising strategy is aligned and optimized.

Effective integration of DSP with your existing advertising efforts also involves adjusting your budget and bidding strategies. As DSP campaigns tend to have a broader reach and more complex targeting capabilities, it's essential to allocate sufficient resources to these efforts. Depending on your business goals, DSP can be used to complement or expand your current campaigns. For example, you may decide to use DSP for upper-funnel brand awareness and display ads, while focusing your Sponsored Product or Sponsored Brand campaigns on bottom-funnel conversion activities. This multi-layered approach ensures that your budget is effectively distributed across the various stages of the customer journey, driving both awareness and conversion.

In addition, utilizing DSP allows you to scale your campaigns based on performance. As your campaigns evolve, DSP gives you the ability to adjust and fine-tune your targeting, creative, and budgets on a granular level. For instance, if you notice that a specific audience segment is performing particularly well in your DSP campaign, you can increase your budget allocation to target that segment more aggressively. Conversely, if a certain segment isn't delivering the desired results, you can shift your focus and reallocate resources to other high-performing areas. This agility and flexibility in campaign management are essential for maximizing the overall effectiveness of your advertising strategy.

Another crucial aspect of DSP integration is creative optimization. As you run campaigns across various platforms and formats, it's important to tailor your creative assets to match the context and medium of the ad. For example, a video ad on Amazon Prime Video should be engaging, concise, and relevant to the content the viewer is consuming. Display ads on third-party websites, on the other hand, may require different creative formats and messaging to align with the browsing experience. By aligning your creative with the specific platform and audience, you can significantly improve the effectiveness of your DSP campaigns.

Lastly, integrating DSP with your current Amazon advertising efforts allows you to leverage Amazon's vast data and insights to refine your targeting strategy continually. The ability to segment audiences based on their purchase behavior, shopping intent, and viewing habits allows you to deliver highly personalized, relevant ads that drive better results. Moreover, as DSP is built on top of Amazon's robust data infrastructure, you can trust that you're accessing high-quality, actionable insights that will guide your advertising decisions.

Integrating DSP with your existing Amazon advertising efforts is a highly effective way to amplify your reach, optimize your targeting, and create a more cohesive and data-driven advertising strategy. By combining the power of DSP with other Amazon advertising solutions such as Sponsored Products and Sponsored Brands, you can build a comprehensive, multi-channel campaign that drives brand awareness, customer engagement, and conversions. Through careful planning, optimization, and data analysis, businesses can fully leverage DSP to maximize the effectiveness of their advertising campaigns and achieve sustained growth on Amazon's platform.

CHAPTER 14
MEASURING AND ANALYZING DSP CAMPAIGN PERFORMANCE

UNDERSTANDING DSP-SPECIFIC METRICS AND REPORTING

Understanding DSP-specific metrics and reporting is crucial for optimizing advertising efforts on Amazon's Demand-Side Platform (DSP). The ability to track, measure, and interpret the data from DSP campaigns enables advertisers to fine-tune their strategies, adjust their targeting, and allocate resources effectively to maximize returns on ad spend. DSP campaigns offer an advanced level of control and customization compared to traditional advertising methods, and understanding the metrics associated with DSP is the key to unlocking its full potential.

One of the foundational aspects of DSP-specific reporting is understanding the core set of metrics that help determine the effectiveness of a campaign. These metrics go beyond traditional impressions, clicks, and conversions, offering a deeper look at user engagement, audience targeting, and ad placement performance. To navigate DSP campaigns effectively, it is essential to understand how to interpret these metrics in a way that aligns with specific business objectives.

The first metric to understand is **impressions**. Impressions represent the number of times an ad is shown to a user, but on its own, this number doesn't provide enough context. It is important to analyze impressions in combination with other engagement metrics to understand how well your ad is performing. High impressions might seem promising, but if they are not leading to other valuable actions like clicks or conversions, then the ad's effectiveness may be limited. Therefore, impressions should be evaluated alongside metrics like **click-through rate (CTR)**, which measures the percentage of users who clicked on the ad after seeing it. A low CTR despite high impressions could indicate that your ad creative or targeting needs to be adjusted.

Next, **clicks** and **click-through rate (CTR)** are pivotal in assessing how compelling your ad is to potential customers. While impressions show the ad's visibility, clicks indicate the level of interest or action taken by users. CTR is calculated by dividing the number of clicks by the number of impressions, and this metric provides valuable insight into the effectiveness of the ad copy and visuals. A high CTR typically suggests that the ad resonates with the target audience and encourages interaction. However, if the CTR is low, it may signal that your targeting needs refinement or that your ad design is not catching users' attention as effectively as it could be.

Conversions are one of the most important metrics to track in DSP campaigns. Conversion is defined as the action that a user takes after interacting with the ad, which could include making a purchase, signing up for a service, or completing another desired action. Conversion tracking allows you to understand how well your DSP campaign is driving real business results. However, it's important to consider **conversion rate**, which calculates the percentage of users who made a purchase after clicking on an ad. This metric can be impacted by factors such as ad relevance, the user experience on your product page, and the overall appeal of the product being advertised.

Another critical metric is **cost-per-click (CPC)**. CPC refers to how much you pay each time a user clicks on your ad. This metric helps you understand how much you are investing in driving traffic to your listings or website. Monitoring CPC allows you to assess whether your ad spend is efficient and if it aligns with your return on investment (ROI). Lower CPC values generally mean that your ad is cost-effective in driving clicks, while higher CPC values could indicate that you are overpaying for the traffic generated by your ads.

Cost-per-acquisition (CPA) is another important metric, and it complements CPC by focusing on the cost of converting a user rather than just getting a click. CPA is the total cost of the campaign divided by the number of conversions it generated. This metric is particularly useful for understanding the overall efficiency of your advertising spend. A high CPA may suggest that although you are driving clicks, those clicks are not converting into sales at an optimal rate. If the CPA is higher than the profit generated from the conversions, it could indicate that the campaign needs optimization to improve its performance.

Tracking **return on ad spend (ROAS)** is essential for determining the profitability of a DSP campaign. ROAS measures the revenue generated for every dollar spent on advertising. It is a direct way of calculating how much money you're making in relation to what you're spending on your DSP campaigns. A higher ROAS means that the campaign is generating more revenue relative to the advertising cost, which is a clear indicator of success. However, if the ROAS is too low, you may need to revisit your campaign's targeting, creatives, or even the overall approach to optimize the return on your ad spend.

View-through conversions are another DSP-specific metric that advertisers should track. This metric captures the number of conversions that occur after a user has viewed an ad but has not clicked on it. The view-through conversion metric is important because it helps to measure the impact of ad visibility even when users don't immediately engage with the ad. It can provide valuable insights into how effective your ad is at generating brand awareness and influencing purchasing decisions, even without direct interaction. By analyzing view-through conversions, you can better understand the longer-term influence of your ads and how they might be helping to move potential customers down the purchase funnel.

Engagement metrics are also worth monitoring in DSP campaigns. These can include metrics like video completion rates for video ads, which show the percentage of viewers who watch the entire video ad. Engagement metrics are especially important when running video or display ads because they provide insight into how compelling and captivating your ad creative is. High engagement rates typically correlate with more effective storytelling or messaging that resonates with the target audience. On the other hand, low engagement rates might suggest that the content isn't resonating with users, necessitating a review of the creative approach or targeting strategy.

Another metric to consider is **frequency**, which refers to the average number of times an individual sees your ad. While higher frequency can improve brand recall and awareness, it can also lead to ad fatigue, where users begin to ignore or become irritated by repetitive exposure to the same ad. Monitoring frequency allows you to find the optimal balance of ad exposure, ensuring that users see your ad enough times to be influenced without overexposing them, which can be counterproductive.

For DSP campaigns that involve multiple ad formats, it's crucial to evaluate the performance of different ad types individually. **Display ads**, for example, may have a different set of performance expectations compared to **video ads** or **audio ads**. Display ads typically focus on creating awareness and driving traffic, while video ads are often used to engage users emotionally and deliver a more immersive brand experience. Each ad type will have different engagement rates, conversion patterns, and cost structures, so understanding how each ad format is performing within the DSP reporting framework is essential for campaign optimization.

Attribution models play a critical role in DSP reporting. Attribution models help you understand the customer journey by attributing credit to different touchpoints in the path to conversion. For example, you may want to use a last-click attribution model, which gives full credit to the last interaction a user had before making a purchase, or a first-click model, which attributes the conversion to the first ad interaction. By experimenting with different attribution models, you can better understand how your DSP ads are influencing customers at various stages of the buying process and adjust your strategy accordingly.

Understanding DSP-specific metrics and reporting is fundamental for any advertiser looking to maximize the effectiveness of their campaigns on Amazon. By focusing on key performance indicators such as impressions, CTR, conversions, CPC, CPA, ROAS, and view-through conversions, you can gain valuable insights into how well your ads are performing. Moreover, tracking engagement metrics, frequency, and ad format performance enables you to fine-tune your strategy and ensure that your DSP campaigns deliver the desired results. With a thorough understanding of these metrics, you can make data-driven decisions that lead to better-targeted campaigns, improved ad spend efficiency, and ultimately, higher returns on your advertising investment.

ANALYZING AUDIENCE PERFORMANCE AND OPTIMIZING TARGETING

When it comes to advertising on a dynamic and competitive platform like Amazon Prime, it's essential to understand the importance of analyzing audience performance and optimizing targeting. The success of any advertising strategy hinges not just on creating compelling ads, but on knowing your audience intimately—what they respond to, when they engage, and how to best reach them. If you're looking to achieve lasting results with your Amazon Prime campaigns, focusing on these aspects is the key to unlocking higher conversion rates and ensuring your budget is spent effectively.

First and foremost, understanding who your audience is and what drives them is the cornerstone of any successful advertising campaign. Amazon Prime offers a vast and diverse user base, so if you want to stand out, you need to zero in on the individuals most likely to be interested in your product. But how do you determine who these people are? It all starts with gathering data. Using Amazon's advertising tools, such as Amazon Marketing Services (AMS), you can access valuable insights about your audience's demographics, purchasing behavior, and viewing habits.

These insights are powerful because they help you identify patterns that reveal key audience segments. For example, Amazon provides data such as age groups, geographic locations, interests, and even the types of products customers are searching for. By understanding these details, you can tailor your campaigns to appeal directly to the audience that is most likely to engage with your content. The key here is segmentation. Not every person who uses Amazon Prime is going to be interested in your product, so dividing your audience into specific segments allows you to target your ads more precisely, saving you both time and money.

Once you have segmented your audience, the next step is to analyze how each group is performing. To do this effectively, it's essential to track the metrics that matter. Amazon Prime provides a comprehensive suite of analytics tools that allow you to monitor your ad campaigns in real-time. Metrics such as click-through rate (CTR), conversion rate, and return on ad spend (ROAS) can help you determine how well your campaigns are performing for different audience segments. For instance, if one segment is showing high engagement but low conversion, it may indicate that while the audience is interested, the landing page or product offering needs optimization. On the other hand, if a particular segment is converting well, this is a signal to double down on that audience and continue creating ads that resonate with their interests.

Optimization doesn't stop at audience segmentation and monitoring performance metrics. You also need to fine-tune your targeting strategies based on the data you gather. This involves testing different ad formats, adjusting your bids, and refining your creative assets to appeal to the specific needs of your audience. For example, you may find that a video ad featuring a product demonstration resonates more with one segment, while a still image ad highlighting product benefits is more effective with another group. Amazon's platform allows for A/B testing, so you can run different ad versions and analyze which one yields the best results. By continually testing and adjusting, you create a cycle of improvement that keeps your campaigns fresh and optimized.

In addition to optimizing the creative aspects of your ads, another crucial factor is the timing and placement of your advertisements. Audience behavior on Amazon Prime isn't static; it changes based on time of day, week, and even season. By analyzing your audience's engagement patterns, you can schedule your ads to run at times when they are most likely to convert. For example, if you're selling fitness equipment, you might find that users engage with your ads more frequently in the morning before their workouts or in the evenings when they're winding down. By running your ads during peak engagement hours, you increase the likelihood of reaching your audience when they are most receptive to your message.

Optimizing ad placement is another essential component of your targeting strategy. Amazon Prime offers multiple ways to serve ads, including on the Amazon website, within Prime Video, and across third-party websites that are part of the Amazon Advertising Network. Each placement comes with its own set of advantages and challenges, and understanding which locations work best for your audience is vital. For instance, if you're advertising a product related to movies or television, ads within the Prime Video environment may be more effective because users are already immersed in the content. On the other hand, if your product is more general, you might find that displaying your ads on the Amazon website itself drives more traffic.

As you continue to analyze and optimize your campaigns, it's important to stay on top of the evolving trends within Amazon's advertising ecosystem. Amazon frequently updates its platform with new tools, features, and targeting options that can enhance the precision of your campaigns. For example, Amazon recently introduced the ability to use machine learning algorithms to predict which users are most likely to make a purchase. These predictive models can improve targeting accuracy and help you reach customers who are at the optimal stage in their buying journey.

Furthermore, while Amazon offers rich insights into audience behavior on its platform, it's also valuable to integrate data from other sources to create a more comprehensive picture of your audience. By leveraging third-party analytics tools or customer feedback, you can gain additional insights that enrich your understanding of who your audience is and how they interact with your brand across different channels.

The ultimate goal of analyzing audience performance and optimizing targeting is to maximize your return on investment. This requires a deep understanding of how your audience behaves, how they respond to different types of content, and how to reach them in a way that leads to conversions. The more you refine your targeting, the more efficient your campaigns become, and the greater your chances of achieving sustained success on Amazon Prime.

Analyzing audience performance and optimizing targeting on Amazon Prime requires a combination of data-driven decision-making, continuous testing, and strategic adjustments. By diving into the wealth of analytics available on the platform and consistently refining your approach, you'll be able to fine-tune your campaigns, reach the right customers, and ultimately drive sales. As Amazon's advertising tools continue to evolve, staying informed about new features and trends will ensure that your campaigns remain at the forefront of the competition, positioning you for success in an ever-changing digital marketplace.

EVALUATING THE ROI OF YOUR DSP CAMPAIGNS

When running a Demand-Side Platform (DSP) campaign on Amazon, it's essential to evaluate the return on investment (ROI) in order to determine whether your efforts are paying off. DSP campaigns allow advertisers to purchase ad space programmatically and optimize their efforts across Amazon's vast network, but without assessing the ROI, it's impossible to know if your campaigns are truly driving value. Evaluating ROI involves more than simply looking at whether you made a profit. It requires an in-depth analysis of several factors, including ad spend, conversion rates, customer engagement, and overall impact on your brand's long-term success. Let's dive deeper into the key elements that will help you effectively evaluate the ROI of your DSP campaigns and fine-tune them to drive even better results.

At the core of ROI evaluation is a clear understanding of what ROI means in the context of a DSP campaign. Unlike traditional advertising, where ROI may be focused solely on direct sales or immediate conversions, DSP campaigns take a more nuanced approach. You might be running a DSP campaign to increase brand awareness, drive traffic to your product listings, or generate sales. Therefore, the ROI metrics will vary depending on your specific campaign objectives.

One of the first steps in evaluating ROI is to establish clear and measurable goals for your DSP campaign. Without clear objectives, it becomes difficult to determine what success looks like. Are you aiming for a specific sales target? Is the goal to increase brand visibility and awareness in a specific region? Perhaps you're working on increasing customer engagement or driving repeat purchases. By setting distinct and measurable goals, you provide yourself with a roadmap to assess whether the campaign's results align with your expectations.

After establishing your goals, you'll need to track the appropriate performance metrics. These metrics serve as the foundation for any ROI evaluation, and they provide the data necessary to measure success. One of the most important metrics to monitor is your total ad spend, which includes the amount you paid for impressions, clicks, and conversions. This figure will help you calculate the cost associated with each action your campaign drives. You'll also need to track the number of impressions your ad receives, which represents how often your ad is shown to potential customers. While impressions alone don't guarantee success, they are a crucial indicator of reach and exposure.

However, measuring ROI is not just about tracking costs and impressions. Conversions are key to understanding how effective your campaign is at moving potential customers from consideration to action. Conversions refer to the number of people who complete a desired action, such as purchasing your product after interacting with your ad. Evaluating the conversion rate allows you to gauge how well your ads are resonating with your target audience. A high conversion rate suggests that your ads are compelling and persuasive, while a low conversion rate indicates that adjustments may be needed, whether in terms of ad content, targeting, or user experience.

In addition to conversions, it's critical to examine your customer's lifetime value (CLV). CLV is a projection of the total revenue you can expect from a customer over the course of their relationship with your brand. This is especially important for evaluating ROI on DSP campaigns because it helps to account for long-term value, rather than just one-off purchases. When evaluating ROI on DSP campaigns, it's essential to factor in how much revenue a customer might bring in over time, beyond their first purchase. Even if a customer doesn't convert immediately, they might engage with your brand in the future, resulting in future sales that contribute to your campaign's overall success.

Alongside conversions and lifetime value, another critical metric is the return on ad spend (ROAS). ROAS measures the total revenue generated by your ad campaign relative to the amount spent on advertising. For instance, if you spent $500 on an ad campaign and generated $2,000 in sales, your ROAS would be 4:1, meaning for every dollar you spent, you earned four dollars in return. ROAS offers a clear, tangible way to measure the profitability of your campaigns. A high ROAS indicates that your ads are generating strong returns, while a low ROAS suggests that you may need to optimize your campaigns to increase efficiency and effectiveness.

While calculating metrics like ad spend and ROAS provides insight into the financial impact of your campaign, evaluating the overall performance of your DSP campaigns requires a more holistic approach. Sometimes, the true value of a campaign may not be immediately apparent. For example, a campaign aimed at raising awareness about a new product may not generate immediate sales but may position your brand to see increased sales over time. This kind of indirect impact can be just as important as direct conversions. A long-term perspective is therefore crucial when measuring ROI, especially in the competitive and fast-moving world of digital advertising.

Additionally, a key factor in ROI evaluation is optimizing your targeting strategy. Amazon's DSP platform allows advertisers to target specific audiences based on factors like their purchasing behavior, interests, demographics, and browsing history. By monitoring the performance of different audience segments, you can identify which groups are most responsive to your ads and which aren't. If certain audience segments are not converting at the expected rate, consider refining your targeting or trying new approaches. Testing different types of creatives, adjusting bids, or shifting targeting parameters may help improve your ROI over time.

Moreover, it's also important to measure the performance of different ad formats and placements. DSP campaigns on Amazon allow you to display ads across various channels, including Amazon's own website, third-party sites, and within Amazon Prime Video. Depending on the nature of your product and your audience's behavior, certain placements may drive higher engagement and conversions. For instance, video ads may perform better for products in categories like electronics or entertainment, while display ads might work well for everyday consumer goods. Experimenting with different ad formats and placements will help you better understand where to allocate your resources for optimal results.

Another crucial aspect of evaluating ROI is ensuring that you're tracking the right attribution models. Attribution refers to the process of determining which touchpoints in a customer's journey influenced their decision to convert. In a DSP campaign, there are many potential touchpoints, including clicks, impressions, and views, and each one may play a role in driving a sale. By employing an accurate attribution model, you can gain deeper insights into how your ads are performing across various stages of the customer journey. Whether you use last-click, first-click, or multi-touch attribution models, understanding how customers interact with your ads at different stages will help you fine-tune your strategy and budget allocation.

It's important to stay informed about industry trends and changes in Amazon's advertising ecosystem. Amazon regularly updates its DSP features, introduces new ad formats, and provides new ways to track performance. Keeping up to date with these changes allows you to adapt your campaigns to maximize ROI and stay ahead of the competition. The world of programmatic advertising is constantly evolving, and staying flexible and responsive to these shifts will help ensure that your campaigns remain profitable and effective over time.

Evaluating the ROI of your DSP campaigns is an essential aspect of digital advertising on Amazon. By focusing on key performance metrics such as ad spend, conversions, ROAS, and customer lifetime value, you can determine whether your campaigns are achieving the desired results. Additionally, adopting a holistic, long-term perspective, optimizing your targeting strategies, experimenting with ad formats and placements, and using the right attribution models will all contribute to a more accurate and comprehensive ROI evaluation. Ultimately, the more you refine and optimize your DSP campaigns, the greater your chances of driving sustained success on the Amazon platform.

WORKING WITH AMAZON MANAGED SERVICES OR SELF-SERVICE DSP

When it comes to advertising on Amazon Prime, one of the most crucial decisions you'll make is choosing between Amazon Managed Services (AMS) or the Self-Service Demand-Side Platform (DSP). Each option comes with its own set of advantages and challenges, and understanding the differences between them is essential to creating a successful advertising strategy. Whether you're a seasoned marketer or just getting started, this choice will have a significant impact on your campaigns, budget management, and overall outcomes. Understanding how these two services work and how they align with your specific goals is key to mastering the platform and driving real success.

Amazon Managed Services (AMS) is a fully managed advertising solution where Amazon's team of experts works directly with you to create, manage, and optimize your ad campaigns. This service is ideal for advertisers who may not have the in-house expertise, resources, or time to manage their campaigns independently but still want to leverage Amazon's advertising tools to their fullest potential. When you choose AMS, you're essentially outsourcing the campaign management to Amazon's skilled professionals, who use their deep knowledge of the platform, algorithms, and customer behavior to craft a strategy that meets your goals.

AMS allows you to tap into Amazon's wealth of data and insights to create highly targeted campaigns. The managed service is particularly beneficial for advertisers who want to avoid the complexities of manual campaign management or don't have the bandwidth to dive into the nuances of programmatic advertising. Amazon's team takes care of the entire process, from setting up your campaigns to optimizing targeting, monitoring performance, and adjusting bids in real-time. This hands-off approach ensures that your campaigns are in the hands of experts who are continuously analyzing performance and refining strategies to maximize your ad spend.

On the other hand, the Self-Service DSP provides advertisers with full control over their campaigns. This platform allows you to purchase ad space programmatically and manage your campaigns directly through Amazon's DSP interface. Unlike AMS, where the management is handled by Amazon, the Self-Service DSP empowers you to create and optimize your own campaigns. This option is best suited for advertisers who have a solid understanding of the advertising ecosystem and the tools necessary to run and manage their campaigns effectively.

The Self-Service DSP offers a great deal of flexibility and autonomy. It allows you to build customized campaigns, choose your target audience, select placements, and adjust bids as needed. With this level of control, advertisers can implement more granular targeting strategies based on demographics, purchase behavior, browsing history, and even in-market signals. Furthermore, you can track your campaigns in real-time and make immediate adjustments to optimize performance. This can be especially valuable for those who prefer a hands-on approach and want to closely monitor how their ads are performing.

One of the major benefits of using the Self-Service DSP is the ability to experiment and test different campaign elements. You can create multiple ad creatives, test different bidding strategies, and adjust targeting to see what resonates best with your audience. This level of experimentation can lead to more refined strategies and higher-performing campaigns over time. For advertisers with the time and expertise to dive into the data, the Self-Service DSP offers greater opportunities for innovation and optimization.

However, this autonomy comes with its own set of challenges. Managing a DSP campaign requires a thorough understanding of programmatic advertising, bid management, and audience segmentation. If you're new to this space or don't have the resources to monitor your campaigns closely, it can be overwhelming. The Self-Service DSP demands a greater investment of time and knowledge to ensure that campaigns are running efficiently and delivering the desired results. Without expertise in ad targeting, bidding strategies, and data analysis, there's a risk of overspending on ads that aren't driving the desired outcomes.

When choosing between AMS and the Self-Service DSP, it's important to evaluate your team's expertise, your budget, and your campaign goals. AMS is an excellent choice for those who prefer a more hands-off approach and want Amazon's experts to guide them through the process. It's also beneficial for businesses that don't have the resources to manage campaigns internally or for those looking for a more streamlined, turnkey solution. AMS offers the benefit of having access to Amazon's knowledge and experience, ensuring that your campaigns are well-executed and optimized for success.

In contrast, the Self-Service DSP offers flexibility, control, and the ability to experiment with various targeting strategies and ad formats. It's best suited for those who have the necessary resources and expertise to manage campaigns independently. If your team is comfortable with programmatic advertising and understands how to track key performance metrics, the Self-Service DSP can offer a more hands-on approach to advertising that may yield even more customized results. Additionally, with the Self-Service DSP, you have direct access to real-time performance data, giving you immediate insights into how your campaigns are performing and what adjustments need to be made.

One important consideration when working with either AMS or the Self-Service DSP is the level of data and insights you have access to. Amazon provides both options with robust analytics tools, but there are some differences in the level of granularity you can access. With AMS, Amazon's team is responsible for monitoring the data and optimizing the campaign on your behalf. While you can still view performance reports, the primary responsibility for analyzing and adjusting campaigns lies with Amazon's experts. This might limit your ability to delve into the details of your campaigns in the same way that you can with the Self-Service DSP.

The Self-Service DSP, on the other hand, provides you with full control over your data. You can track every aspect of your campaign, including impressions, clicks, conversions, and other important metrics. This level of transparency allows you to make data-driven decisions and quickly identify what's working and what's not. The ability to track campaigns in real-time also gives you the opportunity to make swift adjustments, whether it's tweaking your targeting parameters, adjusting bids, or experimenting with new ad creatives.

Another factor to consider is the level of customization available in each service. With AMS, your ad creatives and targeting are optimized based on the strategies that Amazon's team believes will be most effective. While this can be highly effective, it may not always align with your brand's vision or specific requirements. The Self-Service DSP offers much more flexibility in terms of creative freedom, allowing you to develop ads that resonate directly with your brand and customers. You have full control over the creative process, including choosing ad formats, placements, and messages, which can lead to more tailored, personalized campaigns.

Ultimately, the choice between Amazon Managed Services and the Self-Service DSP comes down to how much control you want over your campaigns and how much expertise you have at your disposal. If you're looking for a hands-off solution with expert guidance and management, AMS is the way to go. It provides a hassle-free experience where Amazon's team handles all the heavy lifting. On the other hand, if you prefer a more hands-on approach, want to experiment with different strategies, and have the resources to manage your campaigns, the Self-Service DSP is the better option. Both options offer powerful tools and features, but your decision should align with your business goals, resources, and level of expertise in programmatic advertising.

In the end, both AMS and the Self-Service DSP have their place in an Amazon advertising strategy. The decision comes down to the amount of time and effort you're willing to invest in campaign management and whether you prefer expert guidance or the autonomy to manage your own campaigns. Each option has its strengths and challenges, but by understanding how they work, you can choose the one that best fits your business needs and drives the most success.

BEST PRACTICES FOR LONG-TERM DSP SUCCESS

Achieving long-term success with Demand-Side Platform (DSP) campaigns on Amazon requires a thoughtful and strategic approach. Amazon DSP provides powerful tools that enable advertisers to purchase and manage programmatic advertising, but simply launching a campaign is not enough to ensure sustained success. To truly thrive, advertisers must embrace best practices that focus on optimization, refinement, and continuous learning. Whether you are just starting with DSP or looking to refine your current approach, adopting these best practices can help you build a foundation for long-term success, ensure optimal performance, and maximize your return on investment (ROI).

One of the most critical aspects of long-term DSP success is setting clear and measurable goals from the very beginning. Without defined objectives, it's impossible to evaluate whether your campaigns are meeting expectations or driving the results you need. These goals should go beyond just increasing sales; they should be aligned with your broader business strategy. Are you looking to increase brand awareness, generate traffic to your product listings, or engage a specific audience segment? Establishing measurable and realistic goals helps guide every decision you make, from targeting to budgeting, and provides a framework for tracking success. It's also important to recognize that different campaigns may have different objectives. A brand awareness campaign will look very different from one focused on driving conversions, and your approach should reflect that.

Once your goals are set, you need to continuously monitor and optimize your campaigns. Optimization is at the heart of DSP advertising, and it's an ongoing process that requires attention to detail and agility. One of the most effective ways to optimize your campaigns is by regularly analyzing the performance data and making informed adjustments. Amazon's DSP offers a wealth of data that includes metrics such as impressions, clicks, conversions, cost per acquisition (CPA), return on ad spend (ROAS), and customer lifetime value (CLV). These metrics provide deep insights into how your ads are performing across various touchpoints. Monitoring these numbers in real-time allows you to spot any underperforming areas and adjust accordingly. For example, if you notice that your ads are receiving plenty of impressions but low conversions, you may need to rethink your targeting or ad creatives.

Another important element of optimization is adjusting your bids. Bidding strategies play a crucial role in how your ads are served and can directly impact campaign performance. In programmatic advertising, Amazon's DSP uses auction-based bidding, where advertisers compete for ad inventory based on their bids. One key to long-term success is setting appropriate bids that reflect the value of your target audience and the competition within your niche. Too high a bid can lead to overspending, while too low a bid can cause your ads to be overlooked. Regularly assessing your bidding strategies and adjusting them based on the performance of your campaigns will help maintain an efficient budget and ensure that your ads are reaching the right audience at the right time.

Another best practice is to continuously refine and expand your targeting. Amazon's DSP allows advertisers to target audiences based on a variety of factors, such as demographics, shopping behavior, purchase history, and interests. However, even with these sophisticated targeting options, it's essential to regularly test and experiment with different audience segments. Over time, you may discover new customer groups that are highly responsive to your ads, while others may underperform. Regularly testing different targeting strategies and expanding your audience reach allows you to identify which segments provide the best return on investment. It's also important to take advantage of Amazon's lookalike targeting, which allows you to reach new customers who share similar characteristics to your existing buyers. This approach can be particularly powerful for finding high-converting customers who are more likely to engage with your brand.

Beyond targeting, creative optimization is another essential component of long-term DSP success. Your ad creatives must resonate with your audience and effectively communicate your brand's value proposition. Experimenting with different ad formats, such as display ads, video ads, and interactive ads, allows you to see which formats work best for your goals. Video ads, for example, can be highly effective for storytelling and building deeper emotional connections with your audience, while display ads may be more suitable for driving quick actions like purchases or clicks. By continuously testing different ad creatives and formats, you can refine your messaging, visuals, and calls to action to maximize engagement and conversions.

In addition to creative optimization, it's important to maintain a focus on frequency capping. While it's essential to reach your target audience, bombarding them with the same ads repeatedly can lead to ad fatigue, where consumers become less responsive or even annoyed by your messaging. By setting frequency caps, you can ensure that your ads are shown at the right intervals without overwhelming your audience. This not only helps maintain a positive brand experience but also ensures that your ads remain fresh and engaging over time. Finding the right balance between exposure and repetition is key to sustaining interest and engagement in your campaigns.

One aspect of long-term DSP success that often gets overlooked is the importance of attribution and tracking. Attribution refers to the process of understanding how different touchpoints in a customer's journey contribute to the final conversion. Amazon's DSP allows advertisers to track the customer journey across various channels, providing insights into how ads on Amazon Prime, Amazon.com, and third-party sites interact to influence consumer behavior. By using multi-touch attribution, you can better understand the role of each touchpoint in driving conversions, which enables you to optimize your campaigns more effectively. For example, if you notice that video ads have a significant impact on consumer awareness but display ads drive more conversions, you can allocate your budget accordingly to maximize both short-term and long-term results.

Equally important is building customer relationships beyond the first purchase. Many advertisers focus on acquiring new customers but overlook the potential value of existing customers. Building a long-term customer base through retargeting and remarketing is crucial for sustained growth. By using data from previous campaigns to retarget customers who have engaged with your brand but have not yet converted, you can increase the likelihood of turning one-time visitors into repeat buyers. Additionally, remarketing can help reinforce brand loyalty and increase the lifetime value of each customer. This approach not only drives immediate revenue but also contributes to the long-term success of your DSP strategy by building a more loyal and engaged customer base.

Furthermore, a successful DSP strategy requires an understanding of the ever-changing landscape of Amazon's advertising ecosystem. The digital advertising world is constantly evolving, and staying up-to-date with new features, ad formats, and targeting capabilities is essential. Amazon regularly updates its DSP platform with new tools and functionality, and advertisers who are quick to adopt these changes often gain a competitive edge. Regularly reviewing the latest features and staying informed about updates ensures that your campaigns remain relevant and innovative. It also allows you to leverage the full potential of the DSP platform, enabling you to stay ahead of competitors and continuously optimize your campaigns for success.

Lastly, collaboration and knowledge sharing are vital for long-term DSP success. Whether you're working with a dedicated Amazon account manager, an agency partner, or your internal team, ensuring open communication and collaboration can significantly improve campaign performance. By sharing insights, feedback, and performance data, you can identify new opportunities, solve challenges, and refine your strategy. Regularly reviewing campaign results with key stakeholders and having a feedback loop in place allows you to continuously adapt and improve your approach.

Achieving long-term DSP success requires a commitment to continuous optimization, experimentation, and learning. By setting clear goals, monitoring performance, refining targeting, testing creatives, and staying informed about industry changes, you can build a strong foundation for sustained growth. It's also crucial to focus on customer retention, attribution, and collaboration to ensure that your campaigns deliver long-term value. With these best practices in mind, you'll be well on your way to mastering Amazon DSP and driving success for your brand over the long haul.

PART 6

Driving Success and Maximizing Your Amazon Prime
Advertising ROI

CHAPTER 15

INTEGRATING ADVERTISING WITH YOUR OVERALL AMAZON STRATEGY

OPTIMIZING PRODUCT LISTINGS FOR CONVERSION

When it comes to driving conversions on Amazon, optimizing your product listings is one of the most effective strategies you can employ. Your product listing is the first impression potential customers have of your brand and products, and it serves as a key decision-making point in the buying process. A well-optimized listing not only attracts shoppers but also convinces them to click the "Buy" button. Achieving a high conversion rate on Amazon is an ongoing process that requires attention to detail, a deep understanding of consumer behavior, and the continuous refinement of your listings to match customer expectations.

The foundation of a highly optimized product listing starts with an understanding of what influences a customer's decision to purchase. Customers come to Amazon with an intent to buy, but they also expect a seamless, informative, and engaging shopping experience. A product listing that fails to provide clear, relevant, and compelling information can quickly turn potential buyers away, even if the product is high-quality and competitively priced. Optimizing your product listings for conversion means ensuring that every element of your listing, from the title to the product images, works together to persuade the customer that your product is the best choice.

One of the most important aspects of a product listing is the product title. The title is the first thing customers see, and it must immediately communicate the key attributes of the product while also including relevant keywords. Effective titles are clear, concise, and contain the most important search terms customers would use when looking for a product like yours. A product title that is too vague or overly complicated can confuse customers, causing them to lose interest before even learning more about the product. On the other hand, a well-crafted title not only boosts your product's visibility in search results but also ensures that the right customers are clicking on your listing. Including details such as brand, size, color, and other relevant features will make it easier for customers to understand what your product offers at a glance. It's important to remember, though, that Amazon has specific guidelines regarding title length and formatting, and it's crucial to follow these rules to avoid listing violations.

In addition to a compelling title, high-quality product images are essential for driving conversions. A picture speaks a thousand words, and on Amazon, the product image is often the deciding factor between a potential customer clicking on your listing or moving on to the next option. Customers rely heavily on images to understand the look and feel of a product, so providing clear, high-resolution images that showcase your product from different angles and in various settings is crucial. Amazon allows multiple images, so use this opportunity to show your product in use, highlight key features, and give potential buyers a full picture of what they can expect. Product images should be well-lit, professional, and free of distractions. A cluttered or poorly composed image can detract from the product's appeal and leave customers questioning the quality of the item.

Alongside great images, the product description is a powerful tool in convincing customers to convert. While the title and images give customers the first glimpse of the product, the product description is where you have the chance to fully explain the features and benefits of your product. A product description should be informative, engaging, and easy to read. It's essential to clearly outline the benefits of the product and how it solves a problem or meets a need. While customers appreciate technical details, they are often more focused on how the product will enhance their life or improve their situation. Therefore, rather than simply listing features, focus on showing the value the product brings. It's important to use simple, conversational language that resonates with your audience while also providing enough detail to make an informed purchasing decision.

The product bullet points on Amazon are also an integral part of the listing, offering another opportunity to communicate key information about your product. Bullet points are often used to highlight the most important selling points of the product, such as unique features, size, material, and benefits. These should be concise but impactful, giving customers the essential information they need at a glance. Think of the bullet points as a way to quickly answer any questions a potential customer might have. Including both technical specifications and more customer-centric information—such as how the product enhances convenience, comfort, or lifestyle—helps strike a balance that appeals to a wider range of shoppers.

A critical part of optimizing your listing for conversion is leveraging keywords. Keywords play a major role in driving traffic to your product, but they also impact how your listing is ranked and displayed on Amazon. Conducting thorough keyword research is essential to ensure that your listing appears in relevant searches and attracts the right audience. Use tools like Amazon's search bar, competitor listings, and external keyword research platforms to identify the most relevant search terms for your product. Once you have a list of effective keywords, naturally incorporate them into your product title, description, bullet points, and backend search terms. However, avoid keyword stuffing, as this can make your listing look spammy and hurt your conversion rate. The goal is to use keywords in a way that reads naturally while also providing relevant information to the customer.

Pricing is another crucial factor in the conversion equation. While it may seem straightforward, pricing can be the difference between a customer choosing your product or selecting a competitor's. The price must reflect the value of the product and align with what customers are willing to pay. To optimize for conversion, ensure that your price is competitive within your market and comparable to similar products. Amazon offers a pricing tool that allows sellers to set competitive pricing while considering market trends, competition, and other relevant factors. Additionally, Amazon's dynamic pricing model means that prices can fluctuate depending on demand, inventory levels, and other external factors. Regularly reviewing and adjusting your pricing ensures that you stay competitive without sacrificing your profit margins.

Reviews and ratings are powerful social proof that can significantly impact your conversion rates. Positive reviews act as a seal of approval for your product, reassuring customers that they are making a wise purchasing decision. In fact, customers often rely on reviews to validate their choices, with many shoppers trusting peer recommendations more than product descriptions. Encourage satisfied customers to leave reviews, and actively engage with your customer base by responding to feedback. Addressing negative reviews professionally and offering solutions can also build trust and show potential buyers that you are committed to customer satisfaction. However, while reviews are important, it's equally critical to ensure that your product meets the high expectations that reviews imply. A product with negative reviews or low ratings can lead to decreased trust, lower conversion rates, and potential sales losses.

Another element that can optimize your product listing for conversion is enhanced brand content or A+ Content. This feature allows brand owners to enhance their product descriptions with rich media, including additional images, comparison charts, and detailed product information. Enhanced content helps tell the story of your brand and product in a more visually appealing way, which can increase engagement and boost conversion rates. A+ Content also improves the listing's SEO, ensuring that your product is more discoverable on Amazon. Creating compelling A+ Content that speaks directly to your customers' needs can provide a strong competitive edge, particularly when shoppers are comparing multiple products in the same category.

Consider leveraging promotions and deals as part of your conversion optimization strategy. Amazon offers various promotional tools, such as coupons, lightning deals, and discounts, that can encourage customers to make a purchase. These time-sensitive offers create urgency and can help persuade customers to buy now rather than wait. Incorporating promotions into your listings can increase visibility, attract price-sensitive customers, and drive sales, particularly during peak shopping periods like Amazon Prime Day or the holiday season.

Optimizing your product listings for conversion is not a one-time task but rather an ongoing effort. It requires a deep understanding of your target audience, continuous testing, and the ability to adapt to market trends. A well-optimized listing can be the difference between a high conversion rate and a missed opportunity. By refining your titles, images, descriptions, keywords, pricing, reviews, and promotional strategies, you can ensure that your product listings not only attract traffic but also convert that traffic into loyal customers. Regularly analyzing and adjusting your approach based on performance data will help you maintain a competitive edge and continue driving success over the long term.

LEVERAGING AMAZON PRIME BADGES AND BENEFITS

In the highly competitive world of e-commerce, every tool at your disposal plays a critical role in securing customer trust, driving sales, and enhancing brand visibility. One of the most powerful assets on the Amazon platform is the array of badges and benefits associated with Amazon Prime. These features not only differentiate your products in a crowded marketplace but also offer unique opportunities to maximize your sales potential. Leveraging Amazon Prime badges and benefits requires an understanding of how they work, how they influence customer behavior, and how they can be incorporated into your strategy to achieve sustained success.

Amazon Prime is much more than a subscription service; it's a powerful driver of consumer behavior. Prime members enjoy a host of benefits, from fast shipping to exclusive deals, and these advantages shape their buying decisions. As a seller, gaining access to these benefits and displaying the right Prime badges on your listings can significantly boost your product's appeal, making it more likely to attract clicks and convert shoppers into buyers. In fact, many shoppers filter their search results to show only Prime-eligible products, so having a product that's part of the Prime ecosystem can give you a distinct competitive advantage.

One of the most recognizable and sought-after features of Amazon Prime is the Prime badge itself. This badge signifies that the product is available for fast, free shipping through the Amazon Prime program, which is a major selling point for Amazon's most loyal customers. The Prime badge provides an instant sense of convenience and trustworthiness, which are key factors that influence purchasing decisions. For Prime members, the availability of a Prime badge can be the difference between choosing one product over another. When shopping on Amazon, customers are often seeking fast, reliable delivery, and the Prime badge offers them peace of mind that they can receive their items quickly, often within one or two days. This perceived value of convenience can increase the likelihood of a customer completing their purchase.

There are two primary ways to qualify for the Prime badge: through Fulfillment by Amazon (FBA) or through Seller Fulfilled Prime (SFP). Both methods allow sellers to tap into the vast network of Amazon Prime members, but they require different approaches. FBA involves sending your inventory to Amazon's fulfillment centers, where Amazon takes care of storage, packing, shipping, and customer service. This option provides sellers with automatic access to the Prime badge, as all FBA products are eligible for Prime. FBA is ideal for sellers who want a hands-off approach to fulfillment and are looking to scale quickly. On the other hand, Seller Fulfilled Prime (SFP) allows sellers to fulfill orders directly from their own warehouse while still offering Prime benefits, such as fast shipping, to customers. To participate in SFP, sellers must meet Amazon's performance standards, which include meeting strict shipping speed requirements. However, once approved, sellers can gain access to the Prime badge without relying on Amazon's fulfillment centers, providing more control over inventory and shipping.

Another crucial benefit of being part of the Prime ecosystem is the opportunity to tap into Prime Day and other exclusive events. Prime Day is one of the most anticipated shopping events on Amazon, and it's only available to Prime members. Participating in Prime Day and other exclusive promotions, such as Black Friday and Cyber Monday deals, allows you to offer discounts, bundle deals, or limited-time offers to a massive audience of highly engaged shoppers. The presence of the Prime badge increases the chances of your product being noticed and purchased during these high-traffic events, as Prime members are more likely to trust and prioritize products that come with the Prime designation. Moreover, Amazon often promotes Prime Day and other events heavily in its marketing campaigns, providing additional exposure for Prime-eligible products.

Beyond the Prime badge, Amazon also offers Prime-exclusive benefits that can increase your product's visibility and appeal. For example, Prime Early Access is an exclusive perk that allows Prime members to shop select Lightning Deals and promotions up to 30 minutes before they are made available to the general public. By participating in these events, you're not only providing Prime members with exclusive offers but also gaining an edge in a crowded marketplace. Being able to offer discounts and time-sensitive deals to a loyal, motivated audience can lead to higher sales volumes and greater brand recognition.

The benefits of Amazon Prime extend beyond shipping. Prime Video, Prime Music, and other entertainment offerings are just some of the ways that Amazon engages its subscribers. As a seller, understanding that Prime members are highly engaged and accustomed to receiving high-value perks can help you tailor your strategy to meet their expectations. These members are not just looking for quick delivery—they're looking for premium experiences across all aspects of Amazon. Therefore, products that offer exceptional value, quality, and service are more likely to resonate with this audience. The Prime badge becomes more than just a symbol of fast shipping; it's a badge of trust that signals your product meets Amazon's high standards.

However, leveraging Amazon Prime badges and benefits goes beyond simply qualifying for the Prime badge. Sellers need to take full advantage of the Prime ecosystem by integrating their listings with Prime benefits in a way that enhances the overall customer experience. For example, product listings with the Prime badge should also feature compelling, high-quality images, detailed descriptions, and customer reviews that reinforce the product's quality and value. Adding features like Enhanced Brand Content (EBC) or A+ Content, which allow you to showcase your product's benefits in a more engaging, visual format, can further enhance the credibility of your listing and increase conversion rates. Customers who see a well-designed product page with thorough, compelling information will be more likely to trust your product and make a purchase.

Moreover, participating in Amazon's Subscribe & Save program can help increase the lifetime value of your customers. For products that are consumable or need to be replenished, Amazon's Subscribe & Save program allows customers to sign up for automatic deliveries at a discounted price. This subscription model helps build customer loyalty and increases the chances of repeat purchases, making it an ideal tool for sellers looking to build long-term relationships with Prime members. Prime members are particularly inclined to participate in such programs because they already value the convenience of Amazon's services and appreciate the added savings and reliability that the Subscribe & Save program offers.

It's also important to consider how the Prime badge and benefits fit into your broader marketing strategy. One of the best ways to leverage the Prime badge is by participating in Amazon's advertising programs, such as Sponsored Products, Sponsored Brands, and Display Ads. Prime-eligible listings tend to perform better in these campaigns, as the Prime badge increases the likelihood that customers will click on your ad and complete the purchase. By targeting Prime members with tailored ad campaigns and combining your advertising efforts with Prime's exclusive benefits, you can amplify your product's visibility, attract high-intent shoppers, and drive conversions more effectively.

Another critical advantage of Prime eligibility is the increased likelihood of winning the Buy Box. The Buy Box is a coveted position on Amazon's product pages that allows sellers to be the default seller for a particular product. Winning the Buy Box is crucial for increasing sales, as the majority of customers click on the Buy Box when making a purchase. Amazon takes several factors into account when determining the Buy Box winner, including product price, shipping speed, and seller performance. Since Prime-eligible products are often prioritized in the Buy Box selection process, qualifying for Prime is an essential part of winning this highly competitive space and driving more sales.

Leveraging Amazon Prime badges and benefits requires more than just meeting the eligibility criteria. To maximize the impact of these features, sellers must actively manage their inventory, ensure prompt order fulfillment, and offer exceptional customer service. Prime members are accustomed to a high level of convenience and reliability, so providing them with an excellent shopping experience is paramount. By combining the advantages of the Prime badge with strong product listings, effective advertising, and superior customer service, you can take full advantage of Amazon Prime's capabilities and drive long-term success for your business.

The Amazon Prime ecosystem offers a wealth of benefits that can help sellers drive conversions, increase visibility, and build customer loyalty. By qualifying for the Prime badge, taking advantage of Prime-exclusive events, and optimizing your listings with the right content, you can differentiate your products and create a seamless, compelling experience for Amazon's most engaged shoppers. As Prime membership continues to grow, the importance of leveraging these badges and benefits will only increase, making it a crucial element of any seller's strategy for success on the platform.

UTILIZING AMAZON PROMOTIONS AND DEALS

In the competitive landscape of e-commerce, one of the most effective strategies for boosting visibility, driving sales, and maximizing customer engagement is through the use of promotions and deals. Amazon, being the global powerhouse it is, provides sellers with a range of promotional tools designed to help increase exposure and drive conversions. Whether you are a seasoned seller or new to the platform, mastering Amazon's promotions and deals is a crucial part of optimizing your sales strategy. Leveraging these tools effectively requires a combination of timing, strategy, and understanding customer behavior.

Promotions and deals are invaluable because they tap into the psychology of urgency and scarcity. Shoppers are inherently motivated by a sense of opportunity, and offering limited-time discounts or special offers can create a sense of excitement around your products. When potential customers perceive a good deal, they are more likely to make a purchase, sometimes even outside their original shopping intentions. Amazon's suite of promotional tools, from Lightning Deals to Coupons, offers a wide array of ways to meet customers' needs while aligning with your business goals.

One of the most well-known promotional features on Amazon is the Lightning Deal. These time-limited offers create an immediate sense of urgency by offering deep discounts for a specific period, often only a few hours. This feature is particularly effective during high-traffic times like Amazon Prime Day, Black Friday, and Cyber Monday. Lightning Deals are designed to attract a large volume of shoppers who are specifically seeking out discounted products. They are prominently featured on Amazon's Deal pages, making them highly visible to Prime members and other shoppers. The key to successfully utilizing Lightning Deals is ensuring that your product is not only competitively priced but also stands out among the many other deals that may be available. Sellers who participate in these deals can significantly boost their sales volume and increase their product's visibility. However, there are a few critical requirements for being eligible for a Lightning Deal, including maintaining a competitive price, having sufficient inventory, and ensuring that your product has a strong performance history in terms of reviews and ratings. Sellers must also apply in advance and be selected by Amazon, as only a limited number of deals are accepted.

Beyond Lightning Deals, Amazon offers several other promotional tools that can help attract customers and drive sales. One of these is the Deal of the Day, which is similar to a Lightning Deal but typically lasts for a full 24 hours. Deal of the Day promotions are often featured prominently on Amazon's homepage and are designed to give sellers the opportunity to reach an even wider audience. As with Lightning Deals, the success of a Deal of the Day largely hinges on competitive pricing, strong product ratings, and the ability to fulfill orders promptly. Participating in a Deal of the Day can lead to significant spikes in sales, particularly if your product is placed in front of an audience actively looking for deals. These offers are ideal for high-volume products that have broad appeal and a strong customer base.

Amazon Coupons are another highly effective way to boost sales while encouraging customers to make a purchase. Coupons are easy to set up and can be added to both product listings and search results. When a customer clicks on a coupon, they are typically offered a discount on the product at checkout. This simple, yet highly effective promotion can attract price-conscious shoppers who are more likely to purchase when they see an immediate discount. Amazon Coupons also appear in Amazon's coupon directory, which allows shoppers to browse and discover new deals. Coupons can be customized based on a percentage or dollar amount off the listed price, and they can be targeted to specific products, categories, or even brands. They are an excellent way to build brand awareness and incentivize purchases, especially when paired with strategic marketing efforts such as Sponsored Products or Sponsored Brands ads. Coupons are particularly valuable in competitive categories where price sensitivity is high and customers are constantly searching for the best value.

One of the significant advantages of using Amazon Coupons is that they provide the opportunity to capture more visibility. Coupons appear both on product detail pages and in search results, making them visible to customers who are actively browsing for items in your category. The visibility and potential for engagement are amplified when you incorporate coupons into a larger promotional strategy, such as pairing them with a Lightning Deal or offering them as part of a cross-sell or upsell promotion. The best part is that coupons can be tracked and measured, so you can easily assess their effectiveness and refine your approach to future promotions.

In addition to specific promotional tools like Lightning Deals and Coupons, Amazon also offers promotional credits that allow sellers to offset marketing costs. This can be especially helpful for sellers looking to drive traffic to their listings and boost conversions. For example, Amazon often provides promotional credits for Sponsored Products campaigns, allowing you to advertise your products with additional funding. This is a great way to stretch your marketing budget further, particularly if you're trying to drive traffic to a new listing or promote a seasonal product. These credits can also be used in conjunction with Amazon's other promotional features, such as Lightning Deals and Deal of the Day, allowing you to get the most out of your promotional investments.

Another strategic tool within the Amazon promotional ecosystem is the Buy One, Get One (BOGO) offer. This type of deal allows customers to receive a free or discounted product when they purchase a specific item. BOGO deals are popular for driving higher sales volumes, increasing the average order value, and introducing customers to new or complementary products. This type of promotion is especially useful when trying to clear out inventory, promote a product that needs a boost, or introduce customers to a related item. By offering a Buy One, Get One promotion, sellers can create a compelling reason for customers to purchase more items, thus increasing their overall sales and enhancing customer satisfaction.

Seasonal promotions are another excellent way to leverage Amazon's promotional tools. Certain times of the year—such as the holidays, back-to-school season, or Prime Day—are natural opportunities to offer time-sensitive deals that can drive massive traffic and sales. Amazon's platform allows sellers to tailor promotions to specific times of the year, and aligning your promotional strategy with seasonal trends can help you tap into the buying behavior of customers during these peak shopping periods. Seasonal promotions can include discounts, bundling deals, or flash sales that provide urgency and exclusivity. Whether you are promoting holiday-themed products or offering back-to-school deals, seasonal promotions allow you to capitalize on the heightened buying activity associated with these times of year.

In addition to using Amazon's internal promotional tools, it's important to promote your deals and discounts through external marketing channels. For example, you can integrate Amazon promotions into your social media marketing strategy by announcing limited-time deals to your followers. By directing traffic to your Amazon listings from social media platforms, email campaigns, and other digital channels, you can further amplify the reach of your promotions and drive sales. By utilizing a multi-channel approach, you ensure that your promotions are seen by as many potential buyers as possible, increasing the chances of a successful conversion.

The effectiveness of your promotional strategy can also be improved by carefully analyzing the results of your promotions. Amazon provides detailed reporting tools that allow you to track the performance of your Lightning Deals, Coupons, and other promotional offers. These reports give you valuable insights into how your promotions are performing, including metrics such as sales volume, clicks, and conversion rates. By analyzing this data, you can identify which promotions are most effective, which products are performing well, and where you may need to make adjustments. Continuous testing and optimization are crucial to long-term success in e-commerce, and regularly reviewing your promotional campaigns will help you refine your approach and maximize your return on investment.

Utilizing Amazon's promotions and deals effectively is a key strategy for driving sales, increasing brand visibility, and engaging with customers. From time-limited Lightning Deals to customizable Coupons and seasonal promotions, the opportunities for leveraging Amazon's promotional tools are vast. By aligning your promotional efforts with your broader marketing and business goals, you can create a compelling shopping experience that not only attracts more customers but also boosts your overall conversion rates. Ultimately, success on Amazon requires a strategic approach to promotions, and those who take the time to plan, test, and optimize their deals will reap the rewards of increased sales and customer loyalty.

BUILDING STRONG CUSTOMER RELATIONSHIPS AND REVIEWS

In the realm of e-commerce, the foundation of success is not merely based on the quality of products, pricing, or advertising strategies, but also on the relationships you cultivate with your customers. Building strong, lasting relationships with your customers goes beyond simply fulfilling an order—it's about creating a seamless experience that makes shoppers feel valued, heard, and understood. This personal connection fosters loyalty, generates positive word-of-mouth, and most importantly, drives repeat business. One of the most powerful ways to build these relationships is through excellent customer service and proactively engaging with reviews.

Customer reviews are an integral part of the buying process for many online shoppers. Amazon, with its massive marketplace, is no exception. The platform has created a robust review system where customers can rate and review products they've purchased, providing feedback to potential buyers. The importance of these reviews cannot be overstated. A strong collection of positive reviews not only boosts a product's visibility on Amazon but also increases trust among new customers. Potential buyers often rely heavily on reviews when deciding whether or not to make a purchase, and they are much more likely to choose a product that has numerous positive feedback over one that has little or no reviews. As a seller, you have the power to influence this process and shape your product's reputation.

To begin building strong customer relationships, it's important to foster an environment of open communication. Transparency plays a crucial role in this process. Customers want to know what they are purchasing, what they can expect in terms of delivery, and how their concerns will be addressed if issues arise. When customers feel informed and confident, they are more likely to leave a positive review. Therefore, ensuring your product listings are clear, detailed, and accurate is one of the first steps in developing strong customer trust. High-quality images, comprehensive product descriptions, clear shipping details, and straightforward return policies can all enhance the customer experience and reduce confusion or dissatisfaction.

The importance of exceptional customer service cannot be overstated in the process of relationship-building. It is easy for a customer to become frustrated when they encounter problems with a product, shipping delays, or an unresolved inquiry. Addressing concerns promptly and professionally can turn a negative situation into an opportunity to build a loyal customer. Whether a customer is facing an issue with a defective product or simply has a question about your item, responding swiftly, courteously, and effectively makes a significant difference. The goal is not just to solve a problem but to exceed the customer's expectations in how you handle the situation. If customers feel valued and well taken care of, they are more likely to return to your brand in the future and recommend your products to others.

Beyond reactive customer service, being proactive is equally essential for long-term success. Reaching out to customers after a purchase is an effective way to continue the relationship. A simple follow-up email asking if they are satisfied with their purchase and if they have any questions can help you better understand their needs and preferences. It also opens the door for receiving valuable feedback that can be used to improve your products and services. Additionally, it can provide an opportunity to request reviews in a non-intrusive way. However, it's important to remember that requesting reviews should never feel pushy or forced. Customers appreciate genuine requests that feel authentic and that don't pressure them into writing a positive review.

In addition to communication, delivering on promises is essential for building strong relationships. This means ensuring that products arrive on time, are in good condition, and meet the description in your listing. If there are delays in shipping or if your inventory is running low, it's crucial to keep customers informed. Transparency about such delays and offering alternatives or compensation can go a long way in maintaining customer satisfaction. Consistency in delivering a high-quality experience helps to establish your reputation as a reliable seller, which, over time, can lead to repeat business and more positive reviews.

Once a customer is happy with their purchase, encouraging them to leave feedback is the next step in strengthening that relationship. Positive reviews are critical to building trust with future buyers, and they also provide valuable insights into what your customers love about your products. Reviews, especially positive ones, are an important social proof tool. When potential buyers see that others have had a good experience with your product, they are more likely to trust you and make a purchase themselves. A strong collection of positive reviews also helps improve your product's visibility in Amazon's search rankings, which ultimately drives more sales.

However, gathering reviews isn't as simple as asking for them. It's important to build a process that is respectful and compliant with Amazon's policies. Amazon strictly prohibits incentivizing customers to leave positive reviews in exchange for rewards, discounts, or any other form of compensation. Instead, the focus should be on providing a top-notch product and service that naturally encourages customers to share their feedback. As you continue to deliver exceptional experiences, customers will be more likely to leave reviews without being prompted.

Engaging with reviews is just as important as acquiring them. Amazon provides a platform for sellers to respond to customer reviews, and using this feature effectively can help build stronger relationships with your customers. Responding to both positive and negative reviews demonstrates that you care about your customers' opinions. When responding to positive reviews, express gratitude and appreciation. Acknowledge the customer's feedback, thank them for their business, and show that you value their support. For negative reviews, the goal should be to address the issue respectfully and offer a solution. A quick, courteous response to a negative review can demonstrate your commitment to resolving customer concerns and can help mitigate any damage to your brand reputation. Often, customers will appreciate your willingness to address their complaints and will update their reviews accordingly.

While it's important to engage with all reviews, there are times when sellers might need to dispute reviews that violate Amazon's review policies. For example, reviews that are unrelated to the product or that contain inappropriate content can sometimes slip through the cracks. In these instances, sellers have the ability to report the review to Amazon for further investigation. It's essential, however, to understand Amazon's guidelines on what constitutes a legitimate complaint or issue, as frivolously disputing reviews can harm your relationship with customers and Amazon.

Another strategy to encourage positive reviews and strengthen relationships is through Amazon's "Request a Review" button. This feature allows sellers to send a standardized email to customers asking them to review the product they purchased. It is compliant with Amazon's review policies and ensures that sellers are asking for feedback in a respectful manner. However, it's important to use this tool sparingly and only after a customer has had enough time to use the product and form an opinion. In some cases, customers may choose to leave a review spontaneously if they feel strongly about the product, while others may need a gentle reminder.

Building a strong customer base is also tied to your ability to create customer loyalty. This is where repeat buyers come into play. When you consistently deliver quality products and a great experience, customers will remember your brand and turn to you when they need similar items. A loyal customer base not only provides recurring sales but also becomes an advocate for your brand. This is where reviews and customer relationships intersect: loyal customers are often the ones who are most willing to leave positive feedback, recommend your products to others, and share their experiences.

Furthermore, maintaining relationships with customers and keeping them engaged doesn't end once they leave a review. You can keep in touch through email marketing campaigns, offering new product updates, special promotions, or discounts. With the right strategy, you can transform a one-time buyer into a loyal customer who keeps coming back for more. Personalization plays a key role in customer retention. When customers feel recognized and valued as individuals, they are more likely to return and engage with your brand.

Building strong customer relationships and securing positive reviews is not a one-time task but an ongoing process that requires consistent effort, attention to detail, and a genuine commitment to customer satisfaction. By focusing on clear communication, excellent customer service, and a proactive approach to engagement, you can establish trust with your customers and create a loyal base that will continue to support your brand. These efforts not only lead to better reviews but also long-term business success, allowing your Amazon presence to grow and thrive.

THE IMPORTANCE OF INVENTORY MANAGEMENT FOR ADVERTISING SUCCESS

Effective inventory management is one of the most critical elements of a successful advertising strategy on Amazon. Many sellers often overlook the pivotal role inventory plays in advertising performance, assuming that once their campaigns are up and running, sales will simply follow. However, inventory and advertising are deeply interconnected, and managing inventory properly can directly impact the effectiveness of your ad campaigns, your return on investment, and ultimately your sales success.

When it comes to advertising on Amazon, running out of stock can have disastrous consequences. If your inventory levels drop to zero, your ads can still run, but potential customers will not be able to purchase your product. This results in wasted ad spend and can lead to a poor customer experience. Even worse, if your product is out of stock for an extended period, Amazon's algorithms might penalize you, decreasing your visibility on the platform. Amazon's advertising system relies on the availability of your products to drive conversions. If customers click on your ad and find that the product is unavailable, you risk losing their trust, and they might choose a competitor's listing instead.

The importance of inventory management in advertising goes beyond merely avoiding stockouts. Proper inventory management allows you to plan your campaigns around the availability of your products, ensuring that you're not advertising a product that won't be able to fulfill demand. It also allows you to control your budget more effectively. If you have a limited inventory, you'll want to ensure that your ad spend aligns with the number of units you have available to sell. On the flip side, if you have a high inventory, advertising can help you move products quickly, but careful attention must still be paid to avoid overstocking and tying up resources in products that are not selling well.

Maintaining optimal stock levels is equally important. If you consistently run low on inventory, your ad campaigns will suffer due to missed opportunities for sales, which means your ads may not be as effective as they could be. Running out of stock on a popular product can also trigger a negative feedback loop where your product's ranking drops, and customers become more likely to buy from other sellers who have consistent stock levels. On the other hand, maintaining excessive stock can lead to over-advertising and wasted spend, especially if your product isn't moving at the pace you anticipated. This is why understanding your inventory turnover rates and using this data to inform your advertising strategy is crucial. By using inventory data, you can predict trends and plan your campaigns with better accuracy.

In order to achieve success in advertising on Amazon, it is necessary to strike the right balance between your stock levels and your ad spend. Without proper inventory forecasting, you risk either understocking or overstocking, both of which can result in significant lost revenue. Understocking leaves you unable to fulfill demand, thereby wasting your ad spend, while overstocking may push you to increase your advertising efforts to clear out slow-moving inventory, which can lead to inefficiencies and wasted budget.

Effective inventory management also supports the profitability of your campaigns. When you maintain adequate stock levels, you ensure that you're not driving traffic to a product that isn't available for purchase. This means your click-through rates (CTR) and conversion rates will be higher, as customers will find your product when they click on your ads. This leads to higher sales, which in turn can help improve your product's ranking on Amazon. A well-stocked product with high sales velocity also triggers Amazon's algorithm to prioritize it in search results and ads. This is crucial for sustained advertising success.

Another aspect of inventory management that contributes to advertising success is seasonal demand forecasting. Some products are seasonal, meaning that demand will fluctuate throughout the year. By understanding these trends and planning ahead, you can align your advertising efforts with times when your products are most likely to sell. For instance, if you sell holiday decorations, you'll want to ramp up your ad campaigns months in advance of the holiday season, ensuring you have enough stock to meet the anticipated demand. Conversely, you'll need to adjust your campaigns if you're entering a slow season. Having the ability to forecast demand based on past sales trends can help you manage your inventory and budget in a way that maximizes the effectiveness of your campaigns.

Inventory management tools play a critical role in this process. Amazon's inventory management system provides a wealth of data that can help you track your stock levels, sales velocity, and replenishment needs. Sellers can use Amazon's inventory dashboard to gain real-time insights into their stock levels and track the performance of their products. This allows you to make informed decisions about which products need to be restocked, which items are underperforming, and where to allocate your ad spend for the best return on investment. For example, you might find that certain products are selling faster than anticipated and require restocking sooner than expected. By catching these trends early, you can avoid stockouts and keep your campaigns running smoothly.

Additionally, external tools like third-party inventory management software can provide further insights into your sales trends, supply chain performance, and demand forecasting. These tools allow you to automate processes like stock level monitoring and reordering, making it easier to stay ahead of potential inventory issues. By using these tools to integrate inventory management with your advertising strategy, you can ensure that your ad spend is being directed at products that will generate the highest return on investment, while avoiding wasted spend on items that aren't selling well.

Another important factor to consider in inventory management is the role of Amazon's Fulfillment by Amazon (FBA) service. FBA allows you to store your products in Amazon's fulfillment centers, where they are picked, packed, and shipped directly to customers. This service offers a significant advantage for sellers looking to manage their inventory more efficiently, as Amazon handles many of the logistical challenges that come with maintaining stock. Additionally, using FBA can improve your chances of winning the coveted "Prime" badge, which can increase the visibility of your products. Amazon's Prime customers tend to be more loyal and are more likely to purchase from Prime-eligible listings. This makes FBA an attractive option for sellers who want to streamline inventory management while increasing their products' chances of winning the buy box and receiving higher visibility in search results.

When inventory is managed effectively, it also positively impacts customer satisfaction and seller reputation. The faster a product can be shipped to a customer, the more likely they are to leave a positive review, which in turn influences future sales. If you run out of stock or cannot deliver products in a timely manner, customer satisfaction suffers, and so does your seller rating. Low ratings can harm your ability to advertise effectively, as Amazon favors sellers with high ratings when promoting products through ads. A high rating will result in better ad placements, higher click-through rates, and improved visibility.

Ultimately, the key to inventory management for advertising success lies in planning, forecasting, and using data to inform your decisions. Ad campaigns should be strategically aligned with the availability of your products, and a proactive approach to managing your inventory ensures that you don't miss out on sales opportunities. By maintaining optimal stock levels, forecasting demand, using inventory management tools, and making data-driven decisions, you can ensure that your ad campaigns are both cost-effective and successful.

Effective inventory management is a fundamental pillar of successful advertising on Amazon. Without proper inventory control, even the most sophisticated ad campaigns can fall short of their potential. A product that is frequently out of stock or overstocked may lead to wasted ad spend, poor customer experiences, and lost sales. By maintaining a careful balance between stock levels and advertising efforts, and by utilizing tools that help streamline the process, sellers can ensure that their campaigns are optimized for success. Managing inventory well will not only improve your advertising performance but also lead to a more sustainable and profitable business on Amazon.

CHAPTER 16

MEASURING YOUR OVERALL ADVERTISING SUCCESS AND ROI

CALCULATING KEY PERFORMANCE INDICATORS (KPIS)

In the fast-paced world of e-commerce, particularly when navigating the intricacies of advertising platforms like Amazon, one of the most important tasks is understanding how well your campaigns are performing. Without tracking the right metrics, it's almost impossible to determine whether your advertising efforts are delivering the results you expect. This is where Key Performance Indicators (KPIs) come in. KPIs are the measurable values that provide insight into how well your advertising campaigns are working, helping you make data-driven decisions that can improve your sales, visibility, and overall return on investment.

Calculating KPIs allows you to gauge the effectiveness of your advertising strategies on Amazon, particularly when running campaigns through Amazon Prime or other Amazon advertising services. KPIs give you a clear picture of your campaign's health and help you identify areas for improvement. The metrics you choose to track will vary depending on the goals you've set for your campaign—whether that's increasing sales, generating brand awareness, or driving traffic to your listings. However, regardless of your specific goals, there are a few critical KPIs that can provide you with a comprehensive understanding of how your advertising is performing.

One of the most important KPIs to calculate is the Advertising Cost of Sales (ACoS). ACoS is a metric that helps you understand the relationship between the amount spent on advertising and the amount generated in sales. It is calculated by dividing the total ad spend by the total sales attributed to that ad campaign. For example, if you spend $100 on an ad campaign and generate $500 in sales, your ACoS would be 20%. The lower the ACoS, the more efficient your advertising is, as it indicates that you are spending less to generate more sales. By regularly calculating ACoS, you can monitor the efficiency of your campaigns and adjust your ad spend to achieve a better return.

While ACoS is crucial for evaluating efficiency, it's also important to calculate other metrics that help assess the broader impact of your advertising efforts. One such metric is the Return on Advertising Spend (RoAS), which is essentially the inverse of ACoS. RoAS measures how much revenue you earn for every dollar spent on advertising. If your RoAS is 5, it means that for every $1 spent on ads, you're generating $5 in sales. RoAS helps you determine whether your ads are profitable. The higher your RoAS, the more revenue your ads are driving relative to the cost. While ACoS focuses on the cost side of the equation, RoAS focuses on the revenue side, and both metrics are essential for understanding your overall advertising performance.

Another important KPI to track is the Click-Through Rate (CTR), which measures the effectiveness of your ads in generating interest and engagement. CTR is calculated by dividing the number of clicks your ad receives by the number of impressions (how many times your ad was shown to users). If your CTR is high, it indicates that your ad is compelling and relevant to your audience. Conversely, a low CTR suggests that your ad might need adjustments in targeting, creative, or messaging. A high CTR is a positive signal for Amazon's algorithm, as it indicates that your ad resonates with users and could lead to more visibility and higher placements in search results.

Conversion Rate (CR) is another vital KPI that should be closely monitored. The conversion rate measures the percentage of people who clicked on your ad and went on to make a purchase. In other words, it shows how effective your ad is at driving actual sales. To calculate conversion rate, divide the total number of purchases by the total number of clicks on your ad. If you have a high conversion rate, it indicates that your product listing is appealing and persuasive, and that your ad is successfully encouraging shoppers to complete their purchase. A low conversion rate, on the other hand, might signal that your landing page or product listing needs optimization, as customers may not be finding what they expected once they clicked through.

In addition to the direct sales and conversion-related KPIs, understanding your product's visibility is essential. Impressions and Reach are two important KPIs in this category. Impressions measure how many times your ad has been displayed to users, while Reach indicates the total number of unique users who have seen your ad. These metrics help you understand how broadly your ad is being distributed across Amazon's platform. If your goal is to increase brand awareness, tracking impressions and reach will help you gauge whether your ads are effectively reaching your target audience. However, it's important to note that high impressions or reach alone don't necessarily guarantee sales—what matters is the relevance and engagement of the audience seeing your ad.

Cost per Click (CPC) is another KPI that can provide valuable insight into how much you're paying for each click on your ad. CPC is the amount you pay each time a user clicks on your ad, and it is determined by competitive bidding in Amazon's advertising auction system. If your CPC is too high, it could signal that you're paying more than necessary for clicks, which may reduce your overall advertising efficiency. Tracking CPC allows you to adjust your bidding strategy and optimize for more cost-effective clicks. Lowering your CPC while maintaining or increasing your CTR is a key factor in improving your overall ACoS and RoAS.

It's also important to consider the Lifetime Value (LTV) of a customer when calculating KPIs. While this metric is more long-term, it's valuable in understanding the overall impact of your advertising efforts. LTV refers to the total revenue a customer generates over their entire relationship with your brand. A higher LTV indicates that your customers are not just making one-time purchases but are more likely to return for repeat business. This is particularly important for businesses with products that lend themselves to repeat purchases or subscriptions. Tracking LTV helps you assess the long-term profitability of your customer acquisition efforts, and it can guide your decisions on how much you're willing to spend on acquiring new customers through advertising.

To get a clearer understanding of the effectiveness of your campaigns, you should also track the Cost per Acquisition (CPA). CPA measures the cost of acquiring a customer through your advertising efforts. It is calculated by dividing your total ad spend by the number of new customers acquired through the campaign. Monitoring CPA ensures that you are spending your advertising dollars wisely and not overpaying to acquire customers. By comparing CPA to the LTV of a customer, you can determine whether your customer acquisition costs are sustainable and profitable.

Lastly, you should keep a close eye on your sales velocity. Sales velocity measures how quickly your product is selling over time, which is especially important when managing advertising campaigns for products that need to sell quickly or seasonally. Sales velocity can help you identify which products are resonating with your audience and which may need further promotion. This metric can also inform your inventory decisions, helping you avoid stockouts or overstock situations.

As you calculate these KPIs, it's essential to continuously review and adjust your strategies based on the data. Advertising on Amazon is not a "set it and forget it" process. The landscape is constantly shifting, and your KPIs will change over time as your products, listings, and campaigns evolve. It's critical to monitor your KPIs regularly and make adjustments to your campaigns based on what the data tells you. For instance, if your ACoS is too high, you may need to refine your targeting or bidding strategy. If your CTR is low, you might consider revising your ad creative or testing new keywords to increase engagement.

Calculating KPIs is an essential practice for understanding the success of your advertising campaigns on Amazon. By carefully tracking key metrics such as ACoS, RoAS, CTR, conversion rate, and CPC, you gain insights into the performance of your campaigns and can make data-driven decisions to improve results. The key to maximizing the effectiveness of your ads lies in regularly reviewing and adjusting these

KPIs to ensure you are always optimizing for the best possible return on investment. As you continue to track and analyze your KPIs, you'll have the tools needed to fine-tune your strategy, scale your campaigns, and ultimately drive sustained success in the competitive Amazon marketplace.

ATTRIBUTION MODELING: UNDERSTANDING THE IMPACT OF DIFFERENT AD TYPES

In the world of digital advertising, attribution modeling plays a critical role in understanding how different ad types contribute to a customer's journey and eventual conversion. For sellers on platforms like Amazon, attribution modeling allows you to pinpoint which advertisements—whether they are display ads, sponsored products, or video ads—are driving the most value for your business. The complexity lies in determining how to allocate credit across multiple touchpoints in the customer's buying journey, as each ad type interacts with the customer at different stages.

To effectively optimize your Amazon advertising strategy, it's essential to understand the nuances of attribution modeling and how different ad types impact a customer's decision-making process. Amazon offers a variety of advertising options, and each serves a unique purpose in driving traffic, increasing visibility, and generating conversions. The challenge lies in measuring the true value each ad type brings to the table, especially when a customer interacts with several ads before making a purchase.

Attribution modeling is the process of assigning value to each marketing touchpoint that influences a customer's decision. This is important because, in most cases, a customer will not make a purchase after interacting with a single ad. Instead, they may click on a product display ad, view a video ad, add an item to their shopping cart, and then later return to the site to make the purchase. Understanding how each of these interactions contributes to the final sale can help you allocate your ad budget more effectively and make more informed decisions about where to focus your efforts.

One of the most common attribution models used in e-commerce is the last-click attribution model. This model gives 100% of the credit to the final touchpoint before the conversion. In other words, if a customer clicks on a sponsored product ad and then makes a purchase, the sale is attributed solely to that ad. While this model is easy to understand and provides clear insights into which ad types are driving conversions, it has its limitations. The last-click model fails to account for earlier touchpoints in the customer's journey, such as display ads or video ads, which may have played a crucial role in introducing the customer to your product in the first place.

For this reason, more sophisticated attribution models are often employed to offer a more nuanced understanding of the customer journey. One such model is the first-click attribution model, which assigns 100% of the credit to the first ad that a customer interacted with. This model can be useful for understanding which ads are effective at raising initial awareness of your product. If a customer first interacts with a video ad, for instance, the first-click attribution model will attribute the conversion to that ad. This model helps businesses measure the effectiveness of their top-of-the-funnel ads, which aim to generate interest and bring customers into the buying process.

However, while the first-click model provides insights into the ads that initially engage customers, it also has its shortcomings. Like last-click attribution, it oversimplifies the customer journey. In reality, customers often interact with multiple ads before making a purchase. The linear attribution model, which distributes credit evenly across all touchpoints, can provide a more balanced view of how various ads contribute to a sale. For instance, if a customer clicks on a video ad, follows up with a product display ad, and finally clicks on a sponsored product ad before making the purchase, the linear model will allocate credit equally across all three touchpoints.

While the linear model provides more equitable attribution, it can still be too simplistic for complex customer journeys. To address this, some businesses use time decay attribution, which assigns more value to the ads that are closer in time to the conversion. The logic behind this approach is that the closer an ad is to the actual purchase, the more influence it has on the decision-making process. Time decay attribution recognizes that while initial touchpoints like video or display ads may be important for awareness, the final ad clicked right before purchase plays a more significant role in the actual conversion. This approach helps businesses account for the diminishing impact of earlier touchpoints as a customer moves closer to making a decision.

One of the most sophisticated attribution models is the position-based attribution model, which divides credit between the first and last touchpoints, while also giving some credit to the interactions that occurred in between. Typically, the first and last touchpoints are assigned 40% of the credit each, while the remaining 20% is distributed among the intermediate touchpoints. This model can be particularly helpful for businesses that want to acknowledge both the role of awareness-building ads (like video or display ads) and the final touchpoint (like sponsored product ads) that sealed the deal. The position-based model provides a more holistic view of the customer journey and can help businesses optimize their ad strategies across multiple channels.

Amazon offers a unique advantage when it comes to attribution modeling, thanks to its robust advertising platform and the vast amount of data available. Sellers on Amazon have access to comprehensive reporting tools that help them understand how their ads are performing at each stage of the customer journey. Amazon Attribution, for example, provides insights into how your non-Amazon ads, such as Google or social media ads, are driving traffic to your Amazon listings. With this tool, you can track how customers interact with your ads outside of Amazon, as well as how these interactions lead to conversions on the platform.

By leveraging Amazon Attribution, sellers can gain a deeper understanding of the role that external ads play in driving traffic and conversions on Amazon. This is particularly important in multi-channel advertising strategies, where a combination of Amazon ads, display ads, social media ads, and video content may be used to reach customers at different stages of the buying journey. Attribution modeling allows sellers to connect the dots between these touchpoints, helping them optimize their ad spend across channels for maximum impact.

Another key element of Amazon's advertising ecosystem is the ability to track and measure the performance of various ad types, including Sponsored Products, Sponsored Brands, Sponsored Display, and Video Ads. Each of these ad types serves a unique function and targets customers at different points in their journey. Sponsored Products are highly effective at driving conversions because they target customers who are actively searching for products. Sponsored Brands, on the other hand, are great for building brand awareness and driving traffic to your Amazon Storefront or product listings. Sponsored Display ads allow you to retarget potential customers who have previously interacted with your brand, while Video Ads are excellent for engaging customers at the top of the funnel and building brand awareness.

Understanding the contribution of each ad type to the overall sales funnel is essential for making informed decisions about how to allocate your advertising budget. By using attribution modeling to measure the impact of different ad types, you can identify which ads are performing well and adjust your strategy accordingly. For example, if you find that your Sponsored Brands ads are effective at driving traffic but not as successful at converting visitors into customers, you might consider refining your targeting or adjusting your ad copy to better capture their attention.

The ultimate goal of attribution modeling is to help you make smarter decisions about where to allocate your advertising budget. By understanding how different ad types contribute to conversions at different stages of the customer journey, you can optimize your campaigns to drive the best possible results. Whether you are looking to build brand awareness, drive traffic, or increase sales, attribution modeling enables you to evaluate the effectiveness of your ads and make data-driven decisions that lead to better outcomes.

Attribution modeling is a powerful tool for understanding the impact of different ad types in Amazon's advertising ecosystem. By analyzing the customer journey and assigning value to each touchpoint, you can make more informed decisions about where to invest your advertising dollars. Whether you are using last-click attribution, first-click attribution, linear attribution, or time decay attribution, understanding how each ad type contributes to the sales process allows you to optimize your campaigns and maximize the effectiveness of your advertising strategy. Through careful analysis and the right attribution model, you can drive more sales, improve your return on investment, and ultimately achieve long-term success on Amazon.

UTILIZING AMAZON BRAND ANALYTICS FOR HOLISTIC PERFORMANCE INSIGHTS

To succeed in today's highly competitive e-commerce environment, leveraging the data and insights available through Amazon's comprehensive suite of tools is crucial. One of the most valuable resources for sellers looking to optimize their performance on the platform is Amazon Brand Analytics. This powerful tool provides sellers with an in-depth understanding of their customers' behaviors, product performance, and the competitive landscape. By utilizing Brand Analytics, sellers can gain holistic performance insights that enable them to make data-driven decisions that drive growth, improve sales, and enhance their overall Amazon strategy.

Amazon Brand Analytics is available to sellers who are enrolled in Amazon Brand Registry, which helps protect registered trademarks while giving brands access to key performance data and insights. This tool is a treasure trove of information, offering an array of reports that reveal critical details about consumer interactions, trends, and preferences. As a seller, having access to this wealth of data allows you to better understand your target audience, optimize your listings, and fine-tune your advertising campaigns, ultimately leading to increased conversions and long-term success.

One of the core features of Amazon Brand Analytics is its ability to provide insights into search terms and customer behavior. The Search Terms Report, for example, shows sellers the most popular search queries that led to clicks and conversions for their products. By analyzing this data, sellers can uncover valuable keywords that resonate with their target audience, allowing them to refine their keyword strategy and improve visibility in search results. Understanding which search terms drive the most traffic is essential for optimizing product listings and ensuring that your products appear in front of the right customers.

Beyond search terms, Brand Analytics provides data on the competitive landscape, giving sellers visibility into how their products are performing relative to others in the same category. The Market Basket Analysis report, for example, shows which products are frequently purchased together. This information can help you identify complementary products and cross-sell or bundle items effectively. Understanding what products are often bought in conjunction with yours can also inform your advertising strategies, as you can target customers who are interested in similar products, increasing the likelihood of conversion.

The Competitive Intelligence section of Amazon Brand Analytics is another invaluable feature for sellers looking to gain an edge in the marketplace. This section reveals your competitors' market share, pricing strategies, and performance trends. By understanding how your competitors are positioning themselves, you can make informed decisions about how to differentiate your products and adjust your pricing or promotional strategies. Competitive analysis allows you to identify gaps in the market, capitalize on emerging trends, and adjust your offerings to meet the evolving needs of your target audience.

Brand Analytics also provides deep insights into your product's performance, with reports that help you monitor the health of your listings. For instance, the Amazon Retail Insights report allows you to track key performance indicators (KPIs) such as conversion rates, units sold, and total sales for each product. By analyzing this data, you can identify underperforming products and optimize them to improve performance. Whether it's adjusting your product descriptions, refining your images, or experimenting with different pricing strategies, the insights from Brand Analytics give you the information you need to make impactful changes that lead to higher sales and greater visibility.

Another critical aspect of Brand Analytics is its ability to offer demographic insights about your customers. The Demographics Report provides information on the age, gender, income, and location of your buyers, which is invaluable for refining your product positioning and marketing strategies. Knowing who your customers are and what they care about allows you to tailor your messaging and promotions to better meet their needs. For example, if your product is attracting a specific age group or income bracket, you can create targeted advertising campaigns that speak directly to those consumers, improving your conversion rates and return on investment.

The insights provided by Brand Analytics also extend to advertising performance. The Advertising Report within Brand Analytics allows you to evaluate the effectiveness of your Amazon advertising campaigns, including Sponsored Products, Sponsored Brands, and Sponsored Display ads. By analyzing key metrics such as impressions, clicks, conversions, and return on ad spend (ROAS), you can assess which ad types are delivering the best results and adjust your strategy accordingly. This data is crucial for optimizing your advertising spend, ensuring that you're investing in the right areas to maximize your returns. Whether you're focusing on brand awareness or driving direct sales, the performance insights from Brand Analytics help you fine-tune your ad campaigns to achieve the best outcomes.

Brand Analytics also empowers you to track and analyze your product's performance over time. The Performance Over Time report shows how your sales, traffic, and conversion rates have evolved, giving you a clear picture of trends and patterns. This data can be especially useful for understanding seasonal fluctuations in demand, as well as identifying the impact of marketing campaigns, promotions, and other external factors on your sales performance. By tracking these metrics, you can adjust your strategies to capitalize on peak selling periods and mitigate any dips in performance.

One of the most powerful ways to leverage Amazon Brand Analytics is by integrating it with other data sources to get a complete picture of your business's performance. For instance, combining Brand Analytics with your own inventory data and sales reports can help you align your marketing efforts with your supply chain. If you know which products are selling the best, you can focus your advertising efforts on those items while ensuring that you have enough stock to meet demand. Conversely, if you notice that certain products are underperforming, you can quickly identify the root causes—whether it's due to a lack of visibility, poor reviews, or ineffective pricing—and take corrective action.

In addition to improving your internal operations, Brand Analytics also enables you to enhance your customer relationships. By understanding customer behavior, preferences, and demographics, you can deliver more personalized experiences. For example, by identifying the types of products your customers frequently purchase together, you can create targeted bundle offers or special promotions that increase the likelihood of repeat purchases. You can also use demographic insights to tailor your customer communications, making them more relevant and engaging.

The ability to track and understand product performance through Amazon Brand Analytics ultimately allows you to make data-driven decisions that lead to better business outcomes. The detailed insights provided by Brand Analytics give you the power to optimize your product listings, refine your advertising strategies, and enhance your customer relationships. By leveraging these insights, you can stay ahead of the competition, improve your ROI, and grow your brand on Amazon.

Amazon Brand Analytics offers a wealth of insights that can help you optimize your Amazon business performance. From understanding customer behavior and uncovering valuable search terms to analyzing the competitive landscape and measuring advertising success, Brand Analytics provides the data you need to make informed, strategic decisions. By harnessing the power of these insights, you can improve your product listings, create more targeted advertising campaigns, and ultimately drive better results across the board. Whether you are a seasoned seller or just getting started on Amazon, Brand Analytics is an essential tool for driving sustainable growth and maximizing your potential on the platform.

TRACKING ORGANIC VS. PAID SALES GROWTH

Understanding the dynamics between organic and paid sales growth is essential for any seller looking to thrive on Amazon. As competition continues to grow and the marketplace becomes more saturated, maximizing sales while efficiently managing advertising spend is crucial for long-term success. The relationship between organic and paid sales provides valuable insights into your overall marketing strategy and helps identify which areas need optimization. By properly tracking these two key aspects, you can make more informed decisions that improve not only your sales but also your return on investment.

At the core of any effective sales strategy lies the understanding of what drives traffic to your listings. Organic sales refer to those purchases made by customers who discover your products naturally, often through search results, recommendations, or direct visits. These sales occur without any paid advertising efforts, relying instead on Amazon's search algorithm and organic ranking to bring your products to potential buyers. On the other hand, paid sales are those that are generated through Amazon's advertising platforms, such as Sponsored Products, Sponsored Brands, and Sponsored Display ads. These sales occur because you have invested money into promoting your products, ensuring they appear in front of targeted audiences.

To track the growth of organic versus paid sales, sellers must begin by closely monitoring their sales data over time. One of the first steps in this process is identifying and differentiating between the two types of sales. Fortunately, Amazon's robust reporting tools, such as Amazon Seller Central's advertising reports, provide the data necessary to separate organic sales from those generated through ads. These reports offer valuable insights into key metrics like impressions, clicks, and conversions for paid campaigns, as well as detailed sales data for organic listings. By comparing this data over a specific period, sellers can begin to see the relative growth of both organic and paid sales and make informed decisions based on that information.

To understand the impact of advertising on overall sales, sellers must look at the conversion rate and how it evolves over time. A high conversion rate for paid traffic indicates that your ads are well-targeted and resonating with potential customers. Conversely, a low conversion rate may suggest that your ad copy, targeting strategy, or product pricing needs adjustments. It's important to note that while paid sales often contribute directly to an increase in visibility, this can also have a positive impact on organic sales. For instance, a well-performing paid campaign can drive more traffic to your product listings, leading to more organic clicks and purchases as well. This phenomenon is known as the halo effect, where the increased visibility from paid ads improves a product's organic rank, contributing to long-term sales growth.

Another key factor in tracking organic versus paid sales growth is understanding the customer journey and how it intersects with your advertising efforts. The customer journey on Amazon typically begins with a search query, leading to product listings that are ranked based on relevance and other factors such as reviews, price, and sales history. If your product ranks well organically, it's likely that it will receive more visibility in search results, ultimately leading to more organic sales. However, a strong paid campaign can enhance this visibility even further by placing your product in front of potential buyers who might not have come across your listing otherwise. By analyzing which keywords and search terms drive the most paid traffic to your product, sellers can gain a deeper understanding of how specific ads influence organic sales as well.

Tracking both organic and paid sales growth can also help sellers make better decisions when it comes to advertising spend. For example, if you notice that your organic sales are increasing significantly over time, it may be an indicator that your product is becoming more visible within Amazon's search results. In such cases, you may want to reduce your paid advertising spend, allowing you to focus your budget on other aspects of your business, such as new product launches or seasonal promotions. On the other hand, if your organic sales are stagnating or declining, it may be time to invest more heavily in paid campaigns to boost your product's visibility and rankings.

Another critical aspect of tracking both organic and paid sales is the concept of cannibalization. This occurs when paid ads are directly responsible for sales that might have occurred organically without the ad spend. Essentially, you're paying for sales that would have come in anyway. While this is a natural part of the advertising process, it's important to minimize this effect to ensure that your ad spend is truly contributing to incremental sales growth. To track and minimize cannibalization, sellers can monitor the relationship between their organic and paid sales using tools like Amazon's Advertising Console, which provides a breakdown of performance for each ad campaign and compares it to organic sales growth over the same period. If paid ads are generating the same number of sales as organic traffic would have, it's time to adjust targeting, bidding, or budgets to ensure that you are focusing your spend on new customer acquisition.

There's also the aspect of long-term versus short-term impact when evaluating organic and paid sales growth. While paid sales are often seen as a more immediate, short-term solution, organic sales tend to reflect a more sustainable, long-term strategy. In this sense, a successful paid campaign should not only contribute to an immediate spike in sales but also serve as a foundation for boosting organic growth. For instance, a well-executed ad campaign can improve a product's visibility and, over time, its ranking on Amazon's search results. As your product ranks higher, it can attract more organic sales without further ad spend, allowing your business to grow without depending on continuous advertising. On the other hand, relying solely on paid ads without focusing on organic visibility could lead to a situation where sales plateau once ad spend is reduced or stopped.

To get a clearer picture of the impact of advertising on organic sales, sellers should look at the Amazon Attribution tool. This tool allows sellers to measure how their advertising efforts influence customer actions both on and off Amazon. By tracking how users interact with ads and whether those interactions lead to conversions, sellers can understand how paid ads contribute to organic sales over time. This attribution data can be incredibly valuable when determining the ROI of your ad spend, as it can help you determine whether your advertising dollars are driving incremental growth or simply cannibalizing organic sales.

Lastly, a comprehensive understanding of organic versus paid sales growth also requires periodic benchmarking. Sellers should regularly compare their sales performance against industry benchmarks and competitors to determine whether their growth trajectory is in line with the market. Understanding how your sales are growing in comparison to similar products can provide insights into whether your organic or paid sales strategies are working. If your paid sales growth is outpacing organic sales growth, it could indicate that you need to adjust your organic optimization strategy to support long-term sales sustainability.

Tracking and analyzing the growth of organic and paid sales is an ongoing process that requires careful attention to the data. By understanding the interplay between these two components, sellers can make informed decisions that maximize visibility, improve return on ad spend, and ensure that their business is growing in both the short and long term. Successful businesses on Amazon don't just rely on one form of sales growth over another—they create a balanced, integrated strategy that leverages both organic ranking and targeted advertising to drive sustained success.

MAKING DATA-DRIVEN DECISIONS FOR CONTINUOUS IMPROVEMENT

In the world of e-commerce, making data-driven decisions is not just a good practice—it is essential for sustained growth and success. As the digital landscape constantly evolves, sellers who rely on their instincts and gut feelings alone are at a significant disadvantage. Amazon, as one of the largest and most competitive marketplaces, offers a wealth of data, and the ability to harness this data effectively is the key to staying ahead of the competition. By analyzing key metrics, adjusting strategies based on real-time insights, and continually testing and optimizing campaigns, sellers can ensure that their businesses are always improving and adapting to changing consumer behaviors and market conditions.

The foundation of making data-driven decisions lies in understanding the types of data that are available and knowing how to interpret it correctly. Amazon provides a vast array of analytics tools, including sales performance data, customer behavior insights, advertising performance reports, and inventory analytics, just to name a few. These tools give sellers a comprehensive view of how their products are performing, which ads are driving traffic, and which keywords are generating the most sales. However, it's not enough to simply collect this data; sellers must also know how to use it to make informed decisions that lead to measurable improvements.

One of the first steps in making data-driven decisions is setting clear, actionable goals. These goals should be specific, measurable, attainable, relevant, and time-bound—commonly known as the SMART criteria. For example, a seller might set a goal to increase their return on ad spend (ROAS) by 10% over the next quarter or to reduce their customer acquisition cost (CAC) by 15% within six months. By defining goals that are specific and measurable, sellers create a framework for analyzing data and making decisions that drive results. These goals act as benchmarks, allowing you to track progress and make necessary adjustments as you move forward.

Once goals are in place, the next step is identifying the key performance indicators (KPIs) that will help measure progress. KPIs are the metrics that indicate whether or not your business is on track to meet its goals. For example, if your goal is to increase ROAS, you would need to closely monitor your advertising performance, focusing on metrics like clicks, conversions, and cost per click (CPC). If your goal is to reduce CAC, you would track customer acquisition costs across different channels, ensuring that you are maximizing the efficiency of your ad spend. Amazon's advertising platform provides detailed reporting on all of these metrics, making it easier for sellers to identify areas that need attention.

Tracking these KPIs consistently over time is crucial for making informed decisions. While it may be tempting to focus on short-term results, data-driven decisions require a long-term perspective. It's essential to track performance over extended periods, comparing month-over-month or year-over-year data to identify trends. For example, if you notice that your conversion rate has been steadily declining over the past few months, this could signal a problem with your product listings or advertising campaigns that needs to be addressed. By regularly reviewing your KPIs, you can identify patterns, spot issues early, and make adjustments before they become significant problems.

One of the most powerful aspects of data-driven decision-making is the ability to conduct A/B testing. A/B testing involves comparing two variations of a campaign, listing, or ad to determine which one performs better. This process allows sellers to test different strategies, optimize their campaigns, and fine-tune their listings for maximum effectiveness. For example, you might test two different headlines for a product ad to see which one generates more clicks, or you might experiment with different images or price points on your product detail page to determine which combination results in higher conversions. A/B testing is a continuous process, and by constantly refining your strategies based on real-world data, you can steadily improve your performance over time.

However, making data-driven decisions goes beyond just optimizing your advertising campaigns or product listings. It also requires analyzing customer behavior to understand what drives purchasing decisions. Amazon provides detailed insights into how customers are interacting with your products, including how they are finding your listings, which keywords they are using, and where they are dropping off in the buying process. By understanding these behavioral patterns, you can identify opportunities to improve the customer experience, whether that means refining your product descriptions, adjusting your pricing strategy, or offering more compelling promotional deals. For example, if you notice that customers frequently abandon their carts before completing a purchase, this could indicate an issue with your checkout process, or perhaps you need to offer a more enticing discount to encourage conversions.

Customer feedback is another valuable source of data that can inform your decision-making. Amazon's review system allows buyers to leave feedback on products they've purchased, and these reviews can provide valuable insights into what customers like or dislike about your product. Negative reviews, in particular, should not be ignored; instead, they should be seen as an opportunity to learn and improve. If multiple customers are mentioning the same issue in their reviews, this is a clear signal that you need to address it, whether by improving the product itself or adjusting your marketing approach. By staying proactive and responding to customer feedback, you demonstrate that you value your customers' input and are committed to making continuous improvements.

Another critical aspect of data-driven decision-making is forecasting future performance. By analyzing historical data and understanding market trends, sellers can predict future demand, inventory needs, and sales growth. This allows you to plan your inventory levels more effectively, avoiding stockouts and overstocking situations that can disrupt your business. For example, if you notice that a particular product consistently sees a surge in sales during the holiday season, you can plan ahead to ensure you have enough stock to meet demand. Similarly, by monitoring trends in consumer behavior, you can adjust your marketing strategy to capitalize on seasonal changes or emerging product categories.

It's also important to note that data-driven decisions should not be made in isolation. While it's essential to rely on hard data, it's equally important to incorporate qualitative insights and industry knowledge into your decision-making process. For example, a change in customer behavior may coincide with a broader trend in the market, such as a shift in consumer preferences or a new competitor entering the space. By combining quantitative data with qualitative insights, you can make more well-rounded decisions that take into account both the numbers and the bigger picture.

Making data-driven decisions is an iterative process. Continuous improvement is at the heart of data-driven decision-making, and there will always be room for optimization. The e-commerce landscape is constantly evolving, and sellers who embrace a culture of continuous testing, learning, and adapting are the ones who will succeed in the long run. By staying curious, open to new data sources, and committed to ongoing analysis, sellers can ensure that their business remains agile and well-positioned for growth, no matter how the market changes.

Data-driven decisions are the cornerstone of success in today's competitive e-commerce environment. By utilizing the wealth of data available through Amazon's tools and analytics, setting clear goals, tracking relevant KPIs, conducting A/B tests, and continuously optimizing based on real-time insights, sellers can achieve sustained growth and improve their performance over time. The key to success lies in viewing data not as a static resource but as a dynamic tool that can drive constant refinement and improvement, ensuring that your business stays ahead of the curve in an ever-evolving marketplace.

CHAPTER 17
FUTURE TRENDS AND STAYING AHEAD IN AMAZON PRIME ADVERTISING

EMERGING ADVERTISING FEATURES AND TECHNOLOGIES

The world of digital advertising is constantly evolving, and Amazon Prime is at the forefront of this transformation. As more sellers and brands tap into the platform's enormous potential, Amazon has been rolling out a range of emerging advertising features and technologies aimed at enhancing user experience, boosting conversions, and providing advertisers with deeper insights. For advertisers seeking to stay ahead of the competition and maintain relevance in a rapidly changing marketplace, understanding and embracing these new tools is crucial. In this dynamic landscape, knowing how to leverage these emerging technologies can provide a significant competitive advantage.

One of the most prominent emerging features on Amazon Prime is the growing integration of artificial intelligence (AI) and machine learning into advertising strategies. AI-driven features are revolutionizing how brands target their audiences and optimize their campaigns in real time. These advancements have made it possible for advertisers to automate much of their decision-making, optimizing ad placements, bidding strategies, and targeting based on real-time data analysis. With machine learning algorithms, Amazon Prime can predict which users are most likely to convert, allowing brands to refine their targeting methods and maximize their return on ad spend (ROAS). These intelligent systems not only improve efficiency but also provide a deeper level of personalization, allowing advertisers to reach the right audience with the right message at the right time.

Additionally, Amazon's advancements in AI have led to more sophisticated targeting techniques. Historically, advertisers have relied on broad targeting methods such as keywords and demographics. However, Amazon's AI systems go beyond simple targeting by using behavioral data to understand what users are likely to buy based on their browsing and purchasing habits. This level of detail enables hyper-targeting, where ads are shown to consumers who are highly likely to convert. In the context of Amazon Prime, this means that your ads will appear not just to anyone browsing the platform, but to those who exhibit the characteristics of customers most likely to purchase your product.

Another emerging technology that has garnered significant attention is voice search advertising. With the rise of Alexa and other voice-enabled devices, consumers are increasingly using voice commands to search for products and make purchases. As more people embrace voice technology, Amazon has been working to integrate voice search into its advertising offerings. This integration opens up exciting new opportunities for advertisers to reach consumers through voice-enabled devices, whether it's through Amazon's voice assistants or through devices that support Amazon Prime video content. Voice search advertising requires advertisers to rethink their strategies, as the language used in voice searches is often different from typed queries. Therefore, marketers need to optimize their listings and ad copy to align with conversational search patterns.

Video ads have also become increasingly important in the evolving landscape of Amazon advertising. With the rise of video content consumption on platforms like Amazon Prime Video and other streaming services, video ads offer an engaging and dynamic way to reach potential customers. Video ads can effectively capture attention, tell a story, and convey product features and benefits in a more memorable way than static images or text. Advertisers can take advantage of Amazon's video ad placements to showcase their products in action, share customer testimonials, or even demonstrate how their products fit into consumers' everyday lives. With video becoming a dominant form of content, investing in this advertising format offers a higher chance of connecting with viewers and generating conversions.

Along with video ads, Amazon is also enhancing its capabilities in interactive ad formats. Interactive advertising offers an engaging way for consumers to interact with ads, whether it's through polls, quizzes, or gamified experiences. These types of ads drive engagement and create memorable experiences for users, which can lead to higher brand recall and increased conversion rates. Interactive ads allow advertisers to build a more dynamic relationship with consumers by providing them with a choice or a personalized experience. As user engagement becomes increasingly important, interactive ad formats will likely play a crucial role in driving the success of advertising campaigns on Amazon Prime.

Shoppable video is another technology gaining traction in Amazon's advertising ecosystem. Shoppable video ads allow consumers to purchase products directly from video content, whether it's through Amazon Prime Video or other video platforms supported by Amazon. This technology allows users to skip the traditional browsing process and make immediate purchases from within the video, streamlining the customer journey. For advertisers, this means they can drive direct sales from the video content itself, making it easier for viewers to transition from awareness to purchase. With the power of video combined with the convenience of one-click purchasing, shoppable videos offer a seamless shopping experience that encourages quick conversions.

In addition to these advanced ad formats, Amazon is also investing heavily in improving its programmatic advertising capabilities. Programmatic advertising refers to the automated buying and selling of digital ads using software and algorithms to optimize ad placements in real time. Amazon's programmatic advertising platform uses vast amounts of data to target users based on their behavior, location, and other factors, allowing advertisers to deliver highly relevant ads to the right people. With the ability to analyze data quickly and make instant adjustments, programmatic advertising enables more efficient ad spend and better targeting of high-conversion audiences. For advertisers on Amazon Prime, this technology ensures that their ads are placed where they will have the greatest impact, improving their chances of success.

As privacy concerns and regulations become more prominent, Amazon has also been focusing on data privacy and ensuring that advertisers can continue to reach their target audiences without compromising consumer privacy. With stricter data protection laws such as GDPR in place, Amazon has developed new ways to anonymize and aggregate user data, ensuring compliance while still providing valuable insights for advertisers. This includes tools that allow advertisers to create more secure customer segments and track performance without violating privacy laws. These privacy-centric innovations not only help advertisers stay compliant but also build trust with consumers, who are becoming increasingly concerned about how their data is used.

Augmented reality (AR) is another technology that is likely to become a key player in the future of Amazon advertising. As AR technology advances, it allows consumers to interact with products in a more immersive way before making a purchase. For example, AR ads might enable users to virtually "try on" products, like clothing or eyewear, or see how furniture will look in their homes. This immersive experience enhances the customer's decision-making process, reducing the likelihood of returns and improving customer satisfaction. As Amazon continues to expand its use of AR, advertisers will have the opportunity to incorporate these interactive elements into their campaigns, driving engagement and improving the online shopping experience.

The rise of data-driven advertising tools is also helping advertisers better understand the performance of their campaigns. With machine learning and AI technologies, Amazon has enhanced its analytics platforms, offering sellers deeper insights into customer behavior, campaign performance, and return on investment (ROI). By analyzing customer interactions with ads, reviewing which ads are most effective at driving sales, and refining targeting strategies, advertisers can continuously improve their campaigns. These advanced analytics tools provide real-time insights into which ad types and formats are delivering the best results, allowing sellers to pivot and optimize their strategies quickly.

Emerging advertising features and technologies are transforming the way advertisers engage with consumers on Amazon Prime. By embracing these innovations, brands can create more personalized, interactive, and engaging ad experiences that resonate with their target audience. The growing integration of AI, machine learning, voice search, video ads, and interactive formats is shaping the future of advertising on the platform. For sellers and advertisers looking to stay ahead of the competition, understanding and incorporating these cutting-edge features will be key to driving sales, maximizing ROI, and ensuring long-term success in an increasingly competitive marketplace.

ADAPTING TO CHANGES IN AMAZON'S ALGORITHM AND POLICIES

As Amazon continues to evolve and adapt to the changing landscape of e-commerce and digital marketing, so too do its algorithms and policies. These shifts can significantly impact advertisers, making it essential for them to stay ahead of the curve. Understanding how to adapt to changes in Amazon's algorithm and policies is critical for ensuring that your advertising campaigns remain successful and that you continue to maximize your sales potential. Staying flexible and proactive in the face of these changes can help maintain consistent performance and avoid the pitfalls that come with unexpected shifts.

One of the most important things to recognize about Amazon's algorithm is that it is dynamic and frequently updated. This is done to improve the customer experience, increase the relevance of search results, and better align product listings with consumer expectations. While Amazon does not disclose every detail of its algorithm, certain elements are known to influence how products are ranked and displayed in search results. For example, the algorithm heavily favors products with high-quality content, positive reviews, competitive pricing, and relevance to a customer's search query. However, as Amazon refines its algorithm, it can introduce new ranking factors or adjust the weight of existing ones, which may impact the visibility of your products.

In recent years, Amazon has become more focused on improving the relevance of search results through machine learning and artificial intelligence (AI). This means that the algorithm is now better equipped to understand customer intent and serve more personalized results. As Amazon continually adjusts its algorithm to provide better results, it is crucial for advertisers to stay informed and be ready to adapt their strategies. Changes in the algorithm might lead to shifts in how certain keywords or product categories are ranked. For instance, a keyword that once drove significant traffic to your product may lose relevance, requiring you to revisit your keyword strategy and ensure your product listings are aligned with current search trends.

One of the best ways to adapt to these changes is to closely monitor performance data. By regularly tracking key performance indicators (KPIs), such as conversion rates, click-through rates (CTR), and sales volume, you can quickly identify any dips or anomalies that could be attributed to algorithm changes. If you notice that your ads are not performing as well as they used to, it may be a signal that the algorithm has adjusted how it ranks or displays your ads. This insight allows you to take action, such as refining your targeting strategy, optimizing your listings, or adjusting your bidding approach to regain visibility and improve performance.

Alongside the algorithmic changes, Amazon also periodically updates its advertising policies. These policy shifts can directly affect how your ads are displayed, what types of ads are allowed, and how they can be targeted. For example, Amazon may introduce stricter rules about the type of content that can be included in your ad creatives or impose new restrictions on targeting based on customer data. Policy updates may also include changes in how advertisers can bid for ad placements, what metrics are used to assess ad performance, or even how different types of ads can be positioned across the platform. Understanding these policy changes is essential for staying compliant and ensuring your campaigns are not negatively affected.

To keep up with changes in policies, it is important to regularly review Amazon's official communications and documentation. Amazon typically informs advertisers about policy updates through the Seller Central or Amazon Advertising console, so staying active on these platforms will ensure you do not miss any important announcements. Additionally, joining relevant Amazon seller or advertising forums can provide a community-driven approach to understanding policy changes. Other sellers or advertisers who are experiencing similar challenges can share insights or best practices for adapting to new policies.

The key to adapting to both algorithm and policy changes is flexibility. Instead of viewing these shifts as obstacles, consider them as opportunities for growth. For example, if Amazon's algorithm change affects your visibility in search results, you can use this as an opportunity to optimize your product listings with higher-quality images, better descriptions, and more relevant keywords. Alternatively, if a new policy limits the type of content you can include in your ads, it might force you to become more creative and concise in your messaging. By adopting a proactive and adaptable mindset, you can turn these changes into a competitive advantage.

Another vital aspect of adapting to Amazon's algorithm and policy changes is continuously testing and iterating your strategies. The best way to stay on top of shifting algorithms is through A/B testing. By running different versions of your ads or product listings, you can compare their performance and determine what works best in the current environment. Testing various ad creatives, headlines, targeting strategies, and bid amounts will help you fine-tune your campaigns in response to changes. Additionally, running tests on different seasons or times of year can provide valuable insights into how certain adjustments perform during peak shopping periods, such as holidays or special events.

It is also crucial to diversify your advertising strategies and not rely too heavily on a single approach. For instance, if you're primarily using Amazon's Sponsored Products ads and notice that the algorithm's changes have diminished their effectiveness, you could shift some of your focus to other ad types, such as Sponsored Brands or Sponsored Display ads. Diversifying your ad formats ensures that you are not overly dependent on any one strategy, and it allows you to experiment with different channels to see which ones are most effective in the current environment.

Additionally, it is essential to focus on building a strong foundation for your business on Amazon. Even as algorithms and policies change, the core elements of a successful advertising strategy remain the same. These include maintaining a well-optimized product listing, delivering excellent customer service, securing positive reviews, and offering competitive pricing. A strong reputation and a quality product will always have a positive impact on your ad performance, regardless of algorithm shifts. Therefore, ensuring that your product listings are comprehensive, keyword-optimized, and visually appealing can help safeguard your visibility and sales even during times of change.

As Amazon continues to evolve, it's crucial to understand the broader landscape of e-commerce and digital marketing. Staying informed about trends in consumer behavior, emerging advertising technologies, and shifts in industry standards will help you adapt your strategies to meet the demands of the marketplace. Amazon's platform is not static, and neither should your advertising approach be. By keeping a close eye on industry developments, engaging in continuous learning, and staying open to new advertising features and opportunities, you can remain ahead of the curve.

Adapting to changes in Amazon's algorithm and policies is an ongoing process that requires vigilance, flexibility, and proactive engagement. By staying informed about updates to the algorithm and policy changes, regularly tracking key performance indicators, diversifying your ad strategies, and continuously testing new approaches, you can successfully navigate the ever-evolving landscape of Amazon advertising.

With the right mindset and strategies in place, you can continue to achieve success even in the face of frequent changes. Ultimately, the more adaptable you are, the better positioned you will be to maintain a competitive edge and drive long-term success on the platform.

THE GROWING IMPORTANCE OF VIDEO ADVERTISING

In the evolving landscape of digital marketing, video advertising has emerged as one of the most powerful tools for capturing consumer attention and driving sales. Over the past decade, the internet has seen an exponential growth in video content consumption. As technology improves and the demand for dynamic content increases, businesses and advertisers have realized that video offers an unprecedented opportunity to connect with consumers in a more engaging, memorable, and effective way. This trend is especially prominent on e-commerce platforms like Amazon, where visual appeal and instant engagement can directly impact purchasing decisions.

The growing importance of video advertising lies in its ability to convey information in a format that is both entertaining and informative. Traditional static ads or text-based descriptions can only do so much to convey the value of a product. On the other hand, video allows brands to showcase their products in action, demonstrate features, and highlight real-world applications in ways that words or still images simply cannot. This visual storytelling aspect makes video particularly powerful in grabbing the attention of potential buyers, especially in a world where consumers are bombarded with information from multiple channels every day. The sheer visual appeal of a well-crafted video ad makes it easier for consumers to remember a product, and this is key to turning interest into conversions.

Amazon, recognizing the power of video in influencing buying decisions, has expanded its advertising options to include more video-centric features. Video ads now play an integral role in Amazon's advertising ecosystem, as they provide sellers with the ability to differentiate their products from competitors. With Amazon Prime Video and Amazon's Fire TV being major players in the streaming world, Amazon's platform is uniquely positioned to harness the power of video. For sellers, this opens up vast opportunities to connect with potential customers who may not yet be aware of their products, while also reinforcing brand identity and product messaging.

One of the most significant advantages of video advertising on platforms like Amazon is its ability to capture and hold the attention of consumers. In a world where people's attention spans are shortening due to constant digital stimulation, video provides a more dynamic and immersive experience than static ads. The motion and sound elements of video engage multiple senses, making the viewer more likely to stay engaged and absorb the information being presented. This creates a more impactful impression, making it more likely that viewers will recall the ad when they make purchasing decisions later. Research has shown that consumers are far more likely to make a purchase after watching a product video, as it helps them understand the product better and makes them feel more confident about the purchase.

In addition to engagement, video ads also benefit from the inherent ability to tell a story. The storytelling aspect of video is particularly important in creating an emotional connection with consumers. For example, a well-executed video ad might show how a product fits into a customer's life, highlighting its benefits and solving a problem that the viewer can relate to. This type of emotional appeal can resonate more deeply with viewers, leading to increased brand loyalty and more frequent purchases. The ability to tell a compelling story in just a few seconds can often mean the difference between a consumer scrolling past your ad or clicking to learn more.

Video advertising also allows brands to present more information than traditional ads. For products with complex features or unique selling points, a video is the perfect medium to break down the information in a way that is digestible for the consumer. A video can visually demonstrate how a product works, explain how it solves a specific problem, or showcase its key benefits in action. This kind of in-depth information is far more compelling and easier to grasp than a lengthy text description or a static image. In addition, videos allow advertisers to showcase the product's quality and build trust, making it easier for consumers to make a decision based on what they see.

Another significant advantage of video advertising is its shareability. Videos are inherently more likely to be shared on social media platforms, increasing brand visibility. If a video resonates with viewers, they may share it with their friends and followers, extending the reach of the brand far beyond the initial target audience. This viral potential is particularly valuable in the context of Amazon's advertising environment, where a strong social proof can help sway potential buyers. With more and more consumers turning to social media for product recommendations, the potential for video ads to gain organic traction cannot be overstated.

When it comes to targeting, video ads are highly adaptable and can be leveraged across various touchpoints on Amazon's platform. Sellers can utilize video ads on the Amazon homepage, within search results, and in product detail pages, ensuring that the ads are reaching the right audience at the right time. Video ads can be served to shoppers based on their behavior, search history, and preferences, allowing for more refined targeting than traditional ads. This precision in targeting ensures that the video content is shown to the people who are most likely to be interested in the product, improving the chances of conversion.

As consumers become more accustomed to video content, the expectations for its quality have risen as well. In today's competitive market, simply producing a video is not enough; it must be high-quality, professional, and optimized for the platform. This means that advertisers must pay close attention to the production value of their video content. The visuals must be clear and crisp, the audio must be clear, and the message must be concise and compelling. A well-crafted video ad can establish a brand as professional and trustworthy, while a poorly made video can have the opposite effect, leaving a negative impression on consumers.

Video advertising also plays an essential role in the growing trend of "shoppable" video. This trend allows viewers to interact with the video content in real-time and purchase products directly from the video. Shoppable videos are increasingly common on Amazon, where viewers can watch a product demo and immediately purchase it with just a few clicks. This seamless integration of video and commerce streamlines the buying process, making it easier for customers to make impulse purchases. As this trend gains momentum, advertisers should consider incorporating interactive elements into their video campaigns, such as clickable links or pop-up product information, to encourage direct purchases.

As the e-commerce industry continues to evolve, the importance of video advertising will only grow. It is expected that in the coming years, video will become even more dominant, as it continues to be a preferred format for content consumption. With platforms like Amazon increasingly prioritizing video in their advertising offerings, sellers must adapt to this shift in consumer behavior. Those who fail to incorporate video into their advertising strategies may find themselves at a disadvantage, while those who embrace the format will have a powerful tool at their disposal for boosting engagement, improving brand recognition, and driving sales.

Video advertising is no longer a luxury or a supplementary element of an advertising strategy—it is essential for success in today's digital landscape. The growing importance of video lies in its ability to engage consumers, convey complex messages, and create emotional connections. With the rise of shoppable video and enhanced targeting options on platforms like Amazon, video ads offer immense potential for increasing sales and driving brand growth. As technology advances and consumer preferences evolve, video will continue to play a central role in the future of advertising, and those who leverage it effectively will be well-positioned for long-term success.

LEVERAGING AMAZON MARKETING CLOUD (AMC) FOR ADVANCED ANALYTICS

Amazon Marketing Cloud (AMC) represents a powerful suite of tools designed to offer businesses deep insights into their advertising performance. By leveraging the data available through AMC, advertisers can make data-driven decisions that enhance the effectiveness of their campaigns, optimize their strategies, and ultimately drive greater sales. For businesses advertising on Amazon, understanding how to harness the full potential of AMC is crucial for success.

At its core, AMC allows businesses to collect and analyze large sets of data from various Amazon marketing activities. This cloud-based platform enables advertisers to look beyond simple metrics like impressions and clicks and dive into more granular data, offering a complete view of how their campaigns are performing across multiple touchpoints. With AMC, advertisers can track customer behavior, measure the impact of various ad types, and identify opportunities for optimization in real-time. The key benefit of AMC is its ability to provide advanced analytics that go beyond surface-level metrics, enabling brands to make better-informed decisions and increase ROI.

One of the most significant advantages of AMC is its ability to integrate data from different sources. It allows businesses to combine data from sponsored ads, retail performance, customer demographics, and sales funnels, offering a holistic view of how their marketing efforts are influencing their customers. This integration enables businesses to understand the full customer journey, from initial awareness to final purchase, which is essential for identifying which stages in the funnel require improvement and investment. With this comprehensive data, advertisers can fine-tune their campaigns to target high-value customers more effectively.

AMC's advanced analytics tools allow businesses to measure more than just ad performance. By offering detailed insights into consumer behaviors, purchase patterns, and even lifetime value, AMC provides an invaluable resource for businesses seeking to improve customer retention and optimize their product offerings. For instance, businesses can segment their customers based on purchase history and behavior, gaining an understanding of which segments are most responsive to specific ad types or product categories. These insights allow advertisers to develop more targeted and personalized campaigns, ensuring that their messages resonate with the right audience.

In addition to measuring customer behaviors, AMC provides powerful tools for tracking the performance of different types of advertising campaigns. Whether an advertiser is running sponsored product ads, video ads, or display ads, AMC enables them to track the effectiveness of each ad type. By providing metrics such as return on ad spend (ROAS), cost per acquisition (CPA), and other key performance indicators (KPIs), AMC helps businesses determine which ads are driving the most sales and which are underperforming. Armed with this information, advertisers can reallocate their budgets to optimize their spend and improve the overall efficiency of their campaigns.

AMC's ability to provide granular insights also extends to performance across different device types, locations, and demographics. This level of granularity allows businesses to evaluate how well their ads are performing in various contexts. For example, a campaign may perform exceptionally well on mobile devices but underperform on desktop computers. By identifying these differences, businesses can tailor their ad creatives, bidding strategies, and targeting efforts to better align with the preferences and behaviors of their target audience. Whether it's optimizing for mobile-first consumers or focusing on high-performing geographic regions, AMC enables advertisers to adjust their strategies to maximize results.

Another important feature of AMC is its ability to provide predictive analytics. Leveraging machine learning algorithms, AMC can forecast trends and outcomes based on historical data. This predictive capability allows businesses to identify patterns in consumer behavior and predict the future impact of their campaigns. For example, if a specific type of product is gaining traction in certain regions, AMC can help advertisers identify this trend early on, allowing them to adjust their strategies to capitalize on the growing demand. Predictive analytics also help businesses optimize inventory management, ensuring that products are stocked in anticipation of increased demand.

AMC provides advanced tools for measuring cross-channel performance as well. Many businesses today run multi-channel campaigns, spanning from Amazon's own platform to social media, email marketing, and beyond. AMC helps businesses track how their ads perform across these different touchpoints, providing valuable insights into which channels are driving the most traffic and sales. By having access to a unified view of cross-channel performance, businesses can optimize their campaigns to create a more cohesive and effective marketing strategy.

Moreover, the platform provides robust reporting features that allow businesses to track metrics over time. Whether they are comparing performance week-over-week, month-over-month, or year-over-year, AMC's historical data and trend analysis capabilities are invaluable for identifying long-term shifts in performance. By analyzing trends and historical data, advertisers can determine whether changes in their campaigns are producing the desired outcomes or if further adjustments are needed.

For businesses that rely heavily on seasonal trends or promotions, AMC provides a way to evaluate how time-sensitive campaigns are performing. Advertisers can use AMC to track the effectiveness of Black Friday or Prime Day promotions, monitor the impact of holiday campaigns, or assess the success of limited-time offers. By understanding how these campaigns perform relative to non-seasonal campaigns, businesses can fine-tune their future promotional strategies to achieve better outcomes.

A crucial aspect of AMC's value lies in its ability to integrate with Amazon's broader ecosystem, including Amazon Web Services (AWS) and other Amazon advertising tools. This integration enhances the depth of analytics available to businesses, allowing for more advanced data manipulation and analysis. With AWS, businesses can access more sophisticated data storage and processing capabilities, while Amazon's advertising tools provide additional ad-specific data that can be used in conjunction with AMC's analytics. This integration ensures that businesses can leverage all of their Amazon data in a centralized and actionable way, streamlining decision-making processes and driving improved campaign performance.

To fully maximize the benefits of AMC, businesses must ensure they are collecting the right data and using it strategically. This means taking a proactive approach to data management, regularly reviewing campaign performance, and continuously adjusting strategies based on the insights gleaned from AMC's analytics. Additionally, businesses must invest in the necessary expertise to interpret the data effectively. While AMC offers powerful insights, interpreting these insights correctly requires a strong understanding of data analysis, marketing strategies, and consumer behavior. For many businesses, this may mean hiring data specialists or partnering with agencies that specialize in data-driven advertising strategies.

Amazon Marketing Cloud offers an invaluable tool for businesses looking to optimize their advertising campaigns and gain deeper insights into customer behavior and campaign performance. By utilizing AMC's advanced analytics capabilities, businesses can not only measure the effectiveness of their current efforts but also anticipate future trends and optimize their strategies for long-term success. With the platform's ability to integrate multiple data sources, track cross-channel performance, and provide predictive insights, AMC is essential for any business serious about leveraging data to drive advertising success on Amazon. Those who embrace the full potential of AMC will be well-positioned to make smarter, more informed decisions, ultimately leading to better advertising outcomes and increased ROI.

CONTINUOUS LEARNING AND EXPERIMENTATION FOR LONG-TERM SUCCESS

In the ever-evolving landscape of Amazon advertising, the key to long-term success lies not in rigid strategies but in continuous learning and experimentation. The digital marketplace is constantly changing, with new features, tools, and best practices emerging regularly. For businesses looking to thrive on Amazon, it is essential to embrace a mindset of ongoing education and iterative testing. Rather than relying on a one-time approach or fixed methods, advertisers must be agile and adaptive, continuously refining their strategies to stay ahead of the competition.

The first step towards achieving long-term success in Amazon advertising is understanding that the platform itself is a living, breathing entity. What works today may not work tomorrow, and what worked for one product or campaign might not apply to another. This dynamic environment requires advertisers to stay informed and flexible, constantly seeking out new insights, techniques, and approaches to maximize their effectiveness. This ongoing process of learning can come from various sources, including Amazon's own updates and features, as well as industry trends, competitor analysis, and customer feedback. By remaining informed and adaptable, businesses can adjust to shifting trends and maintain a competitive edge.

One of the most powerful tools for fostering continuous learning is data. Amazon's advertising platform provides a wealth of data on ad performance, customer behavior, and sales trends. However, the mere collection of data is not enough; it's how businesses interpret and act on that data that truly makes the difference. Successful advertisers recognize that data is a reflection of what is happening in the marketplace, and it is through careful analysis that they can uncover actionable insights. Regularly reviewing data allows advertisers to identify which strategies are working and which are not, giving them the information they need to make informed decisions. By continually tracking metrics such as return on ad spend (ROAS), click-through rates (CTR), conversion rates, and customer lifetime value, advertisers can assess the impact of their campaigns and adapt their tactics accordingly.

In addition to tracking data, experimentation is crucial for discovering new ways to improve advertising efforts. The practice of experimentation involves testing different approaches, such as new ad formats, bidding strategies, keywords, or targeting methods, and analyzing the results to determine which elements lead to the best outcomes. This experimentation process allows businesses to fine-tune their strategies and identify high-performing tactics that may not have been evident at first. For example, an advertiser may experiment with video ads for the first time and discover that they significantly outperform traditional static display ads in terms of engagement and conversions. Alternatively, an advertiser might test various keywords and discover that certain long-tail keywords yield a higher conversion rate than more generic terms.

Through these ongoing tests and refinements, businesses can continuously evolve their strategies and discover what works best for their unique products and audience. This approach is much more effective than simply relying on one-size-fits-all solutions, as it allows advertisers to tailor their efforts to the specific nuances of their brand and customer base. It also helps mitigate the risks of following trends blindly, as advertisers are making data-backed decisions based on real-time performance rather than guesses or assumptions.

Experimentation is not only about discovering what works—it also involves learning from failures. Not every test will lead to a successful outcome, and that's okay. In fact, some of the most valuable lessons come from experiments that don't produce the expected results. A campaign may fail to generate the anticipated return on investment, but it can still offer valuable insights into customer behavior, ad performance, or competitive dynamics. By viewing each experiment as an opportunity to learn, rather than as a failure, advertisers can create a culture of experimentation that fosters growth and improvement over time. This mindset encourages businesses to take calculated risks and push boundaries, knowing that the results—whether positive or negative—will ultimately lead to better insights and a stronger strategy.

The importance of continuous learning and experimentation is particularly evident when it comes to adapting to changes in the advertising platform itself. Amazon frequently updates its advertising features and tools, and it is crucial for advertisers to stay up-to-date on these changes in order to remain competitive. For instance, Amazon may introduce new targeting options, changes to the bidding structure, or new ad formats that can offer additional opportunities for advertisers to optimize their campaigns. By keeping an eye on these updates and experimenting with new features as they become available, businesses can stay ahead of the curve and gain a competitive advantage over those who may be slower to adopt new strategies.

Furthermore, continuous learning extends beyond just technical skills or platform-specific knowledge. It also involves staying informed about industry trends and consumer behavior. Understanding shifts in consumer preferences, seasonal patterns, and emerging trends can provide valuable context for optimizing advertising strategies. For example, a change in consumer shopping behavior—such as an increased preference for sustainable products—could present an opportunity for advertisers to adjust their messaging and targeting to align with this new trend. By staying informed about broader industry movements, advertisers can ensure that their campaigns are always relevant and in tune with consumer needs.

One of the most effective ways to stay informed and continue learning is through collaboration. Joining industry groups, attending webinars, participating in forums, and networking with other advertisers can provide a wealth of insights and ideas. Learning from the experiences and successes of others can help businesses avoid common pitfalls and discover new strategies that may not have been considered otherwise. Collaboration can also foster a sense of community and support, allowing advertisers to share tips, tricks, and best practices for navigating the complex world of Amazon advertising.

In addition to collaboration, continuous learning also involves developing a deeper understanding of the customer journey. This means going beyond the initial click and conversion to track how customers interact with the product over time. By understanding the entire lifecycle of a customer—from the initial ad impression to post-purchase behavior—advertisers can gain insights into how to improve customer retention and foster long-term loyalty. Learning to interpret and act on data from customer reviews, feedback, and repeat purchases can be a powerful tool for optimizing not only ads but the entire customer experience.

For businesses that are serious about long-term success, a commitment to continuous learning and experimentation is non-negotiable. The digital marketplace is too fast-moving and competitive to rely on static strategies or outdated knowledge. Advertisers must constantly seek new information, test new ideas, and refine their approach based on real-time data and customer feedback. By adopting a culture of experimentation and embracing ongoing learning, businesses can stay adaptable, innovative, and competitive in the ever-changing world of Amazon advertising. Over time, this commitment to learning will lead to more effective campaigns, better customer engagement, and sustained growth.

Long-term success in Amazon advertising is built on a foundation of continuous learning and experimentation. By embracing data, testing new strategies, adapting to changes in the platform, and staying informed about broader industry trends, advertisers can optimize their campaigns for maximum effectiveness. Experimentation allows businesses to discover new opportunities and refine their tactics, while a commitment to learning fosters innovation and adaptability. By making learning an integral part of their advertising strategy, businesses can stay ahead of the competition and achieve sustained success on Amazon's dynamic platform.

CONCLUSION

Mastering Amazon Prime advertising is not a one-time achievement, but rather an ongoing journey that requires dedication, adaptability, and a proactive approach. As the digital advertising landscape constantly evolves, especially on platforms like Amazon Prime, advertisers must continue to hone their skills, refine their strategies, and stay ahead of the curve. Success in this competitive space comes from a deep understanding of the platform's intricacies, a commitment to data-driven decision-making, and the ability to adapt and innovate in response to emerging trends and technologies.

One of the most essential components of advertising success on Amazon Prime is understanding the platform's unique features and tools. It's not enough to simply launch ads and hope for the best. To truly excel, advertisers need to tap into the platform's sophisticated targeting options, utilize its advanced analytics tools, and leverage various ad formats to ensure they are reaching the right audience with the right message. Whether using video ads to capture attention or employing Sponsored Products to boost visibility, each advertising option must be carefully selected and optimized to align with specific business goals.

Additionally, the ability to analyze and act on data is paramount. Amazon Prime advertising provides a wealth of data, offering deep insights into customer behaviors, sales trends, and campaign performance. However, the true value lies not in collecting data, but in analyzing it, understanding its meaning, and making informed decisions based on that analysis. By regularly reviewing key performance indicators (KPIs) such as conversion rates, click-through rates, and return on ad spend (ROAS), businesses can identify which tactics are working and where improvements are needed. The more adept an advertiser becomes at interpreting data, the better equipped they will be to optimize their campaigns and make real-time adjustments that can lead to increased performance and higher ROI.

Of course, advertising on Amazon Prime is not a static endeavor. It requires an ongoing commitment to learning, experimentation, and adaptation. The digital landscape is continuously evolving, with new features, tools, and changes to algorithms. Successful advertisers know that standing still is not an option. Instead, they embrace the need for constant innovation and are not afraid to test new strategies, experiment with different ad formats, or adjust their targeting methods to see what works best. Whether it's exploring new technologies, such as Amazon's growing suite of video ads, or adapting to shifts in consumer behavior, remaining flexible and open to change is key.

Beyond experimenting with different ad formats and strategies, advertisers must also pay close attention to their overall business and marketing strategies. Successful advertising is deeply intertwined with a strong product offering, an optimized product listing, and a deep understanding of the target audience. High-quality listings, with detailed product descriptions, compelling images, and competitive pricing, will always enhance the effectiveness of advertising efforts. It's also critical to recognize that Amazon is more than just a marketplace—it's a dynamic ecosystem where brand reputation and customer trust play significant roles in driving sales. Building strong relationships with customers, responding to feedback, and maintaining a high level of customer satisfaction all contribute to the long-term success of advertising campaigns.

As businesses scale their Amazon Prime advertising efforts, the importance of a strategic approach becomes even more pronounced. Running effective ads on Amazon is not about spending more money, but about spending smarter. Successful advertisers know how to budget effectively, optimize campaigns for maximum reach and impact, and strategically allocate resources to areas that drive the most significant results. Whether it's managing ad spend across multiple products or deciding which types of ads will bring the most value to a specific audience, a well-thought-out approach is necessary for sustainable growth.

Ultimately, mastery of Amazon Prime advertising is an ongoing pursuit that requires patience, persistence, and the willingness to evolve. As you continue to refine your strategies, remember that advertising success is not solely about immediate results—it's about long-term value. The goal is to build campaigns that not only generate short-term sales but also create lasting brand visibility, customer loyalty, and sustained growth. This can only be achieved by embracing a mindset of continuous improvement, analyzing performance data regularly, experimenting with new ideas, and staying informed about platform changes.

The path to mastery involves more than just understanding how to launch ads; it's about learning how to maximize every opportunity that Amazon Prime offers. It's about crafting compelling, relevant campaigns that resonate with your audience and adapting your strategies based on real-time feedback. With the right tools, insights, and approach, you can make the most of your advertising efforts and drive meaningful success on Amazon Prime.

The journey to Amazon Prime advertising mastery is a dynamic and rewarding one. It requires a combination of strategic planning, data analysis, creativity, and an unwavering commitment to adapting to changes in the marketplace. By staying informed about new features, continuously testing and refining your campaigns, and focusing on delivering value to your audience, you can ensure that your advertising efforts yield long-term success. Success on Amazon Prime is not about quick wins, but about building a solid foundation for sustainable growth and profitability. By adopting a mindset of continuous learning and improvement, you can navigate the complexities of Amazon advertising and unlock the full potential of the platform to drive your business forward.

APPENDIX

Navigating the world of Amazon advertising can sometimes feel like diving into a sea of complex terms, policies, and best practices. To make the process easier, this section serves as a comprehensive resource for understanding key advertising terminology, discovering recommended tools that can optimize your campaigns, and adhering to Amazon's advertising policy guidelines. Each of these aspects plays a crucial role in ensuring that your advertising efforts are successful, efficient, and compliant with Amazon's standards.

Glossary of Amazon Advertising Terms

Understanding the language of Amazon advertising is the first step in mastering the platform. Here's a rundown of the most important terms you will encounter:

1. **Sponsored Products**: These are the most common ad format on Amazon. Sponsored Products are keyword-targeted ads that appear in search results and product detail pages, helping to boost visibility for individual listings.

2. **Sponsored Brands**: These ads feature a brand logo, a custom headline, and a selection of products. Sponsored Brands appear at the top of search results and help drive brand recognition in addition to product sales.

3. **Sponsored Display**: These are display ads that appear both on and off Amazon, aimed at retargeting audiences who have shown interest in similar products. Sponsored Display can appear on Amazon product detail pages, the homepage, and other websites that Amazon has partnered with.

4. **A+ Content**: This is a premium content feature that allows brands to enhance their product detail pages with rich media, including high-quality images, videos, and detailed descriptions. A+ Content helps improve conversion rates by providing shoppers with more engaging information.

5. **Cost Per Click (CPC)**: This is the amount you pay each time someone clicks on your ad. CPC is a key metric for measuring the efficiency of your ad spend, and it's particularly important in paid search advertising.

6. **Click-Through Rate (CTR)**: The ratio of users who click on an ad compared to the number of times the ad is shown. A high CTR indicates that your ad is compelling and relevant to your target audience.

7. **Conversion Rate**: This refers to the percentage of clicks on an ad that result in a purchase. A higher conversion rate typically

signifies that your ad and product listing are both well-targeted and appealing to potential buyers.

8. **Return on Ad Spend (ROAS)**: A crucial metric, ROAS measures the revenue generated for every dollar spent on advertising. This is an essential tool for understanding the financial effectiveness of your advertising campaigns.

9. **Bid**: A bid is the maximum amount you are willing to pay for a click on your ad. The bid helps determine how competitive your ads are in the auction system used by Amazon.

10. **Targeting**: This refers to the process of selecting the audience you want your ads to reach. Targeting can be done based on keywords, product categories, interests, or demographic data, among other factors.

11. **Impressions**: The number of times your ad is shown to potential customers. Impressions are important because they give you insight into how often your ad is being exposed to the target audience, although they do not necessarily correlate with clicks or conversions.

12. **Dynamic Bidding**: A feature in Amazon advertising that automatically adjusts your bid for individual clicks based on the likelihood of conversion. Dynamic bidding can help maximize your ad spend by ensuring you are bidding competitively while maintaining cost efficiency.

13. **Ad Group**: An ad group contains one or more ads that share the same set of targeting criteria. Organizing ads into ad groups allows for better performance tracking and budget management.

14. **Product Targeting**: This type of targeting focuses on specific products, categories, or brands. It helps advertisers target customers who are browsing similar products and are more likely to convert.

15. **Amazon Marketing Cloud (AMC)**: A set of advanced analytics tools that allows advertisers to track, analyze, and understand data across different marketing channels and customer touchpoints on Amazon. AMC is invaluable for gaining deep insights into advertising performance and customer behavior.

Recommended Tools and Resources

To fully harness the potential of Amazon advertising, having the right tools at your disposal is essential. Below are some of the most effective tools and resources to optimize your campaigns and maximize results:

1. **Amazon Seller Central**: This is the central hub for managing your seller account on Amazon. Through Seller Central, you can create and manage your ads, view performance data, and track

your ad spend. It also allows you to access key metrics and make adjustments to your campaigns in real time.

2. **Amazon Advertising Console**: The Advertising Console is where you create, manage, and optimize your sponsored ad campaigns. This platform provides valuable insights into your campaigns' performance, as well as advanced features like bid management, audience targeting, and reporting.

3. **Amazon Marketing Services (AMS)**: AMS is Amazon's paid search advertising platform that allows you to create targeted ads for products on Amazon. It includes Sponsored Products, Sponsored Brands, and other ad formats, and provides tools for optimizing campaigns based on performance data.

4. **Amazon Attribution**: This tool gives you insights into how non-Amazon marketing channels are impacting sales on Amazon. Amazon Attribution helps advertisers measure the effectiveness of their off-Amazon marketing efforts and optimize cross-channel strategies.

5. **Helium 10**: This is an all-in-one software suite designed for Amazon sellers. It offers a range of tools for keyword research, product listing optimization, market analysis, and ad campaign management. Helium 10 can help improve your Amazon advertising strategy by providing valuable insights into search trends and competitor activity.

6. **Sellics**: Another popular Amazon advertising tool, Sellics provides a complete solution for PPC management, keyword tracking, and competitor analysis. It helps sellers optimize their Amazon ads through detailed reporting and real-time insights into performance.

7. **Jungle Scout**: Known for its product research capabilities, Jungle Scout also offers tools for optimizing ad campaigns. It provides data-driven insights into product trends, keyword opportunities, and advertising strategies, helping sellers make informed decisions.

8. **Google Analytics**: While Amazon's advertising tools provide detailed insights, using Google Analytics in combination with your Amazon ads can help you track customer behavior across multiple platforms and gain a deeper understanding of your target audience.

9. **Google Keyword Planner**: For keyword research, Google Keyword Planner can help identify popular search terms and trends. This tool is especially useful when selecting keywords for your Amazon ads to ensure you're targeting high-converting terms.

10. **Canva**: Visual content plays a crucial role in Amazon advertising, particularly for Sponsored Brands and display ads. Canva is a free, user-friendly design tool that allows advertisers to create professional-quality graphics for ad creatives.

Amazon Advertising Policy Guidelines

Ensuring that your ads comply with Amazon's advertising policies is crucial for maintaining a positive relationship with the platform and avoiding any potential issues with your account. Amazon has strict guidelines regarding the types of ads allowed, the content displayed, and how products should be presented. Some key policy areas to keep in mind include:

1. **Ad Content**: All ads must accurately represent the products being advertised. Misleading claims, false product descriptions, or any form of exaggeration are strictly prohibited. Additionally, Amazon requires that the ad content be appropriate, respectful, and free of offensive material.

2. **Prohibited Products**: Amazon has a list of products that cannot be advertised. These include illegal items, hazardous materials, and certain restricted goods like tobacco or alcohol. Make sure to review the full list of prohibited products on Amazon's policy page before launching ads.

3. **Trademarks and Copyright**: Ads must not infringe on third-party intellectual property rights, including trademarks, copyrights, and patents. Advertisers should be cautious when using logos, images, or names that may belong to other brands.

4. **Keyword Targeting**: Keywords used in ads must be relevant to the product being advertised. Using irrelevant or inappropriate keywords to attract clicks or impressions is a violation of Amazon's policies.

5. **Ad Placement and Format**: Amazon has specific rules about where and how ads can appear. For example, Sponsored Products must adhere to certain guidelines regarding image quality, product categorization, and ad placement in search results.

6. **Pricing and Discounts**: Ads that promote discounted prices must accurately reflect the actual price of the product. Any discrepancies between the price shown in the ad and the price on the product page can lead to policy violations.

7. **Customer Reviews**: Amazon prohibits the use of customer reviews in ads, whether positive or negative. Reviews must be sourced organically through customer interactions and not manipulated for marketing purposes.

By staying well-versed in Amazon's advertising terms, utilizing the right tools, and adhering to Amazon's policies, advertisers can improve the effectiveness of their campaigns and maintain compliance with Amazon's standards. These resources help ensure that every ad you run is optimized for success, enabling your brand to thrive in the competitive Amazon marketplace.

www.ingramcontent.com/pod-product-compliance
Lightning Source LLC
LaVergne TN
LVHW051222050326
832903LV00028B/2217